"*Physicians cannot survive the practice of medicine with just a focus on patient care. Scope Forward is a study allowing providers to grasp and conquer the previously shadowy realm of the complete business of medicine. Praveen Suthrum's deep dive into multiple phases of the medical industry required countless hours of research, interviews, and his astute ability to organize meaningful discoveries into an objective syllabus. Scope Forward will be a definitive resource for healthcare teams as we struggle to become proficient healthcare businesses placing best patient pathways first and at the same time creating enjoyable, efficient, and financially viable enterprises. This text is a must for healthcare leaders charting their course to success.*"

—DR. REED B. HOGAN, GI ASSOCIATES AND
ENDOSCOPY CENTER, MISSISSIPPI

"*Most doctors are not very good at the business side of medicine, and as a gastroenterologist, I can say it's no different in GI. What Praveen has done in his book Scope Forward is to illuminate us (in great detail) about a whole range of issues pertinent to the future of GI, from artificial intelligence to private equity to disruptive technologies. Specifically, in relation to AI, he makes the topic very relevant and real-world - assessing both near and longer-term opportunities for AI in GI. This is a very welcome entry into the 'must read' category for all those involved in gastroenterology. You will learn a lot!*"

—DR. MICHAEL BYRNE, CEO AND FOUNDER OF SATISFAI
HEALTH, AND FOUNDER OF AI4GI, VANCOUVER, CANADA

"Scope Forward offers a refreshing perspective on many aspects of health care within and outside of GI. Narrative also allows readers to access views of many GI thought leaders."

—DR. LATHA ALAPARTHI, GASTROENTEROLOGY CENTER OF CONNECTICUT, VICE PRESIDENT, DHPA, CONNECTICUT

"Scope Forward may at first appear to give a foretelling of the GI landscape in the distant future. Instead, Praveen gives an accurate, unbiased and thoughtful assessment of changes occurring right before our eyes. We need to thoroughly understand and embrace these changes so that we can prepare for the immediate future. Particularly striking is the recognition that digitalization and emerging technologies will rapidly transform the way we practice gastroenterology."

—DR. MICHAEL DRAGUTSKY, CHAIRMAN OF ONE GI AND BOARD MEMBER, DHPA, TENNESSEE

"There's no one way to describe Scope Forward. It is a treasure trove of insights for anyone in the field of gastroenterology. The book helps you understand the changes that are rapidly affecting medicine from the lens of GI. Among several other topics, Scope Forward succeeds extremely well in explaining the wave of business consolidation in private practice and the forces influencing it. I strongly recommend this book."

—DR. KENNETH RUBIN, THE GASTROENTEROLOGY GROUP OF NORTHERN NEW JERSEY

"Sir William Osler, one of the fathers of modern medicine, said he who studies medicine without books sails an uncharted sea. Praveen's book is an essential map for those who seek to navigate the future of GI without hitting icebergs."

—DR. NARESH GUNARATNAM, HURON GASTROENTEROLOGY AND CHAIR, DATA ANALYTICS, DHPA, MICHIGAN

"As physicians, we have spent our entire training in sharpening clinical acumen to optimize patient care. Scope Forward gives great insight on the intersection of the business side of medicine with the clinical aspect. Praveen Suthrum's book is a must read for physicians to sustain financially viable practices. It will serve as a valuable resource for healthcare leaders."

—DR. MEHUL LALANI, US DIGESTIVE HEALTH
AND TREASURER, DHPA, PENNSYLVANIA

"Navigating the surreal environment we currently face with COVID is challenging, yet we don't have to be alone. In this climate, work efficiency and positioning ourselves for the future with restructuring is needed. Fresh ideas and different perspectives on addressing challenges make a welcome guide. Praveen Suthrum's focus on gastroenterology, the challenges and how others are adapting is timely, insightful and invaluable. A must read!"

—DR. J STEVEN BURDICK, ADVANCED ENDOSCOPY, TEXAS

"We are in amazing times where exponential technologies like digital health and AI can enable us to deliver scalable and highly efficient care like never before. The COVID pandemic has given us a glimpse into the future of care. What is missing is how to align technology with the new business models. Scope Forward does exactly that by providing a roadmap to all in the field of GI and healthcare."

—DR. ASHISH ATREJA, ASSOCIATE PROFESSOR AND CHIEF
INNOVATION OFFICER, MEDICINE, MOUNT SINAI AND SCIENTIFIC
FOUNDER AND BOARD MEMBER, RX.HEALTH, NEW YORK

"*Gastroenterology is an industry that is rapidly changing as new technologies and business models emerge. Scope Forward is a comprehensive guide that will serve as a key navigation tool for physicians as they learn to operate in and find success in the new healthcare environment. I commend Praveen's unbiased evaluation and objective commentary throughout the book as well as his ability to draw parallels between gastroenterology and other industries that may seem unrelated on the surface. I highly recommend this book to anyone in the gastroenterology field.*"

—ABE M'BODJ, PROVIDENT HEALTHCARE PARTNERS, CALIFORNIA

"*This is a prescient piece of work. In the face of the COVID-19 pandemic, it seems like Praveen had a crystal ball when he wrote Scope Forward. His message to disrupt yourself before getting disrupted is more relevant than ever for gastroenterology today. The importance of investigating new technology and new business structures is critical to a successful career. This book is recommended reading for every gastroenterologist wanting to stay relevant in the future.*"

—DR. MICHAEL WEINSTEIN, PRESIDENT & CEO, CAPITAL DIGESTIVE CARE, PAST PRESIDENT, DHPA, MARYLAND

SCOPE FORWARD

SCOPE
FORWARD

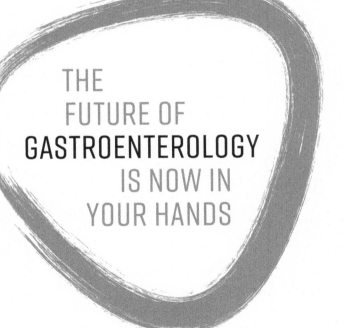

THE
FUTURE OF
GASTROENTEROLOGY
IS NOW IN
YOUR HANDS

PRAVEEN SUTHRUM

AUTHOR OF *PRIVATE EQUITY IN GASTROENTEROLOGY*

LIONCREST
PUBLISHING

SCOPE FORWARD
The Future of Gastroenterology Is Now in Your Hands

ISBN   978-1-5445-0885-6 *Paperback*
          978-1-5445-0886-3 *Ebook*

For C. K.

Thank you for putting that monkey on my back.

Fifteen years later, your trick is still working.

CONTENTS

AND THEN THE PANDEMIC HIT

Scope Forward was written before COVID-19 to help gastro-enterologists create a future on their terms. By amplifying trends that were underway, I wanted to draw the industry's attention to what seemed obvious to me. If gastroenterology (GI) practices didn't disrupt themselves, something else would.

Once the COVID-19 pandemic exploded, an early reader of the book commented, "It's actually crazy that *Scope Forward* was written well before the pandemic hit and how things are even more relevant now."

We'll look back at 2020 as the year that healthcare was compelled to shift gears. The industry adapted to telemedicine almost overnight. Restrictive laws changed in a matter of days. Cloud technology scaled up. Doctors and patients suddenly found themselves inside each other's homes. More importantly, we could no longer look away from the mirror that the pandemic was showing us. With widespread infections and deaths, our healthcare system's failures have been too hard to ignore.

Recent changes are not limited to telemedicine. As you'll find out in the following pages, there are many technology and business trends that are changing gastroenterology. They have been intersecting and multiplying quietly until now. Disruption was brewing under the surface. What COVID-19 has done is *accelerate* that disruption by throwing most limitations out the door.

The pandemic is creating a new void in gastroenterology, leaving us no choice but to think differently. Patients are delaying or canceling elective procedures, fearing risk of infection in medical facilities. Today's business of gastroenterology relies on electives such as colonoscopy. Further, social distancing, staff absences (or furloughs), and additional costs of personal protective equipment (PPE) are making unprecedented demands on GI offices and surgery centers.

Before we can imagine a future after COVID-19, we must understand gastroenterology from the lens presented in *Scope Forward*. I've resisted the temptation to make changes to the book *because of* COVID-19. It's important to see things as they were. A tsunami was already on its way. What the pandemic has done is crunched the time we had at hand. Now we are in the midst of it all.

I've added an afterword on the impact of COVID-19. Through the pages that lead up to it, it'll become apparent to you—as it is to me—that the future of gastroenterology will change. Such a future will not resemble the past. Whether that's a good thing or not depends on what we do with the information that follows.

INTRODUCTION

Ninety-five percent of private practices in the region were gone. There were hardly any independent physicians left to refer patients around. Two health systems dominated the landscape by buying up practices. People who showed up at the remaining independent facilities usually had low-paying insurance plans. Then there were those willing to pay cash for opioids.

I was visiting a private medical practice in the area to understand why they were bleeding money. The physician owner had returned from retirement to manage the practice. The administrator of the facility said she was "stuck in this job." The owner's son, also a physician, gave up on medicine to work on the business. Wasn't it just a matter of time before they would spin out of control?

That experience served as a poignant reminder of what healthcare would become if we let industry forces dominate us. Out of respect for the region and the facility, I won't tell you where it is. But doesn't some of it already sound familiar to you? In truth, couldn't it be Anytown, America? Couldn't at least some aspect of it be Yourtown, America?

You know it already. Gastroenterology is in the midst of massive structural disruption. Stool DNA tests for colon cancer are disrupting screening colonoscopy. If that technology fails, then there are many companies working on liquid biopsy. These are blood tests that look for not one but many cancers at the same time. If that doesn't disrupt, then there's artificial intelligence (AI). AI has the potential to classify cancerous polyps and spot what endoscopists might miss.

Most gastroenterology (GI) practices are too busy to worry about technology. They've been more concerned about business consolidation led by private equity. In 2019, there were at least 16 private equity transactions in gastroenterology. Compare that to two deals in 2018. There's a race to get bigger faster.

But taking private equity for the wrong reasons is like playing with fire. In the 1990s, Physician Practice Management companies (PPMs) burnt billions of dollars. They tried to merge practices and went bust. In the end, doctors and PPMs sued each other.

Leaving that aside for a moment, look at Big Brothers who want a piece of gastroenterology. Hospitals want to hire you. Big insurance companies are acquiring medical practices. Big Tech wants to lead healthcare using algorithms. Even Walmart is entering the game of healthcare.

Note: GI is an abbreviation for gastrointestinal. However, for the sake of readability, I'll be using GI to refer to the field of gastroenterology or gastroenterologists.

Meanwhile, patients are changing their expectations from GI. Some are biohacking their way into the microbiome. Some others want their colon cleansed to showcase a flatter belly. Not exactly reasons doctors went to medical school.

When I talked about these emerging trends, gastroenterologists had these responses: Some felt threatened. Some brushed them away. Some got excited. But many were in a state of confusion.

Now, that's a problem.

When we take action in a state of fear or confusion, we regret those decisions later. In such a state, we tend to be reactive, we follow the trend of the herd for safety, or we simply go where others want us to go out of our own indecision.

When a large cohort like GI takes action in a state of disarray, the industry risks implosion. Hospitals laying off doctors with limited notice. Private equity (PE) deals going bust. Technology changes catching the industry off guard. At its worst, implosion can mean doctors rebuilding their practices from scratch. That would put countless people at risk, including patients. Once, a doctor told me, "Distracted doctors do more harm than good."

To make more empowered choices, we must first understand the future with an open and curious mind. We must be willing to look at every area—be it clinical, technological, or business—without judgment. We must take stock of our own situation. And then we must take action in defined timelines.

I began writing this book as a way of inviting gastroenterologists to peek into the future. I conducted over 30 interviews in various parts of the country. From Minnesota to Mississippi and from California to New York. Gastroenterologists in various phases of their journey generously shared their time and perspective. More importantly, they shared their views so candidly. Their concerns about PE or hospital consolidation or DNA testing. Their dreams about a better future for healthcare. The challenge for me was to reflect and connect the dots as objectively as possible.

You can say this book will serve as your tour guide to the future of gastroenterology, but I have to caution that my aim isn't to be exhaustive. For example, I'm not covering several important topics, such as the pharmaceutical industry, policy, or the mounting costs of healthcare. Instead of talking about all the sights on this tour, I wish to give you a decent slice to help you develop your perspective across technology and business. Also, if you are a hospital or insurer, you'll find I'm unabashedly biased toward doctors. Doctors come first and the rest of the industry after. In their success lies the success of healthcare. Their failure risks a total collapse of the system.

If there's any cohort of medicine I understand, it would be gastroenterology. Through NextServices, the company I co-founded, I have worked with GI doctors since 2005. We help gastroenterologists with billing, technology, compliance, and more recently, private equity. My team and I built a cloud-based software platform called enki.

Once, a gastroenterologist asked me, "How do you know the inside stories? Do you have any family members who are gastroenterologists?"

I said, "No, but I have friends who are."

Then he mused, "Oh, then in your past life, you must've been a gastroenterologist!"

I'll take that.

I contributed to two books by C. K. Prahalad, a management guru and my teacher at the University of Michigan. *The Fortune at the Bottom of the Pyramid* and *The New Age of Innovation* (coauthored with M. S. Krishnan) both became management best sellers. That experience provided a method for me to not only *see* the future but to *connect* the dots for others.

More recently, I wrote *Private Equity in Gastroenterology: Navigating the Next Wave* (Amazon #1 New Release in Private Equity and Gastroenterology). The book offered much-needed clarity on the subject.

They say writers use writing as a way to work out topics they wish to understand. You can say that's what happened to me through this book. I learned a lot through the interviews and research.

Reading *Scope Forward* will give you enough depth to develop your own point of view of the future. By the end of these pages, you will come away excited about the way forward because you'll develop a clearer vision. You'll have a sense of what to do next and how to direct not only yourself but others.

My vision is for the GI industry to use this book to shift the course of gastroenterology. We must come together and align.

We must change the space for good. To not only help us thrive in our professional lives but to sleep well at night, knowing we've made healthcare better for those who need it the most.

By picking up this book, you've set something into motion for yourself and the industry. That *something* is to take the future head-on and be willing to shape what's to follow in the next decade.

Let's scope forward.

A QUICK NOTE ON PROFESSIONAL ADVICE

This book is not intended to provide financial or legal advice or steer you in a particular direction. It won't answer all your questions. Rather, it'll help you ask the right questions to make decisions that work for you. All opinions expressed belong solely to me as the author and do not belong to the organizations I may be associated with. This book isn't a substitute for professional expertise from attorneys, accountants, or investment bankers.

PART 1

WHERE ARE WE GOING?

In this section, we'll explore where the gastroenterology industry is headed. In particular, our conversation will center around four themes:

1. Exponential technologies
2. Business consolidation
3. Big Brothers
4. Patient behavior

Exponential technologies are technologies that have the capacity to double in performance every few years. Computers are the most common example of exponential technologies. Once room-sized mainframes, computers now snugly fit into our pockets. There are many advanced technologies accelerating today, such as DNA testing, artificial intelligence (AI), synthetic biology, robotics, and 3D printing. In chapter 1, we'll explore the future of GI through the lens of these technologies. We'll especially consider DNA testing and AI.

Fueled by private equity, the business of gastroenterology is consolidating. In chapter 2, we'll take stock of the state of consolidation. We'll also learn the underlying reasons for this consolidation. And we'll look back at the PPMs of the 1990s.

Gastroenterology is under tremendous pressure from health systems and big insurances. If that were not enough, big technology companies are entering healthcare. Healthcare is now an important vertical for Amazon and Walmart. In chapter 3, we'll look at the strategies of these Big Brothers.

Finally in chapter 4, we'll explore an unusual trend: changes in patient behavior. Today's patients are seeking more than a solution to sickness. They expect healthcare to make them look good, feel good, and even live forever. And they are willing to try out new solutions if healthcare isn't equipped to answer them. That chapter will help you explore strategies to continue engaging your patients in the future.

This part of the book serves as the basis for understanding the convergence of trends that will shape GI over the next decade. It'll prepare you for later chapters where you'll get to *scope forward* on your terms.

CHAPTER 1

EXPONENTIAL TECHNOLOGIES

The best way to understand exponentials is through a story. Apparently, chess originated in India several hundred years ago. When its creator showed off the game to the king, he was asked to name any reward in appreciation. To which, the creator asked for a grain of rice for the first square of the board and double that thereafter. One grain for the first, two for the second, four for the third, and so on. *Doubling with every square.*

The king laughed, "Are you sure you want such a small reward?"

The creator responded, "Yes, just a few grains of rice are enough."

Surely the king did not understand the power of exponentials. Exponential growth is very deceptive in the beginning. We think it's small, but it's really not. As you reach half the chessboard—the 32nd box—you reach 2,147,483,648 grains of rice. When we double that for the 33rd box, we reach 4.3 billion grains. When we finally reach the end of all 64 boxes on the chessboard or $2^{64} - 1$, we arrive at 18.5 trillion grains of rice. That's more than the global production of rice today.

Obviously, the king didn't see this coming. Both he and the kingdom went bankrupt in trying to fulfill the promise. That's how exponentials work. They are slow to start but multiply in impact as you go along.

THE SHIFT TO DIGITAL

Before we go further, it's important to understand what makes something exponential. To grasp that, we must be clear about the shift to *digital*.

Over a decade ago, many of us still used landline phones, watched cable TV, rented DVDs, called for taxis, took photos using cameras, and drove over to Borders to browse and buy books. During the past 10 years, we watched each of these fields permanently getting altered. Today, we stream movies on Netflix, call Uber to get somewhere, and we keep buying new phones to take better photos. We can't think of what not to use Amazon for. It's true—our life has turned *digital*. Most of us are so hooked to a device that to disconnect digitally is considered being mindful now.

Whether we realize it or not, we are living in exponential times. We are part of a grander, digital game.

How does a field become digitized? By finding a way to convert itself into zeros and ones, the basic language of computers. When music became digitized, we could more easily transmit a song as zeros and ones through the internet. When photography became digitized, we could convert pixels into zeros and ones. When books became digitized, we could access it via Amazon Kindle, a digital device.

Peter Diamandis, the founder and chairman of XPRIZE, says that when a field becomes digitized, it becomes information enabled. It's easier to access, share, and distribute information or data. Once you can represent something in zeros and ones, then it enters an irreversible phase of exponential growth. When a field goes digital, it has the potential to steadily double in performance. (Recollect the story of chess we began the chapter with.) Industries and companies failing to recognize that shift are inevitably disrupted.

With $16 billion in annual revenues, Kodak's leadership position was unquestionable in 1996. Maybe that's why its executives didn't see (or didn't want to see) the wave of digital photography. When photography became digital, it moved from a physical setup of bulky cameras with film rolls to a more virtual environment—a smartphone in your pocket. Moving to digital, photography became cheaper and cheaper to the point where it became virtually free. You could distribute your photos infinitely. Companies like Instagram built apps that made average people take cool photographs. Meanwhile, Kodak went bankrupt in less than 20 years from its peak in mid-1990s.

Ironically, a Kodak engineer invented the digital camera back in 1975, but his bosses shut him up. Kodak's bread and butter was camera film. But going digital meant making no money on its cash cow. Don't you see that it was actually their mindset that led to the fall?

Other industries have experienced their own "Kodak

moments" by ignoring the shift to digital, whereas new entrants capitalized on the move. iTunes disrupted music. Amazon disrupted retailing and books. Airbnb gave us an alternative to hotels. Uber changed our commute. Amazon Web Services helped us rent servers. (We will delve deeper into the topic of disruption in part 4 of the book.)

Unlike Kodak, today's leading companies are transforming themselves faster than ever, riding one exponential wave to the next.

SELF-DRIVING CARS

Back in 2012, I sat in a very different-looking Lexus—it was one of Google's early self-driving cars. Wires ran from a laptop to the steering wheel and into the mechanics of the vehicle. A gray-looking device called the LIDAR scanner sat on top of the car. It rotated all the time and scanned the entire environment. The LIDAR served as the eyes of the self-driving car. From what I gathered, it cost $200,000 to convert the Lexus into a self-driving unit. The LIDAR itself cost $75,000. The automotive industry dismissed Google's effort as a research project. Well, it *was* one.

Photo credit: Binod Bawri

The Google Self Driving Car Project started in 2009. A decade later, Google's self-driving car, called Waymo, is a Chrysler Pacifica minivan. On their website, the company says that they are "building the World's Most Experienced Driver." They can make that claim because when one Waymo car drives a mile, the *entire* Waymo system learns. Through 2018 and 2019, the company started to serve the Phoenix area with a self-driving, ride-hailing service called Waymo One.

Recent announcements say a production-ready LIDAR scanner will cost as little as $500. Meanwhile, Elon Musk thinks visual recognition via cameras is better than LIDAR scanners. Tesla's upcoming robotaxis don't even plan to use LIDAR. Think about it: LIDAR that resulted in disrupting cars in the last decade are already somewhat obsolete. (We'll revisit this point later in chapter 11.)

We can clearly see that exponential technologies are disrupting cars and phones. So why wouldn't these technologies find their way into healthcare and gastroenterology?

STOOL DNA TESTS AND SELF-DRIVING CARS

What do stool tests have to do with self-driving cars? We'll soon find out. But let's first go back to the discussion we had earlier on the shift to digital. Screening for cancer through colonoscopy, while a gold standard, reminds me of a field that's at the crossroads of disruption—much like music or photography was before iTunes or smartphones.

If you consider the argument for a moment, a colonoscopy is largely limited to one doctor and one patient at a time. When a doctor performs a colonoscopy, he or she can't scale beyond the procedure. With each procedure, the learning happens within the capacity of that one doctor. To put that into context, only a very small percentage of doctors become endoscopists. And an even smaller percentage achieve mastery in endoscopy. Statistically speaking, we are talking of a very few highly qualified individuals who can reliably screen for cancer using sophisticated methods.

Ask yourself what could make the field of cancer screening go digital? Something that can accelerate cancer screening and give control to the nonexperts. I'm sure you might have arrived at DNA testing or artificial intelligence. We'll explore them both in this chapter.

Now ask yourself these five questions:

1. Can stool DNA testing be ultimately represented in zeros and ones, the language of computers?

2. iTunes allows musicians to reach millions of people. With DNA testing, is it technically possible to screen millions of people for colon cancer?
3. The more Google's self-driving car drives, the more it learns as a system. Could it be technically feasible to reduce screening error rates with more screening data?
4. Smartphones made the average user into a photographer. Could a DNA testing kit (backed by a sophisticated lab) simplify screening to a point where the patient has more control?
5. Amazon made it easier for people to buy books. Could DNA testing make cancer screening dramatically more convenient?

By going digital, we would take a physical environment (endoscopy room to detect cancer) and convert it into a virtual, information-enabled, machine-driven environment (DNA testing to detect cancer).

In 2019, I wrote an article comparing Cologuard to self-driving cars. Cologuard (owned by Exact Sciences) is the commercial name of the stool DNA test for colon cancer screening. Many GI industry readers expressed their displeasure with that comparison. Here are a few pointed comments on the Cologuard from social media.

"I bet you 100 bucks it will be a class action lawsuit in 3 years"

"What does a Google car have to do with it?"

"Colonoscopies are very safe and the gold standard by far"

"First off, Mayo Clinic is a major partner in the development and promotion of Cologuard. Second, as a gastroenterologist, I call BS on the 8% false positive rate, more like 20%+ in my patient population, 60+ years primarily. Of course my patient population is likely skewed. Nevertheless, it is hardly the panacea it is touted to be. Colonoscopy remains the gold standard in skilled hands and proper preparation."

"Well, one problem that I have is that the initial part of the test is a stool hemoccult. If that's positive, it's a positive test. They don't do the DNA part of the test, but still charge $600 for a $2 dollar test. They also just jammed you for a copay on a diagnostic colonoscopy that would have been fully covered as a screening colonoscopy. They do not report if heme positive vs DNA positive. Why not? Maybe because it's hard to justify $600 for a stool hemoccult. They do this every 3 years. Not every 10 as in a screening colonoscopy. Finding a cancer is fine. Wouldn't you rather prevent a cancer by removing a polyp? Sure. It picks up 30% of polyps. Hence the 3 year screening. I like the concept of Cologuard. It's not there yet."

These comments made me wonder if clinicians were trapping themselves in a mindset like that of auto manufacturers. In the beginning, auto companies found self-driving cars dangerous. Today, most of them need an autonomous vehicle strategy to stay relevant.

It's also not my place to comment on the clinical pros and cons of one approach versus the other. I'm a technologist, not a doctor. All I want you to take note of is that stool DNA testing displays characteristics of a field gone digital. When an area becomes digital and information-enabled, it scales exponentially. It opens doors to newer opportunities.

COLORECTAL CANCER SCREENING OPTIONS

There are two main testing categories for colorectal cancer screening: stool-based tests and visual (structural) examination. The American Cancer Society provides this outline of the testing categories. All are followed by colonoscopy for further investigation.

Stool-based tests include:

- **Fecal immunochemical tests (FIT).** The objective of the test is to look for colorectal cancer in hidden or occult blood in stool. The test responds to hemoglobin protein found in red blood cells. A positive test result is usually followed up by a colonoscopy for more direct investigation.
- **Guaiac-based fecal occult blood test (gFOBT).** When you apply feces to a guaiac-quoted (a plant substance) paper, it reacts. The test can't differentiate between blood from colon or other parts of the digestive tract. A colonoscopy is performed to identify the reasons for blood in stool.
- **Stool DNA test (also, multitargeted stool DNA test).** The test looks for DNA mutations because of colorectal cancer. The test looks for cells with these abnormalities in stool samples. The product Cologuard tests for both blood in stool and DNA mutations. If the test is positive, a colonoscopy is performed for further examination.

Visual (or structural) examination includes:

- **Colonoscopy.** A doctor examines the entire length of the colon and rectum, looking for polyps and removing samples for biopsy.
- **Virtual colonoscopy.** This examination is a CT scan of the colon and rectum. A computer puts together several images taken during the scan. The resulting visual provides more detailed images of the organs.

WITH DIGITAL, COLON CANCER SCREENING BECOMES A SOFTWARE PROBLEM

Software is essentially our ability to program something. At its core, software programming is about manipulating zeros and ones. When you screen colon cancer with the aid of a DNA test, it ultimately distills down to data. We can analyze data and come to understand the patterns we discover. As with self-driving cars, DNA testing belongs to a constantly improving digital system. It has the potential to become a *software problem*. And the way to solve software problems is to have programmers and scientists work on them. With more cases and more data, they will get more accurate results.

Exact Sciences, the maker of Cologuard, has screened 3.5 million people as of this writing. That's more data on colon cancer screening than any single group of endoscopists generate or analyze—anywhere in the world. It's possible that with each test of Cologuard, the entire system of DNA-based screening improves.

Mark Stenhouse, general manager of screening for Exact Sciences, said, "For colorectal cancer, too many people are currently unscreened. Experts agree that having a choice of screening options is helpful in increasing patient participation."

As a public company, Exact Sciences has given several positive indications to Wall Street. They've repeatedly said that they plan to capture 40% of the colon cancer screening market (they have a 5% market share as of this writing).

I wanted to know how this might impact gastroenterologists.

Here's what Stenhouse said: "We appreciate that there's

concern, and we're committed to continue gathering data from real world studies, modeling analyses, and other sources in partnership with the GI community. Nearly 50% of Cologuard patients who responded to a survey are previously unscreened. Our relationship with gastroenterologists should be viewed as collaborative, not competitive."

That's how Jerry Tillinger, CEO of US Digestive Health seems to view the risks and opportunities of stool DNA testing. US Digestive Health is a private equity–funded platform based in Pennsylvania. This is what he had to say: "We expect DNA tests will continue to improve, but we also expect colonoscopies to improve through the application of artificial intelligence and other emerging technologies. With both of these tools in our arsenal to help improve screening of colorectal cancer patients, we believe we will dramatically improve screening percentages in our communities. Identifying and treating these patients before they develop colorectal cancer is our number one mission." (You can read his complete interview in chapter 9.)

If companies like Exact Sciences collaborate with gastroenterologists to draw up a path to the future, there's an opportunity for a win-win. More patients can be screened quickly. We can get people earlier to the endoscopy room. With more meaningful collaboration between industry and GI practitioners, could the field of gastroenterology progress to its next iteration? A digital phase that helps us save more lives sooner. We will discuss more on the topic of convergence in chapter 12.

Read the complete interview with Mark Stenhouse and Dr. Paul Limburg (from Exact Sciences) at the end of the chapter.

In May 2018, the American Cancer Society revised its guidelines for colorectal cancer screening. They lowered the screening age from 50 to 45 years. The next year, the FDA approved Cologuard for ages 45–49. That change expanded the market for Exact Sciences to 19 million more Americans. In preparation for their expanded opportunities, the company built a lab facility to process seven million tests annually.

Study these two graphs. One represents sales of Cologuard and the other shows the company's stock price from 2015 to 2019. Both resemble exponential curves.

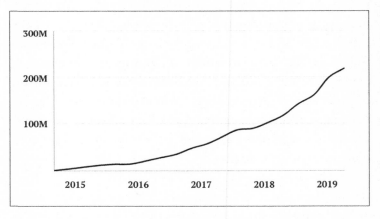

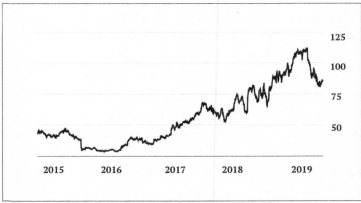

Exact Sciences revenues (top) and stock since 2015 (bottom)

It shouldn't be surprising then that the company projects a revenue of $1.6 billion for 2020. Cologuard itself generates over one billion dollars. Exact Sciences has acquired other biotechnology companies, like Genomic Health, Paradigm, and Viomics to bolster their offerings for a $20 billion cancer diagnostics market. The company has built a sales force of 1,000 people to ensure that their products are consistently prescribed in doctors' offices.

Whether clinicians approve the usage of stool DNA tests to detect cancer or not, this wave is rising. Market behavior, sales growth, and the company's indications in quarterly earnings calls illustrate the exponential potential of Cologuard. Further, the progress of cancer testing will not be limited to stool-based tests. Blood-based tests that can detect multiple cancers will prove dramatically disruptive to traditional, linear ways of cancer screening.

COLOGUARD 2.0 AND A CANCER BLOOD TEST

I asked Mark Stenhouse about Cologuard's next version.

He said, "The overarching objective of Cologuard 2.0 is to improve specificity. And to definitely reduce false positives. We shared some data published in ACG (American College of Gastroenterology). We've initiated a prospective trial. But beyond that, it is premature to comment before FDA submission."

Dr. Paul Limburg added, "We would also consider if there's anything we can do to make the test more convenient."

The future of gastroenterology scopes well beyond colon

cancer, as well. Exact Sciences is due to launch a liver cancer test. Eventually, its goal is to have a stool test to detect gastrointestinal cancers and have a blood test for other types of cancers. In the future, the company plans to arrive at a cost of $100 per test.

On ClinicalTrials.gov, Exact Sciences is listed under a study to obtain whole blood specimens. The goal is to evaluate biomarkers associated with cancer. Conditions mentioned include breast cancer, lung cancer, colorectal cancer, prostate cancer, pancreatic cancer, liver cancer, stomach cancer, and more.

Here's what Dr. Limburg had to say on the blood-based cancer test: "With the collaboration between the Exact Sciences and Mayo Clinic, the marker discovery is ongoing for about 15 of the top fatal cancers. We are trying to understand how we could use a blood-based assay to detect cancer earlier and/or in some cases, identify high-risk conditions like premalignant lesions. The marker discovery research looks very promising."

Liquid biopsy (or blood tests to detect disease), as the field is known, is aiming to redefine cancer detection. The holy grail is to detect multiple cancers using a blood sample.

CancerSEEK, a test originated at Johns Hopkins, can detect eight different cancers. It includes ovarian, liver, esophageal, pancreatic, stomach, colorectal, lung, and breast cancer.

Exact Sciences has to compete with many other companies in the race to lead the liquid biopsy market. According to a report, there might be 175 companies competing in this space. Here are a few:

1. **Personal Genome Diagnostics.** The company is developing two pan-cancer panels under the name elio for tumor profiling and other therapies.
2. **Sysmex Inostics.** The company has a product called OncoBEAM for RAS mutation detection in colorectal cancer.
3. **Thermo Fisher Scientific.** The company has a liquid biopsy assay using digital PCR (dPCR) and NGS technology, which detects cancer and monitors it.
4. **Genomic Health.** The company has diagnostic tests for early detection of breast, colon, and prostate cancer.
5. **Menarini Silicon Biosystems.** The company has a liquid biopsy product called CELLSEARCH. It detects circulating tumor cells (CTCs) in metastatic breast, prostate, and colorectal cancers.
6. **Guardant Health.** Its liquid biopsy assay Guardant360 includes 73 genes associated with cancer. A newer assay GuardantOMNI is a 500-gene panel meant for genetic profiling.

Exact Sciences bought Genomic Health (#4 on the list above) in 2019 for $2.8 billion in cash and stock. Genomic Health CEO Kimberly Popovits called it a "one plus one equals three" opportunity, indicating strategic value from the sale.

Also, take note of Guardant (#6 in the list) in particular. The company registered a 10,000-subject study called LUNAR-2, a blood test for adults with an average risk of colorectal cancer. The trial is expected to be completed by 2022.

Even if one technology fails in improving its accuracy, there's enough momentum for digitizing the field of cancer screening. There will be other companies investing their time and energy to find ways to make noninvasive cancer screening a dominant reality.

Looking at it differently, the demand for early cancer screening will continue to rise. According to the World Cancer Research Fund, colorectal cancer is the third most commonly occurring cancer in men and the second most in women. It's an expanding need. By taking advantage of exponential tools, gastroenterologists can screen more patients than they have in the past.

We must find ways to ride and harness this digital wave to *scope forward*. Not fight or escape it.

IF YOU CAN GENETICALLY ENGINEER BABIES, CAN'T YOU TWEAK THE GUT?

In November 2018, the scientific community went berserk with the birth of two babies. Lulu and Nana were no ordinary twins.

He Jiankui, a biophysics researcher in China, altered them as embryos and planted them in their mother's womb. He used a genetic editing tool called CRISPR/Cas9 to disable a gene. That gene, CCR5, is needed to make a protein that HIV needs.

He basically edited human DNA in an attempt to reduce the risk of HIV in those twins. In an interview, he said, "Society will decide what to do next."

The story of Lulu and Nana offers insights into the direction of where DNA testing could go in gastroenterology. If DNA testing allows us to gather enormous data about our gut, then could it pave the way for tinkering our DNA to treat GI problems? Could DNA editing offer a way to eliminate the occurrence of cancer in a patient's future? That's not that too far-fetched to imagine. In 2017, the FDA approved the first gene therapy for cancer. Known as CAR-T therapy, the method involves reprogramming a person's own cells to attack cancer.

TAKEAWAYS (DNA TESTING)

I'll leave you with a few takeaways on DNA testing.

1. Controversies aside, we are firmly in the frontier of digital biology. This wave has begun, and there's no stopping it.
2. It's not just Exact Sciences. Many companies are venturing into the cancer screening space through DNA testing.
3. Exact Sciences is capitalizing on Cologuard with a heavy sales and marketing push. If the company doesn't keep up with itself, newer technology options might disrupt Cologuard.
4. Some parts of the GI industry are arguing that Cologuard is not reliable. If exponentials are anything to go by, the sensitivity of DNA tests will improve. Other cost-effective alternatives might drop the price of overall DNA testing.
5. If liquid biopsy becomes mainstream, it'll disrupt many types of income streams for gastroenterologists. Consider fees from screening colonoscopy, pathology reimbursements, and imaging studies. How would traditional screening compete with a blood test that can detect 15 types of cancers?
6. When we have more data on colorectal cancer screening, we will be able to visualize and draw out newer correlations. For example, consider links between colorectal

cancer and ethnicity. Instagram was built on top of the wave of digital photography. Similarly, newer digital GI applications will sprout on the foundation of DNA testing.

Stool DNA testing isn't the only exponential technology that's disrupting GI. There are several others. Up next is artificial intelligence.

AI IN GI

Artificial intelligence (AI) is driving the development of many exponential technologies. It's the underlying force behind the formation of many industries of the future, such as digital biology. The ultimate vision for AI is to outperform human intelligence—a point that's known as "singularity." According to Ray Kurzweil, an inventor and futurist, machines will beat human intelligence by 2045. Kurzweil often refers to the merger of machine and human intelligence at that point of singularity. If AI plays out without disastrous effects (think terrorism, massive job loss, warfare, etc.), then it could expand human potential. It could be a powerful tool that accelerates our ability to solve the biggest problems of our day.

In healthcare and gastroenterology, AI offers us the ability to shape a new digital future. It can help us reach patients at a scale and depth that would've been unthinkable in the past. For now, let's go back to the example of self-driving cars to explore what's possible with AI in GI.

Self-driving cars are defined by various levels of sophistication, from Level 1 (driver assistance) to Level 5 (full automation). Today, most auto manufacturers are gearing toward Level 4 automation. At Level 4, a vehicle is capable of handling most complex driving situations unless there's very low visibility.

In his book *Deep Medicine*, Dr. Eric Topol compares self-driving cars with AI-based medicine. He says, "While Level 4 for cars may be achievable under ideal environmental and traffic conditions, it is unlikely that medicine will ever get beyond Level 3 machine autonomy." According to Dr. Topol, we will never get to Level 5. That level entails a lack of oversight by doctors for "all conditions, all the time."

To better understand the context for AI in gastroenterology, I went to an expert source. Dr. Michael Byrne is a well-known leader of the field (read his interview at the end of the chapter). He's the founder of Satisfai Health Inc. and founder of a joint venture with Olympus called ai4gi. Dr. Byrne is also a practicing gastroenterologist at Vancouver General Hospital in Canada.

DIFFERENCES: ARTIFICIAL INTELLIGENCE, MACHINE LEARNING, DEEP LEARNING

Artificial intelligence (AI) is the vast ocean of imparting cognitive abilities to a machine.

Machine learning is the distinct ability of an AI system to recognize patterns. Using machine learning, a computer can analyze vast amounts of data and identify patterns within.

Deep learning is a subset of machine learning. Here, algorithms resemble neural networks of our brains. It's a more sophisticated way to teach a computer.

For our purposes, we will use AI in broad terms.

A few years ago while reading a paper on how to train the human eye for optical biopsy, Dr. Byrne had a question: "There was already AI for facial and fingerprint recognition. Could we not employ some form of AI for optical biopsy?"

As a result of people asking questions like Dr. Byrne's, companies like Satisfai are moving from using AI to "see" polyps to using them to arrive at more complete diagnostics. Gastroenterologists will soon use AI algorithms to identify polyps and classify them. The algorithms will then combine this information with other forms of data, such as genomic, demographic, and lifestyle. AI will put all of that together to come up with prognostic answers. In the future, real-time AI will even help endoscopists decide what kind of forceps to use.

To understand what's likely to happen with AI in GI, we only need to look at experiments already run with breast cancer or lung cancer. In 2019, the FDA cleared QuantX as the first-ever computer-aided breast cancer diagnosis system. In a clinical study, the software led to a 39% reduction in missed breast cancers and a 20% improvement in diagnosis.

In another study, MIT researchers developed algorithms that can predict breast cancer up to five years ahead of time. The algorithm used 90,000 mammograms to detect patterns too subtle for the human eye. The images shared by researchers were surprising. The first image showed a red box identifying a tiny dot of cancer in a scan of the patient's breast. In the second image—a scan taken four years later—the tiny dot was a much bigger, easily visible dot. This was a shocking example of how AI could be used to detect what the human eye cannot. We can use our knowledge, empowered by technology to more effectively screen for cancer.

LEVELS OF AI SOPHISTICATION IN ENDOSCOPY

If we were to come up with an AI guideline for endoscopy, it might look like this. Dr. Byrne reviewed these five levels of endoscopy automation.

- **Level 0:** No automation
- **Level 1 (low automation):** Assists the endoscopist during a procedure with basic features, such as recording time of scope insertion and withdrawal.
- **Level 2 (partial automation):** Identifies polyps at a broad level.
- **Level 3 (conditional automation):** Identifies most polyps, classifying them. The system shows what's cancerous and what's not.
- **Level 4 (high automation):** The system identifies all possible polyps. It shows with 100% accuracy those polyps that are cancerous and need removal. Doctor is required mainly to navigate the scope and remove polyps.
- **Level 5 (full automation):** The system performs endoscopy with no assistance of a doctor. And at all times. Think of this as a GI med bay like the one in the movie *Elysium*.

With breast cancer, AI cannot only examine mammograms, but it can also learn from disparate input data such as age, BMI, number of pregnancies, pre- or postmenopausal, GCPII C1561T gene, RFC1 G80A gene, cSHMT C1420T gene, folate, B2, B6, B12. And then it can come up with the likelihood of breast cancer in a certain patient. As you can imagine, it's challenging for a human to cull out dynamic insights from such large amounts of data.

Similarly, Google researchers applied artificial intelligence algorithms to CT scans to detect lung cancer. Usually, radiologists review CT scans to identify the presence of cancerous lesions. Missed cancers are not unusual. Google taught its AI about lung cancer using various types of scans and a large dataset. The system was 94% accurate across 6,716 cases. When compared to six radiologists, the system performed better than doctors. That's when researchers provided no previous scans. When a previous scan was available, AI and doctors performed at similar levels. What could the implications of early detection be for detecting and managing lung cancer? Could machine-based detection free up doctors to focus more deeply on patient care? Could it create an opportunity for early screening of populations?

According to the *Medical Futurist*, there are 16 FDA-approved AI algorithms for radiology as of mid-2019. Fields like radiology lend themselves to pattern recognition. That's because radiology requires a mastery of finding abnormalities in imaging (X-rays, CT scans, ultrasounds, and MRIs). It's an area that neural networks can get good at quickly, especially with the aid of large datasets.

I spoke to Ira Bahr, chief commercial officer of AliveCor, about technology disruptions in medicine. AliveCor develops wearable EKG devices and competes with the Apple Watch.

He said, "There is a growing consensus that machines are actually not just doing a competent job in reading X-rays, but they do a superior job."

Finally, a Brooklyn-based startup called auggi is using deep learning to classify poop photos. The startup aims to classify these photos using the Bristol stool scale. The Bristol stool scale classifies feces into seven types—from sausage-shaped to hard lumps. Using stool images, auggi becomes a digital coach for gut health. Yes, we are entering a strange, new world where even poop has the potential to be digitized, transmitted, and analyzed.

TAKEAWAYS (AI IN GI)

You are already deeply immersed in AI. Google Maps tells you about traffic that you can't see. Uber finds a cab near you. Netflix recommends movies that you are likely to enjoy. Amazon predicts your buying patterns. Siri plays your favorite songs. Alexa switches off lights before you go to sleep.

With applications like Maps, AI is so pervasive that you don't even notice the technology. Startups like Waze built themselves on top of Google Maps to even tell you where a traffic cop is standing. Waze is now owned by Google.

According to Dr. Byrne, there are more than 100 AI applications in the works for gastroenterology. In 2020, we will see the first set of FDA approvals for AI solutions in GI. That's when the rubber meets the road.

Meanwhile, in Europe, Medtronic plans to distribute an AI-based colonoscopy system called GI Genius. The product acts as a "second observer" during polyp detection. The company expects to roll out the product in the US during the second half of 2020.

It's likely that you'll soon get to test-drive AI in an endoscopy room somewhere. It might tell you to slow down your scope time. It might show you a polyp you missed and urge you to improve your ADR (adenoma detection rate). Even before you do, the tool might classify a polyp and indicate what it might be. You might like it or you might not. But that won't stop AI from embedding itself deeply into the field of endoscopy.

With these initial experiments, more researchers will venture into AI in GI. The GI tract is huge and covers many organs. Solutions that are in the works barely scratch the surface of what's possible. According to Dr. Byrne, the following areas show promise: polyp detection, differentiation, Barrett's esophagus, early gastric cancer, IBD mucosal healing and dyspepsia, pancreatic cysts/cancers, robotic/endoscopic surgery, and capsule endoscopy.

Say insurance companies start paying for colonoscopies based on ADR. Then AI in GI would accelerate. That's because most endoscopists would then rely on a tool to guide them toward improving their ADR. If that happens, then AI in the endoscopy room would be as pervasive as Google Maps in an Uber cab. It will become so ubiquitous that you will no longer notice the technology.

Ask yourself, How could you take advantage of AI to consistently deliver a high ADR outcome in your surgery center? How could you use high ADR scores as proof of quality to negotiate better insurance rates or improve your positioning in the market? Explore AI tools that are pervasive in other specialties. Look into AI tools that automate repeatable administrative transactions that could save you money. Or tools for image recognition—something that could read a doctor's handwritten notes and save you time. Review Amazon Comprehend Medical, a machine learning tool that extracts information from unstructured text. Read through healthcare use cases of Microsoft Azure's machine learning capability. Connect these dots back to GI and to your practice.

That's how you *scope forward*. By changing the questions you ask. By experimenting and building familiarity with new technology. By moving from a feeling of concern about the future to a feeling of excitement. We will delve more deeply into asking the right questions in part 4 as we progress toward Gastroenterology 2.0.

THE MICROBIOME TO INGESTIBLES

Exponential technologies don't stop with DNA testing and AI. There's plenty more. In their latest book, *The Future Is Faster Than You Think*, Peter Diamandis and Steven Kotler talk about three aspects of medical treatment being reinvented. First, sensors, networks, and AI are changing medical diagnostics. Second, robotics and 3D printing are changing procedures. Third, AI, genomics and quantum computing are transforming care itself.

As you read through this roundup of exponential technologies, ask how you could take advantage of these developments. Could your future practice revenues come from the microbiome or virtual reality? At a minimum, what steps could you take to implement telemedicine for chronic GI disease patients?

THE MICROBIOME

Directly relevant to gastroenterology is the microbiome. It's only recently that we've discovered that 90% of our DNA is bacterial. In 2018, 2,400 clinical trials tested microbiome-connected therapies. The industry itself is expected to expand to $3.2 billion by 2024.

Take a look at these microbiome startups in the GI space:

- Eligo Bioscience—a biotechnology company that develops biotherapeutics for editing the microbiome
- EpiBiome—a microbiome engineering company that tackles the challenge of antibiotic resistance
- Symbiotic Health—a biotechnology company that develops novel therapies for C. difficile (inflammation of the colon) by restoring the protective bacteria
- Biosys Health—a company modulating the gut microbiome by developing oral immune therapies
- Evolve BioSystems—a company developing products to establish, restore, and maintain the infant gut microbiome
- SciBac—a company strengthening the microbiome by creating live biotherapeutics that treat antibiotic resistance
- Finch Therapeutics—a company that develops novel and advanced microbiome-based therapies
- Synthetic Biologics—a company that works to preserve the microbiome and restore patient health

As with genetic editing, the future may offer the possibility to alter the microbiome. For more, read Josiah Zayner's biohacking story in chapter 4.

SENSORS

In 2018, a group developed an ingestible sensor to detect GI bleeding. Ingestibles are pill-sized electronics. Some aim to track gut gases as a proxy for bacterial biomass and even

Crohn's disease. Researchers are working on a wearable device that tracks electrical activity of the digestive system. Algorithms then listen to these electrical signals and flag abnormalities.

A team funded by the National Institutes of Health is developing magnetic colonoscopy. In this approach, an endoscopist uses a magnet to control a camera-equipped device inside the gut. Proteus, an FDA-approved sensor, keeps track of a patient's medication adherence from inside the stomach. Ask in what types of cases you might prescribe an ingestible?

ROBOTICS

At Intuitive Surgical's training center in California, I got to play with a surgical robot. The "training" involved picking up colorful rings and placing them on spikes. Robotic arms with haptic feedback (related to the sense of touch) and magnified lenses supported the activity. I felt like a hybrid Iron Man with upgraded human abilities.

Advances in robotics help surgeons do what is otherwise challenging. Sophisticated mechanics make procedures such as Natural Orifice Transluminal Endoscopic Surgery (NOTES) possible. As the name indicates, NOTES helps you navigate using natural orifices of the body. Minimally invasive procedures such as this are on the rise because, among other things, they reduce hospitalization. Consider a procedure such as Peroral Endoscopic Myotomy (POEM) that relies on sophisticated endoscopy technology to make incisions in the inner lining of the esophagus.

Fields of robotics, microinstrumentation, sensors, and

mechatronics are converging. As this happens, we will see further advancements in endoscopic surgery.

IMAGING

One of the biggest announcements at the latest CES was the 8K TV. An 8K display resolution is the next generation after 4K. And somewhere between 4K and 8K pixels, the human eye can't tell the difference between real and virtual. Imagine what 8K technology could mean for endoscopic surgery. In case you are wondering if there are already such endoscope systems, the answer is yes. A Japanese startup, Kairos, launched the 8K endoscope in 2017, but it is yet to roll out.

A drop in the cost of electronics will advance imaging technologies further. The progress of imaging will increase the scope of endoscopic surgery.

VIRTUAL REALITY AND AUGMENTED REALITY

A few years ago, my team tinkered with Google Glass. We extended our EHR enki's access to Glass before dropping the idea. We experimented with extracting stored endoscopic images onto Google's augmented reality glasses. The problem was that seeing endoscopic images via Glass wasn't a pressing need for our clients back then.

Virtual reality (VR) and augmented reality (AR) are growing exponentially. VR is a fully immersive digital experience. AR is about seeing virtual elements in a physical world. As sales of VR headsets increase and costs drop, we will see rapid growth in this field.

In gastroenterology, expect to see active use of VR and AR in endoscopy training. The technology also helps in visualizing diseased organs before surgery. VR applications help in therapy adherence too. When patients see what's wrong and what effect a certain treatment can have, they tend to comply better. Finally, VR/AR is known to rewire neural pathways for recovery. This helps in not only changing behavior but also how patients respond to pain.

TELEMEDICINE

Mobile technology, VR, AR, imaging, and telephony accelerate telemedicine. One of the first moves of Amazon Care was to launch a virtual clinic for its employees.

A recent article by Lancet revealed that only 7.9% of gastroenterologists reported using telemedicine. Yet, in a review of 20 studies in GI, half reported significant improvements based on telemedicine use. Telemedicine serves as low-hanging fruit for those of us in GI to embrace exponential technologies.

FOOD

Doctors prescribe diets such as the low FODMAP for irritable bowel syndrome (IBS). But how do patients ensure they are eating the right foods? Well, now there are food scanners in the market to analyze the food that goes into your mouth. For patients with celiac disease, there are gluten sensors. Then there are plenty of apps to help you track what you consume. Food-tech is hot—especially in the space of plant-based meat (look up "Beyond Meat") and 3D printed food. Advances in food will impact what patients expect from a GI consultation. As patient expectations from healthcare evolve, more and more patients will seek therapy via food to manage GI conditions. (We will discuss more about patient behavior in chapter 4.)

3D PRINTING

Three-dimensional printing is going beyond printing models or even beyond printing food. The field aims to print tissue of organs. Gastroenterologists are currently experimenting with 3D, printing custom endoscopic caps. These are accessories that attach to a scope in order to remove difficult-to-target lesions. Expect 3D printing to play a role in four areas: bioprinting of tissue, modeling before surgery, printing surgical instruments, and custom prosthetics.

DRONES

Healthcare logistics is a $70 billion market. There are many drone startups that are working on the delivery of medical samples. From blood, stool, medicines, and first aid to organs. Some drones even plan to deliver humans.

In May 2019, Zipline, a drone company that started by delivering blood in Rwanda, was valued at $1.2 billion. In October 2019, UPS gained FAA approval to deliver biological samples via drone across a hospital campus. Google's Project Wing plans to use drones to deliver medical supplies in conjunction with Walgreens.

PRESCRIBE AN APP

There'll soon be apps that can listen and diagnose your cough.

Meanwhile, in GI, Rx.Health helps you prescribe an app to patients. Many times, inadequate bowel prep by patients aborts endoscopies. To avoid the problem, Arizona Centers for Digestive Health "prescribed" an app called Rx.Health's Digital Endoscopy Pathway. It reduced their aborted procedures by 50%. The app digitally guides patients through a series of steps to improve bowel prep. In partnership with the American Gastroenterological Association (AGA), Rx.Health is expanding this initiative nationally. We will see more such targeted apps across the GI spectrum.

IMPLICATIONS FOR GASTROENTEROLOGY

As you can see, exponential technologies don't scale in an isolated fashion. One technology accelerates the other. They *converge*. For example, the LIDAR scanner dropped in price and increased in performance. Improvement of LIDAR itself led to self-driving cars becoming a reality.

Thinking about convergence, I wondered how DNA testing and AI would converge.

Here's what Dr. Byrne said: "I don't see DNA testing and AI as parallel fields. I see them as hopefully evolving in tandem and complementing each other. If you have a high level of accuracy in something that could be a truly robust mass screening tool, something that's much less invasive than doing an endoscopic procedure, then you could filter patients appropriately based on that test. With more tests, we'd assume that accuracy and performance is only going to get better."

DNA testing and AI will settle into a common workflow.

That thinking applies to not just DNA testing and AI, but many of the technologies we examined in this chapter. Gastroenterology as a field is in its early stages of implementing these exponential technologies. People who take advantage of these technologies will *scope forward* and build practices of the future. If you ignore them now, it becomes increasingly difficult to catch up later. Ultimately, that'll hurt patient care. Exponential technologies are moving targets. They don't wait. They keep doubling in performance.

Let's look at a few implications:

1. Liquid biopsy will accelerate based on DNA testing. Optical biopsy will accelerate based on AI and imaging. That, in turn, will disrupt the field of cancer screening.
2. Improvement of power supply in sensors makes ingestibles feasible. It also accelerates magnetic colonoscopy and makes drone delivery possible.
3. Greater computing capacity makes machine learning possible. That, in turn, accelerates our ability to program genes. Improvement in genetic editing could influence how we manipulate the microbiome. It'll accelerate the field of genetic engineering. It can help us develop personalized drugs.
4. Improvements in resolution and imaging will improve virtual reality hardware. That'll change what constitutes endoscopy training.
5. Demand for noninvasive procedures will accelerate the progress of robotics and imaging. Acceleration of robotics will advance the field of endoscopic surgery.
6. Big data analysis will help us crunch vast amounts of disparate data. That will change how we arrive at medical diagnosis.

7. Improvements in deep learning will disrupt pattern recognition. That will disrupt fields of pathology and radiology that rely on interpreting patterns.
8. Smaller sensors will help us capture more data from our bodies. More biodata will improve sensitivity of algorithms. Better algorithms will change our use of AI in medicine.

Today's GI practices largely rely on colonoscopies and associated ancillary revenues (anesthesia and pathology). I've found that the dominant thinking amongst most GI doctors is that this model will continue into the future. But as we saw throughout this chapter, the older GI models are likely to be disrupted. When new technology becomes dominant, older models will go the way of Kodak. Moreover, it'll happen faster than you might imagine.

The task ahead of you is to reimagine the future of GI over the next decade. Ask, How do you take advantage of these exponential technologies and not be disrupted by them? Fold that future back to the present. Move in the direction of what you'd like to see happen. That's how you *scope forward*. (More on this in part 4 of the book.)

Not too long ago, I was trekking around Sequoia National Park. I was taken in by those gigantic trees. Over thousands of years old, they seemed like humanity's ancestors. What was most fascinating was the link between fire and sequoia regeneration.

The sequoias do everything to protect themselves from fire damage. For example, they develop thick barks. But it is the fire that causes them to release and germinate seeds. The seeds that will bring the next generation of sequoias and ensure the survival of the species. The fire also kills competing plants and helps with the growth of the young sequoia seedlings. The same fire that can destroy the sequoias is also needed to sustain them. That sounds a lot like what's happening in gastroenterology today. We need disruption to protect ourselves, no matter how much we might dislike the idea of the "fire."

While these exponential technologies seem disruptive, they can result in fresher growth. I explored the idea with Ira Bahr, chief commercial officer of AliveCor. The company developed the Kardia, a single lead EKG device. Using AI, their platform ended up detecting hyperkalemia (elevated potassium) from electrocardiograms.

He said, "What we found in cardiology, for example, is that practitioners can benefit financially because you are finding more cases that require intervention."

Wouldn't the same thinking apply to gastroenterology? Could these disruptive technologies hold the key to the next iteration of GI?

By avoiding disruption, the field of gastroenterology risks becoming a forest that can't survive. By embracing disruption like a forest fire, gastroenterology will protect itself. In turn, it'll save more lives.

What follows now are two interesting interviews from the industry. I asked Mark Stenhouse and Dr. Paul Limburg from Exact Sciences the questions you might have about Cologuard—about the present and future and how their growth might impact gastroenterologists. Similarly, I was curious to know Dr. Michael Byrne's take on how quickly and deeply artificial intelligence will penetrate gastroenterology. Dr. Byrne is an expert in AI and interventional endoscopy. His interview freewheels into the ethics of AI and stitching DNA testing and AI into everyday GI workflow.

INTERVIEW WITH MARK STENHOUSE AND DR. PAUL LIMBURG, COLOGUARD

Mark Stenhouse is the General Manager and Dr. Paul Limburg is the Chief Medical Officer of the Screening Business Unit at Exact Sciences.

Q: How's Cologuard 2.0 going to be different from the existing Cologuard test?

Mark Stenhouse: The overarching objective of Cologuard 2.0 is to improve diagnostic accuracy. We shared promising data with a novel panel of molecular markers at ACG 2019. We have also initiated a prospective trial to generate additional data needed to establish the performance of a next-generation Cologuard test.

Dr. Paul Limburg: The Cologuard 2.0 prospective trial is registered on ClinicalTrials.gov. Exact Sciences is committed to ongoing quality improvement. We want to make sure that Cologuard's performance is as good as it can be.

Q: In your 2019 Q3 earnings call, you mentioned that you are working on a blood test. Is that a liquid biopsy test that can detect multiple cancers at the same time?

Stenhouse: In the prospective clinical trial we are currently enrolling, we will be collecting both stool and blood from consenting patients. That evidence will allow us to continue to advance our research for a blood-based colorectal cancer screening test. At the same time, we have continued confidence in Cologuard because of its ability to detect early-stage cancer and precancer.

Dr. Limburg: With the longstanding collaboration between Exact Sciences and Mayo Clinic, marker discovery efforts are well underway for about 15 of the deadliest cancers. The marker discovery research looks very promising. We plan to use the best-performing markers to develop clinically impactful, blood-based assays, such as the HCC surveillance test we plan to launch in the second half of 2020.

Q: How does your approach vary from that of a company like Guardant? In the future, would multiple approaches to liquid biopsy coexist?

Dr. Limburg: There are wonderful scientists and several companies all trying to develop tests to reach and screen even more patients. We are all trying to understand cancer detection at a biological level and ask the question: can we do this in a better way than we do today? There's a strong sense of collaboration in terms of trying to figure out the high-level road map for liquid biopsy. Obviously, each group is taking a little bit different tact in terms of marker discovery and assay development. We are confident that the knowledge we gained in the development of Cologuard makes us well-positioned to develop innovative, blood-based assays that help to change the status quo in cancer screening. Ultimately, our goal is to develop new tests that have performance characteristics that are attractive to both patients and physicians.

Q: There are announcements that you plan to capture 40% of the colon cancer screening market. What are the implications of that growth for gastroenterologists in practice today?

Stenhouse: Our mission at Exact Sciences is to reduce the cancer burden. For colorectal cancer, too many people are currently unscreened. Experts agree that having a choice of screening options is helpful in increasing patient participation. In that context, we believe that Cologuard and colonoscopy are both complementary and necessary to reach our shared goals with gastroenterologists. All patients with a positive Cologuard need to have a diagnostic colonoscopy, so in order to effectively realize the benefits of Cologuard-based screening, we need to continue working closely together to improve public health.

We appreciate that there's concern and we're committed to continue gathering data from real-world studies, modeling analyses, and other sources in partnership with the GI community. Nearly 50% of Cologuard patients who responded to a survey are previously unscreened. Our relationship with gastroenterologists should be viewed as collaborative, not competitive.

Dr. Limburg: The stark reality is that approximately one-third of the US population over the age of 50 is eligible for screening and hasn't yet been screened. If you add in patients between the ages of 45 to 49 as some guideline groups recommend, there are another 19–20 million screen-eligible individuals. So, say there are 50 million people who need to be screened.

Research studies and clinical experience clearly demonstrate that there's not a one-size-fits-all in colon cancer screening. Cologuard is endorsed by all major guideline groups and has met the highest evidentiary standards that the federal government employs. It's important to recognize that the DeeP-C study involving 10,000 individuals was a major undertaking. These data show that Cologuard has high sensitivity in detecting cancer, early stage cancer and premalignant lesions. However, no test is perfect. Even colonoscopy has its own limitations. The key message is that more people need to be screened, and there is more than one option.

We really need to work as a community to increase screening with the ultimate objective of serving patients.

Q: Exponential technologies in other fields come down in price when performance improves. For example, full genome sequencing has dropped to $1,000. This year, Veritas Genetics priced it at $600. It'll soon be $200. Genetic testing seems to be at an inflection point. However, Cologuard continues to price itself at a $600 price point. What's the underlying thinking with the pricing model?

Stenhouse: We think our price position makes sense based on the value Cologuard brings relative to other noninvasive tests. Embedded within that price is our patient navigation service, which includes compliance reminders and 24-7 support.

Q: What are some steps that Exact Sciences and the GI community could take to work collaboratively and make this a win-win for everyone?

Dr. Limburg: We are actively working to build stronger relationships with all the major GI societies to find opportunities for increased collaboration, with a mission-first focus. Our common objective is to get more people screened using appropriate, effective strategies.

There are some near-term opportunities—the first one is education and awareness. We both want to educate on the endorsed options for average-risk screening. When they should be applied and when they shouldn't be applied. We must ask how we can work with our primary care colleagues to make sure that conversations happen in a way where a patient's choice can be also followed.

There's also more to be done to remove legislative barriers involving patient cost-sharing policies. There are also research activities and clinical testing of new technology advances where we can work on together. In summary, education, awareness, and legislation supporting access to screening would be areas where we see urgent needs for Exact Sciences to work more closely with the gastroenterology community.

Stenhouse: We are trying to reach out to the GI societies broadly to focus on what the primary challenge is. Choice matters. Having a choice of a stool test brings unscreened people into the fold. From my perspective, our focus is to work in collaboration. We are educating millions of patients about the importance of colorectal cancer screening through our Cologuard television ads. That has raised awareness of colorectal cancer. That's also beneficial to the GI community.

Dr. Limburg: We are committed to the mission of getting more patients screened. We are delighted to work more closely with our gastroenterology colleagues and advance our shared goal of reducing the colorectal cancer burden.

INTERVIEW WITH DR. MICHAEL BYRNE, SATISFAI HEALTH, AI4GI

Dr. Michael Byrne is CEO of Satisfai Health and Founder of the ai4gi joint venture. He's also a Clinical Professor of Medicine and an Interventional Gastroenterologist at Vancouver General Hospital. Satisfai applies artificial intelligence to medical image analysis and other areas in gastroenterology.

Q: How did you get started with your startup, Satisfai, and the initiative with Olympus, ai4gi?

Dr. Michael Byrne: By training, I'm a GI physician with particular interest in interventional endoscopy. About seven or eight years ago, I was reading about training the human eye better to do an optical biopsy. Then there were already groups who were working in AI. I thought, why are we trying to improve the human eye? We already have facial and fingerprint recognition. Surely, we can employ some form of AI in optical biopsy.

I was able to form a collaboration with AI experts maybe about five years ago. That's the ai4gi group, which is a joint venture between my company, Satisfai, and an AI group in Montreal called Imagia—ai4gi is also the group working with Olympus.

Independently at Satisfai we are working on many other areas of GI. As you know, GI is huge—not just in terms of anatomy but also in the disease spectrum. There are so many pathologies and anatomies to interrogate with AI. Even just from an imaging standpoint. A lot of our focus has been endoscopic imaging. But if you look through the whole GI tract from top to bottom, you've got precancerous lesions in the esophagus—Barrett's, esophageal cancer—small bowel disease such as Crohn's. Then you have colon polyps, colon cancer and of course IBD. Beyond that, there's all the pancreatic and liver pathology opportunities. I know there's ongoing work to use AI in real-time EUS evaluation, for example.

The gastrointestinal anatomy is huge, and the array of pathology is huge too. It's a great space to be in. There's so much opportunity.

Q: What's "the forest from the trees" view of AI in gastroenterology? Where are we going?

Dr. Byrne: AI is already here. We've progressed from the point of using AI to look at still images and perfect images. We are at the point of using AI to arrive at some sort of diagnostic solutions. Now we have tools for real-time diagnosis in GI.

In the next few years, it'll move toward disease detection and differentiation, or optical biopsy. We'll be able to use a lot of the patient data that right now is hard for humans to interpret. We will be able to put all that data together. Genomic data, patient characteristics, lifestyle, diagnostic and imaging data, and so on. Then we can feed that data into a supercomputer algorithm and come up with current and future prognostic answers.

For example, in the field of IBD, we're moving quickly from being able to use imaging data with other metadata. We can predict how that patient is going to do on drug X in 12 months and in five years. Compare that to how we prescribe right now. These advances will play a big role in precision medicine.

In gastroenterology, AI will revolutionize endoscopic surgery. Future endoscopic surgeons will benefit from real-time tissue visualization, lesion detection, and differentiation. AI will also guide surgeons on what tools to use, what position to choose. For example, AI might guide on using the right kind of snare or forceps, and also to look at resection margins and so on.

Q: What's the extreme version or sci-fi version of where everything is going?

Dr. Byrne: The extreme version, which to many is the frightening version, is where robots or computers will take over our position as doctors. In gastroenterology, decisions around which drugs to use, whether somebody has a particular type of cancer or not will be made by computers without physician involvement.

We keep hearing about robotic surgery. Experts say that about 10–20% of surgeries will be performed by surgical robots. Will that be an assisted surgery? Or will that be a dedicated robot operating on a patient? That would be the sci-fi version. Who knows, maybe that's where it'll go. A lot of experts suggest strongly that we must always have a human in the loop. For medicine, that means having a physician in the loop to make decisions during a procedure or diagnosis or in training the algorithms.

Q: What kind of ethical challenges do you see as we advance to an AI future?

Dr. Byrne: If you consider an analogy with self-driving cars, there's a situation where a car guided by a computer has to make a decision in a snap moment. For example, the car has to make a choice between hitting 10 children on one side and killing the single occupant of the car on the other. There's no scenario where nobody gets hurt. So who makes that decision? Is it ethical for a computer to make that call?

There are scenarios where a computer has to decide whether a patient should be on drug A or drug B. Is that appropriate for a computer to make that choice? Is that decision based on cost of drugs or overall benefit to a particular individual?

There's also the concern of data security and traceability that we have to be careful about.

These are real ethical debates that we haven't even gotten close to solving yet.

It's a topic that needs to have input from physicians, regulatory authorities, ethics experts. As physicians, we are not experts in ethics. We haven't had to deal with these kinds of questions a lot. At least, not so far. Today, we will sit with our individual patients and make good and informed and human decisions with that patient. If we move that to the domain of computers, then of course that's a paradigm shift in terms of ethics. Are we as a society ready to use standalone decisions by AI, or are we taking its advice in the context of the patient and using our own thinking?

Q: From what you know, how many groups are working on AI in GI? Are we talking 10 or more?

Dr. Byrne: No, no, we are talking 10s or more, you know... maybe a 100, depending on how you define a group.

Given how much I've been writing in AI in the last few years, I get a lot of requests to review papers in the AI space. I get four or five review requests a month in various aspects of AI in the GI space. In a year alone, probably, I review about 50 to 60 papers in AI. That gives you an idea as to how many people are working in the GI space with artificial intelligence. Maybe even 100 initiatives is significantly lower than the true number. The appetite and the engagement in GI has exploded in the last two or three years.

Q: What's likely to happen in 2020?

Dr. Byrne: In terms of readiness for clinical reviews, we will see some AI-based solutions in the marketplace. We will move away from academic debates around what AI can do in GI to actually having some tools.

There'll be hurdles and I'm sure some issues. But there are already two or three or more tools in AI that will be approved by, for example, the FDA or by the European or Japanese regulatory authorities. It could be in the areas of colon polyps or Barrett's esophagus in particular.

When we finally see some of these solutions ready for us to use, that's when the lid comes off and we start to truly see the ramifications. Because as soon as people get their hands on these devices, we get real-life experiences. That's when we can improve the solutions, we can examine the barriers, figure what we need to add on. We need to start using these tools so that we can map out the future.

Q: Are the fields of DNA testing and AI going to merge and result in some kind of an accelerated exponential effect?

Dr. Byrne: I don't see DNA testing and AI as parallel fields. I see them as hopefully evolving in tandem and complementing each other. If you have a high level of accuracy in something that could be a truly robust mass screening tool, something that's much less invasive than doing an endoscopic procedure, then you could filter patients appropriately based on that test. With more tests, we'd assume that accuracy and performance is only going to get better. And of course, companies in that space are not sitting still. They are evolving their work.

You can use those tools (such as DNA tests) as triage type tests, and then for higher-risk patients, you can employ AI solutions that we've been working on. You could perform a colonoscopy with AI assistance to help detect lesions and polyps in the colon, for example.

Everything that helps us increase our Adenoma Detection Rate [ADR] benefits the patient. Then you can further determine what kind of tissue you're actually looking at using AI. Then that, in itself, opens up another realm of possibilities. As we go to the future, if there are better high-definition scopes with better lighting, if there's better magnification, we can add AI to it.

I work in Canada, and a lot of colonoscopy here is based on results of a FIT test. If the FIT test is negative, they come back in two years and repeat it. They don't automatically go for colonoscopy. If you have an even more accurate and predictive stool-based tests that are better than a FIT test, why would we not use that? And reserve interventions such as colonoscopy for patients who truly need it? We can also use algorithms to predict how a patient might do in the future based on DNA test results.

I don't see the technologies going in parallel or competing. What I see is really—ultimately—all of these things as part of one big workflow. It's all complementary.

Q: What advice do you have for those who might be opposed to AI?

Dr. Byrne: AI is coming. Certainly, AI is coming to medicine. AI is coming to our space of GI and, in particular—right now—to endoscopy. To those who are concerned about AI, I would see the reasons behind the concern. Is it territorial impact or threat to their practice? During one of my talks, a physician asked if AI would slow him down during colonoscopies because it's looking for different types of polyps and so on. We must ask, Why is ADR variable from one endoscopist to the other in the first place? We have a recommended metric. You should be aiming at an ADR that's greater than 35% or 40%. The AI might tell you to slow down, look behind folds, and have a minimum withdrawal time of six minutes.

When something's not mandated, nobody is really supervising or implementing any measures based on those targets. AI can clearly help. In my opinion, in the near future, the paying authorities will mandate payment based on certain performance metrics. For example, if your ADR is 20%, they may not pay unless performance improves. Using an AI tool can help you achieve that.

If you can improve an endoscopist from a 20% ADR to 25%— that still may not be a great ADR—but it's still a win. We know that even a 1% increase in ADR decreases mortality for colon cancer by 3%.

The community needs to be educated about what AI can do. But you also have to see that some people are threatened because it impacts billing. And maybe they now would also need to review their performance.

For those who are threatened by AI, I'd say that it's coming anyway. So let's embrace it. Let's be real here. This is the 21st century. AI is already embedded in many aspects of our lives—for example, every time you use Siri on your phone.

If we let AI handle routine stuff, then you and I can have more time for patient interaction. We can be more involved.

CHAPTER 2

———

BUSINESS CONSOLIDATION

We are in the midst of a massive wave of consolidation in gastroenterology. Often when we are immersed in a wave, we don't realize what it's about. We need to zoom out and look around. Not only that—we must also understand how we got here and where we are headed so that we can make more conscious decisions about the path we take, as individuals, and as an industry. That's the discussion we'll have in this chapter.

In the beginning, gastroenterologists formed solo or small practices. Like Dr. Kadirawelpillai Iswara in Brooklyn, New York. He started a private practice with his mentor at a hospital and later branched off as a solo practitioner. Over time, his referral base grew. Doctors valued the outcomes of the procedures he performed. They kept him busy by sending patients his way. As he says, he was "at the right place at the right time."

I've known Dr. Iswara for more than a decade. His patients love him. His staff loves him. Even his vendors love him. Well into his 70s, he's as busy as ever. He loves what he does.

Once, he told me excitedly about the "big, big polyps" he removed that day at Maimonides Medical Center, where he serves as the director of gastroenterology. Another time, he talked about his trip to Ecuador. He'd often drop me off at the subway in a metallic-blue Tesla.

I'm sure you know a doctor like Dr. Iswara. They seemed to have gotten it right. They are the ones who've usually inspired others to join medicine. Like Dr. Iswara's nephew, Dr. Naresh Gunaratnam, who also became a gastroenterologist.

By the time Dr. Gunaratnam joined gastroenterology, the specialty was already on its next iteration. For several years, he's been part of Huron Gastroenterology, a group of 18 physicians in Michigan. He's the chair of data analytics for the Digestive Health Physicians Association (DHPA). He also runs an orphanage called Grace in Sri Lanka. Recently, he started a subscription-based wellness initiative within his practice to tackle obesity (which we'll discuss more in chapter 4).

In 2019, the American Gastroenterological Association (AGA) honored Dr. Gunaratnam with a distinguished clinician award. While accepting his award, he spoke of the impact that Dr. Iswara had on him and his friends: "Ironically, there were five kids that played together. All from Sri Lanka. All of us became gastroenterologists because of him! I'm here because of him."

In previous eras, Dr. Gunaratnam might have opened his own private practice, but even older doctors who went that route can see how things have changed. I asked Dr. Iswara if he would go solo in New York in today's environment.

He responded, "You can't open a practice with your name today. Because most of the referrals start in the hospital and flow into your private practice. HMO plans won't take you in. There's intense competition."

So how did things change so much in just one generation of doctors? To share costs, solo practices became small groups with two or three doctors. Those groups became midsize practices, such as Dr. Gunaratnam's group, Huron Gastroenterology in Michigan. A few midsize groups became larger, like GI Associates in Mississippi or MNGI Digestive Health in Minnesota (covered in chapter 8). In the last few years, private equity entered the market by investing in large groups. To make them even bigger.

That changed the game.

In 2016, Audax Private Equity became the first fund to step into gastroenterology. They invested in Gastro Health. That same year, they exited their investment in a dermatology company called Advanced Dermatology. They had held onto the investment in the dermatology company for five years. If you observe, what Audax did was reapply its investment philosophy to GI from other specialties, such as dermatology or dental.

A few years ago, I chatted with Dr. James Leavitt. He's one of the main leaders behind the expansion of Gastro Health. He had dropped by my company's booth at a conference. Dr. Leavitt pulled up a barstool and shared his vision for a larger—much larger—GI group. Back then, there was no word of private equity.

AUDAX'S PORTFOLIO, FROM WOMEN'S HEALTH TO UROLOGY

1. Great Expressions Dental Centers. Dental. Invested in 2008. Exited in 2011.
2. Vision Group Holdings. Refractive surgery. Invested in 2014. Exited.
3. Meridian Behavior Health. Addiction treatment. Invested in 2015.
4. Solis Mammography. Mammography. Invested in 2015. Exited in 2018.
5. United Urology. Urology. Invested in 2016.
6. Axia Women's Health. OB-GYN. Invested in 2017.
7. Phoenix Rehabilitation and Health Services, Inc. Physical therapy. Invested in 2018.

When I interviewed him recently for this book, his vision had already become a reality by taking steady steps toward consolidation. Talking about the current environment, he quoted Sun Tzu. In *The Art of War*, he says, "Strategy without tactics is the slowest route to victory. Tactics without strategy is the noise before defeat." (You can read Dr. Leavitt's interview in chapter 9.)

War or not, the private equity–funded platforms are rapidly consolidating the market. Here are the major deals as of early 2020.

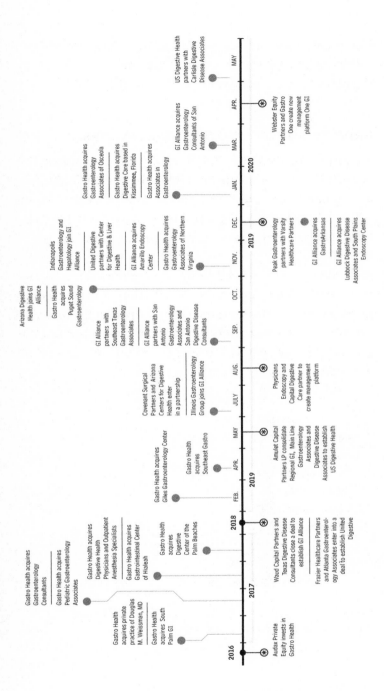

Gastro Health acquires Gastroenterology Consultants

Gastro Health acquires Pediatric Gastroenterology Associates

Gastro Health acquires private practice of Douglas M. Weissman, MD

Gastro Health acquires South Palm GI

Gastro Health acquires Digestive Health Physicians and Outpatient Anesthesia Specialists

Gastro Health acquires Gastrointestinal Center of Hialeah

Gastro Health acquires Digestive Center of the Palm Beaches

Gastro Health acquires Giles Gastroenterology Center

Gastro Health acquires Southeast Gastro

Covenant Surgical Partners and Arizona Centers for Digestive Health enter in a partnership

Illinois Gastroenterology Group joins GI Alliance

GI Alliance partners with Southeast Texas Gastroenterology Associates

GI Alliance partners with San Antonio Gastroenterology Associates and San Antonio Digestive Disease Consultants

Arizona Digestive Health joins GI Alliance

Gastro Health acquires Puget Sound Gastroenterology

Indianapolis Gastroenterology and Hepatology join GI Alliance

United Digestive partners with Center for Digestive & Liver Health

GI Alliance acquires Amarillo Endoscopy Center

Gastro Health acquires Gastroenterology Associates of Northern Virginia

Gastro Health acquires Gastroenterology Associates of Osceola

Gastro Health acquires Digestive Care based in Kissimmee, Florida

Gastro Health acquires Associates in Gastroenterology

GI Alliance acquires Gastroenterology Consultants of San Antonio

US Digestive Health partners with Carlisle Digestive Disease Associates

Audax Private Equity invests in Gastro Health

Waud Capital Partners and Texas Digestive Disease Consultants close a deal to establish GI Alliance

Frazier Healthcare Partners and Atlanta Gastroenterology Associates enter into a deal to establish United Digestive

Amulet Capital Partners LP consolidate Regional GI, Main Line Gastroenterology Associates and Digestive Disease Associates to establish US Digestive Health

Physicians Endoscopy and Capital Digestive Care partner to create management platform

Peak Gastroenterology partners with Varsity Healthcare Partners

GI Alliance acquires GastroArkansas

GI Alliance acquires Lubbock Digestive Disease Associates and South Plains Endoscopy Center

Webster Equity Partners and Gastro One create new management platform One GI

2016 2017 2018 FEB. APR. MAY JULY AUG. SEP. OCT. NOV. DEC. JAN. MAR. APR. MAY
       2019   2019   2020

Gastroenterology isn't isolated in its movement toward consolidation. As you'll soon see all of healthcare is. Let's review the play of private equity in other medical specialties.

PRIVATE EQUITY IN OTHER SPECIALTIES

We must look over the shoulders of other specialties. Not because the specialties are like GI but because their investors are similar. Thus, investment philosophies and exit horizons will be similar. As of Q3 2019, there have been 187 M&A transactions in the physician practice and dental areas.

According to an article in the *Journal of the American Medical Association* (JAMA), the distribution of private equity investments in 2018 is outlined below. Apparently, 14% of all private equity investments are in healthcare. That's sizable given that private equity invested $63 billion into businesses in 2018.

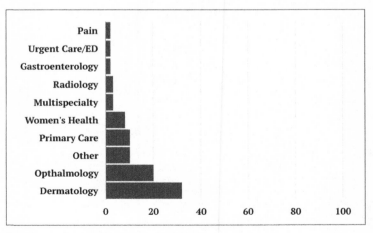

Distribution of private equity across specialties

As you can see, dermatology and ophthalmology led the pack. According to another paper in JAMA, 17 private equity–backed platforms acquired 184 dermatology practices between May 2012 to May 2018. These acquired practices represented 381 dermatology clinics. In 2012, there were only five acquisitions in dermatology. That increased to 59 in 2017. By the first half of 2018, there were already 34 acquisitions.

Dr. Sailesh Konda is an assistant clinical professor of dermatology at the University of Florida Health System. He wrote a paper in a dermatology journal that implied that private equity firms acquired practices that perform procedures with high billing. The *New York Times* said that Dr. Konda's paper made private equity "furious." Per his analysis, there were 33 private equity–backed dermatology groups as of November 2018. Two of which failed.

When you review ophthalmology, there was one acquisition in 2012. By 2016, there were 13 and by 2017, there were 37. As of October 2018, the specialty had seen 50 acquisitions. That's a total of 123 acquisitions, according to Physicians First Healthcare Partners.

Let's now compare early private equity led M&A activity in dermatology and ophthalmology with gastroenterology.

	DERMATOLOGY	OPHTHALMOLOGY
2012	5	1
2013	7	2
2014	13	3
2015	26	4
2016	40	5
	GASTROENTEROLOGY	
2016	1	
2017	2	
2018	2	
2019	16	

There were 16 private equity transactions in GI in 2019, compared to two in 2018. You can't help but notice that the pace is different with GI.

My sources tell me there are at least 20 deals in the works in gastroenterology as of early 2020. Most of the large groups are nearly locked in. What remains are several midsize and small practices. We will no doubt continue to hear announcements throughout 2020 and beyond. Several GI groups will join existing private equity–backed platforms. There will also be newer types of platforms that will take shape.

PRIVATE EQUITY BEYOND 2020

Private equity will do what private equity does. They will buy, build, reshape, and resell practices within a three- to seven-year horizon—all with the goal of making a return on their investment. At that point, a private equity fund is likely to recapitalize the platform with another private equity fund.

The newer private equity fund will repeat the process from that point to the next three- to seven-year transition point. That's how private equity works.

If that were to happen with GI, we can expect the first set of exits from 2022 to 2026. That's when newer players will enter the market.

Jerry Tillinger, CEO of US Digestive Health, one of the more recently formed PE platforms, said this about private equity: "It's a value creation vehicle that helps bring doctors together economically. In a way that those personalities and personal philosophy issues don't necessarily drive the business, at least not in the same way as it used to. So I see this model having legs. I see more and more doctors joining this kind of structure for the duration of their careers." (You'll find his interview in chapter 9.)

THE PPM DEBACLE OF THE 1990S

While talking about private equity, many doctors bring up physician practice management companies (PPMs). It's important to be aware of this topic so that the GI industry avoids the same mistakes that PPMs made.

The PPM space imploded around 1998 and took a few more years after to almost disappear. Oddly, the reasons that PPMs boomed are similar to the reasons private equity is proliferating now. PPMs aimed to consolidate fragmented medical practices. Several doctors sold out to them. The PPMs brought in fresh capital and management talent. They added new ancillaries and tried to negotiate better contracts with insurance companies.

Several of the PPMs were listed on Wall Street. Doctors were given stock in the PPMs, and everyone expected a large exit when the company launched an IPO. But the PPMs overpaid for the practices they acquired. They were in a rush to add new practices so they could demonstrate growth and higher revenues to the market. And while PPMs charged hefty management fees (around 15%–20% of net income), they struggled to run medical businesses. They used confusing accounting practices, like amortizing the cost of acquisition over decades so they could make the company look more profitable than it actually was. In the end, they struggled to execute on their business plans. The market didn't take that lightly. PPM stocks tanked. They ran out of money. When doctors started leaving, they were sued by the PPMs.

Many attorneys and consultants drafted post-PPM-era business plans to help doctors rebuild their lives. Doctors wanted to buy back their practices. They raised capital from hospitals, real estate trusts, and national finance companies to do so. Everyone moved on. A *Medical Economics* article called "Physician Practice Management Companies...Going...Going..." from March 2001 had this to say: "If nothing else, PPMs will be remembered years from now for their sheer destructiveness."

I asked Dr. James Leavitt of Gastro Health the question that must occupy you right now. *Is this current private equity wave going to turn out like the PPMs of the 1990s?*

This is what he said: "PPMs in the 1990s were different. At that time, the PPMs were buying groups randomly. They didn't have the types of platforms and technologies that we have today that could consolidate the back-end office. They didn't have EHRs. They didn't have sophisticated cloud-based practice management and revenue cycle systems. They couldn't really get economies of scale. They weren't really consolidating in a way that consolidation really means— *building something better*. Not just putting things together, but to get better. That's why you can't compare what's happening now with what was happening then."

I asked him what could go wrong with private equity.

Dr. Leavitt said, "When a PE platform just stacks EBITDA, adds doctors, adds groups, without trying to build a better company, that could cause a problem in the future."

I took that to mean if we make the same mistakes as the PPMs without a clear strategy, private equity will run the risk of failure.

I asked a similar question to Dr. Lawrence Kosinski, the former managing partner of Illinois Gastroenterology Group (IGG). He was one of three members to facilitate its private equity transaction. IGG joined GI Alliance in July 2019. What could go wrong with private equity?

This was his reaction: "When you're in private practice, you're a doctor, and your mission is to provide quality care and be attentive toward your patients. But if you're an owner in a PE-funded Management Service Organization (MSO), and you're also practicing in that MSO, you have to make sure to keep your ducks in line. Because your mission may change. You want to make sure this thing gets sold off in a few years and you get a major multiple. That's when there will be potential conflicts between the business side and the clinical practice side."

Business consolidation in gastroenterology is taking many other forms. Capital Digestive Care, a large GI group in the Maryland area plans to expand via strategic partnership with Physicians Endoscopy (chapter 10). Yet another GI group (de-identified as MGG in a later chapter) is expanding as a multispecialty group. They brought doctors on board from nephrology and internal medicine. OptumCare Specialty Practices plans to create joint partnerships with GI practices (chapter 3 and chapter 10). There are few groups in the Midwest that have decided not to take private equity in the near-term. They plan to consolidate regionally and become larger independent entities. There are other types of consolidation underway as well, and you'll read about them in more detail in later chapters.

BIG PICTURE: SYSTEM VS. CONSUMER

To understand the big picture of this wave of consolidation, I called on Sid Sahni, the Chief Strategy and Corporate Development Officer of Prime Therapeutics, a PBM based in Minneapolis. Before his current job, he played a role on both sides of the CVS-Aetna deal. That deal was one of the largest transactions in the history of healthcare.

He explained, "To understand what's happening across healthcare, we must understand what the two biggest aggregators in the country are up to. CVS Health and UnitedHealth Group. CVS has been taking the consumer route. They are thinking, 'Let's cover all the touchpoints of patients to influence consumer behavior. Somewhere the benefits to the company will accrue if I focus on changing patient behavior.' UnitedHealth Group is taking a system approach. They are thinking, 'The system is out of whack; let's fix that first.

Let's reduce costs of hospitals by moving care to clinics, out-patient centers.' Maybe they are building a Kaiser of sorts—a closed system. They are thinking, 'Somewhere, the benefits will accrue if I have the right system.'"

The rest of healthcare is falling into one of these two camps: *system* or *consumer*. It's not just UnitedHealth Group that's building a closed-loop system. There are other Big Brothers. Health systems, technology companies, and retailers are attempting to do the same. We'll examine this more in the next chapter. But, for right now, we must keep asking ourselves, What is the impact of all this on gastroenterology? Are we system- or consumer-driven? Or a blend of both? Are there more options?

IMPLICATIONS FOR GASTROENTEROLOGY

Consolidation is fundamentally restructuring the practice of gastroenterology. The future of gastroenterology will entail mega-platforms, the size of which GI hasn't seen to date (think 500 to 1,000 GIs). And then there will be several niches, including digital GI companies. Here are a few take-aways to consider from this chapter.

TAKEAWAYS

1. The biggest driver for structural consolidation is stemming from the consolidation of health systems. These systems are getting together to ward off competitive pressures from regional hospitals.
2. There's no telling how big is big enough. In metropolitan regions, even groups as large as 60–80 GIs are struggling to get the attention of insurance companies.

3. The industry will keep consolidating through the next decade and beyond. In the form of private equity, hospital-owned practices, multispecialty groups, and so on. Roll-ups won't end anytime soon.
4. Even with the best intentions, a few MSOs (management services organizations) might fail as they did in other specialties. We just don't know which ones. Reasons for failure might be cultural, financial, execution, or market factors. It's best to think through backup options if things don't go as planned and you have to restart.
5. It's best to plan for unexpected turns of events. The biggest threat to the success of GI consolidation could come from outside of healthcare. For example, leveraged private equity–funded GI platforms will be vulnerable to market conditions, such as a recession or an unexpected technological disruption.
6. Practically speaking, only a few independent GI practices will remain. Many of whom will consider a concierge model. Most gastroenterologists will be in under some sort of a corporate structure.

It's pointless to think that one consolidation option is evil and another is virtuous. Private equity may be good *or* bad. Consolidating independently may be good *or* bad. Once a group plants its flag in a certain direction, I've observed that that option becomes the best one there is. Everyone approaches a situation from an angle that's best suited to them at that time. And that's a good thing.

For example, say a group in a region fails, that's really no cause for "see, I told you so" glee to others who didn't join them. Because a regional failure makes everyone vulnerable. It opens doors for external parties, such as a hospital system, to dominate. It's in the collective interest of the industry to make all possible options work.

It's time for gastroenterology to align its interests and *scope forward*. As Dr. Leavitt said, "The real competition is out there."

In this chapter, we examined the future of gastroenterology from the lens of business consolidation. What follows are interviews of two gastroenterology leaders, Dr. Lawrence Kosinski and Dr. Michael Dragutsky, who are scoping forward in different ways. Dr. Kosinski was instrumental in the growth of the Illinois Gastroenterology Group (IGG) and its recent merger with GI Alliance. His candid interview throws light on the big risks that gastroenterology faces as an industry and why he retired ahead of the deal to focus on SonarMD, his GI startup. Meanwhile, Dr. Dragutsky underscores the importance of industry partnerships. As part of the leadership team at Digestive Health Physicians Association, he has the advantage of seeing changes that are underway at a national level.

INTERVIEW WITH DR. LAWRENCE KOSINSKI, SONARMD

Dr. Lawrence Kosinski is the Chief Medical Officer of SonarMD, which develops chronic care management for patients with high beta chronic disease. The company is funded by Blue Cross Venture Partner Fund and Arboretum Ventures. Dr. Kosinski was previously the Managing Partner of Illinois Gastroenterology Group in Chicago.

Q: Where is GI headed?

Dr. Lawrence Kosinski: First, GI has old service lines, like colonoscopy. When 80% of your revenue is coming from one type of procedure, that's vulnerability rather than an asset. There are many competitive products under development. There will be margin compression in colonoscopy. The commoditization of colonoscopy will continue.

The second major force is consolidation. A few years ago when I sat at the governing board meetings of AGA, we were looking at over 50% of practices being less than five doctor groups. That's drastically changing with the infusion of private equity. Gastroenterologists are no longer going to be in control of their practices. Their practices will be rolled up with larger entities.

The third force is competition of risk-bearing entities. Insurances like UnitedHealth Group want to lower their risk. They are vertically integrating and employing physicians. If you look at hospital driven ACOs, they want to control the risk as well. That diminishes the ability of specialists like gastroenterologists to remain independent.

Q: What's likely to happen five to ten years from now?

Dr. Kosinski: I see very large national entities that would employ a majority of gastroenterologists. They will no longer be owners/operators. They either will be employed by large, risk-bearing entities or by entities that are assisting risk-bearing entities. But I don't see independent gastroenterologists very long in the future.

Q: Is there a percentage that comes to mind?

Dr. Kosinski: I would be totally speculating on a percentage. But I could easily see 70–80% of gastroenterologists in the country being employed.

Q: How did Illinois Gastroenterology Group go about its decision to join the GI Alliance? What was the process?

Dr. Kosinski: I was on the board of managers for the Illinois Gastroenterology Group. It was back at the end of 2016, I think, when we initially began our investigation of PE. We engaged Deloitte to educate us. Then we put together a financial book.

Beginning of 2018, we submitted our book to 200 PE firms and 84 of them reviewed it and about 21 actually made bids.

By June 2018, our group interviewed 16 of them, and we had them all rebid. They rebid in July, and in August, we limited our list to six PE firms. A couple of strategic platforms and four pure PEs.

Then we interviewed again. We had long interviews. Then we limited it to three. We had further negotiations. And it was in November 2018 that we signed our LOI with the GI Alliance.

We began due diligence after the holidays in January 2019. That took six months and we finally closed on July 24, 2019.

Q: I understand the economic rationale of narrowing PE funds. What were the psychological factors influencing your decision?

Dr. Kosinski: Well, when you look at a big group like ours, we had quite an age disparity. When you talk of psychological motivations, the older doctors were looking for a payout! The younger doctors were certainly looking for a payout but also security. Those in the middle were following one or the other.

Then there was a very small number of us that were mostly concerned that the practice be left in a good strategic position. I put myself in that category. I didn't get any money out of this deal, and I retired ahead of the deal. Because I had decided to do that, my motivations were pure. I just wanted to make sure that when I walked out of the door of that practice, I was leaving it in a situation that was stable, and it was what the doctors wanted.

We went with the GI Alliance because of a few reasons. The physicians in the group felt that we were not only entering a PE deal but also bolstering on to something that already had significant infrastructure and direction. It was encouraging for the younger doctors.

Q: Did the deal offer the security the doctors were looking for?

Dr. Kosinski: What it's offering them is strategic security. That they're part of the largest GI practice in the country. GI

Alliance has already demonstrated the ability to be centrally managed and organized. It's going to be a powerful, significant force going forward. If you believe in the independence of gastroenterology, then this is probably your best opportunity. To maintain some independence even though you are also giving up control.

Q: Why did you retire ahead of the deal?

Dr. Kosinski: You know SonarMD is my future. I'm 67 years old and can retire now. I have enough money, but I've no interest in retiring my brain. I was going to retire from IGG a year earlier when SonarMD received its first investment. I stayed on because of the PE deal.

I felt I owed it to my group, to stay on and help negotiate the deal. If I would've signed that PE deal, then I would basically be telling the investors that I was going to continue to practice. Ethically, I can't say this and that. I know it sounds crazy that I would give up money like that. But I felt it was the right thing to do. It ended up okay for me. I'm happy!

Q: What would make PE deals fail?

Dr. Kosinski: Lots! It starts with one word, and it begins with C, and that's *culture*!

The challenge that the governing board is going to have is maintaining a culture. When you're in private practice, you're a doctor. And your mission is to provide quality care and be attentive toward your patients. But if you're an owner in a PE-funded MSO, and you're also practicing in that MSO, you have to make sure to keep your ducks in line. Because your mission may change. You want to make sure this thing gets sold off in a few years and you get a major multiple. That's when there will be conflicts between the business side and the clinical practice side. That will happen!

The challenge will be maintaining the culture and the focus when a very, very significant percentage of the revenue and EBITDA of the organization is being siphoned off to the MSO for growth. That, to me, is the biggest concern. You are converting yourself from the mission of patient care into a mission of making your investment return in three to five years.

Q: How would you have dealt with the dilemma of clinical mission versus business goals had you continued being part of the system?

Dr. Kosinski: Let's say I was in a leadership position. My goal would be to build clinical infrastructure. The clinical infrastructure of a successful PE-funded physician group should be as complex as the business infrastructure.

Right now, there's a lot of complexity on the business side. Layers of organizational infrastructure. On the clinical side, it's lacking. No matter how they are owned, the future of a successfully managed organization is to be able to have a clinical infrastructure. Something that will drive uniformity in outcomes. It enables the entity to handle risks.

You can't have heterogeneous practice habits. Not that it has to be a cookbook, but you've got to have some uniformity in the way medicine is being practiced. And I've not seen that in any of the organizations yet. We can remain powerful players at the table. But the only way I can see that happening is if we focus on the clinical infrastructure and build an outcomes-oriented infrastructure. That way, you can bear risk and provide a valuable component in the value chain.

Q: What are some challenges for the GI industry?

Dr. Kosinski: Some of the immediate challenges are to do with changes in the organizational structure. Practices are being purchased and managed externally. There's going to be a significant disruption there. Then, there will always be reimbursement challenges.

Long term, the challenge is for practices to prepare themselves for the dismantling and the diversification from the colonoscopy. GI practices are colonoscopy factories. Everything they do—everything—is oriented toward cranking the colons. Keeping those ambulatory surgery centers busy. Cranking the colonoscopies in and out. That's the number one focus area of every GI practice. It's the focus of every PE fund that's going into GI.

But they are going to be catching a falling knife. If they're trying to maintain revenue streams and EBITDA with a full dependency on colonoscopy.

So if GI is going to succeed in the future, GI has to embrace more care management and more value-based care. If I was a younger physician in my 30s and 40s, that's where my focus will be. Because I know that the colonoscope will not carry me up to age 65.

Q: Isn't that a problem that we don't talk as much about technology disruptions in GI?

Dr. Kosinski: Absolutely! FIT is $20. Twenty dollars! I'm having conversations with Blue Cross Blue Shield's research team. Believe me, this is in their major focus. They want their star ratings improved for colorectal cancer, but that doesn't mean it has to be a colonoscopy. It can be a FIT, and in fact, I don't know why it's not a FIT. Because if you repeat that stool test, over a few years, annually, you will replicate the sensitivity of a colonoscopy.

Then combine that with the fact that most patients don't get their first colonoscopy until they are over 55. You could be using FIT at age 50 instead of having everybody get one. So believe me, the payers know this. Out of the million colonoscopies performed every year, how many of those are necessary?

Q: How does the industry get this disruptive phase right?

Dr. Kosinski: I would imagine you'd start with demographics. If you look at the demographics, it looks like a Mrs. Butterworth's bottle. The millennials are at the bottom and are actually bigger than the baby boomers. But they are far away from the need for colonoscopy. And the baby boomers are moving off. The narrow section is 50. There will be less 50-year-olds than there have been in the last 10 years.

Secondly, there is increased competition from lower-cost, noninvasive tools for screening. Thirdly, reimbursements keep getting compressed. The government has only so much money.

The one thing that the GI community has on its side is that they have been able to screen a large number of patients who now need surveillance. They've had polyps removed; now they've got to come back.

A positive force is care management, and if you embrace it and keep them healthier, that could be a new revenue stream.

Q: How can care management be a revenue stream? Would insurances pay for it?

Dr. Kosinski: Well, the only way care management becomes a revenue generator is if it's combined with risk. I'm not saying there's any payer out there that's going to pay a doctor for care management. If you're willing to bear downside risk along with shared savings, if you can play in a narrow space, there's money to be made. That's our focus at SonarMD.

At SonarMD, we understand certain chronic conditions that have some common characteristics. We call them high beta illnesses. Early detection or mobilization of patients at earlier signs of deterioration is where things can be provided less expensively. Serious complications can be avoided. That's our niche. That's the place we're focusing on.

INTERVIEW WITH DR. MICHAEL DRAGUTSKY, GASTRO ONE

Dr. Michael Dragutsky is the President and Managing Partner of Gastro One in Tennessee. He's also on the board of the Digestive Health Physicians Association (DHPA). In April 2020, Gastro One partnered with Webster Equity Partners to form a practice management platform called One GI. Dr. Dragutsky became the chairman of One GI.

Q: What's the future of gastroenterology? What's likely to happen over the next five years?

Dr. Michael Dragutsky: There will be a move toward subspecialization. Medical information is getting so robust that there will be fewer and fewer general GIs. There will be specialization in IBD, liver procedures, and so on. Practices will develop centers of expertise with certain GI areas. Primary GIs will first see patients and direct them to the right expert within the practice. Advanced endoscopy, such as EMR, pancreatic procedures, POEM, or ESD would become routine down the road.

Next, there will be increased use of technology and an increase in noninvasive tests (e.g., in the detection of colon cancer). Further, there'll be regional consolidation in the specialty. Most small groups will need to aggregate. A system will evolve with hospital-owned groups, payor or PE-funded groups, and large independent practices.

Q: What are some of the challenges for GI today?

Dr. Dragutsky: Physicians tend to resist change. It's important to be proactive and prepared. To be able to scale and provide services needed for the changing market. Also, a change in mindset is needed on the business side of a practice. There's a large need for better tools to manage data and infrastructure.

Physicians need partners from business, finance, technology, infrastructure, human resources, and compliance. The keyword is *alignment*. Everyone's alignment will play an important role in overcoming challenges.

Right now, for my practice, establishing a direction of consolidation and the best route forward is of key importance. Also, it's challenging to help young doctors understand that the system ensures independence into the future.

Amidst a changing environment, the whole medical community has to continue ensuring that patients are a priority. Finally, we must continue to find ways to provide excellent healthcare services and watch out for rising costs.

Q: What could go wrong with what's happening in GI now?

Dr. Dragutsky: A single-payor system could change everything. Increased regulations or potential reimbursement cuts could also cause uncertainty.

Next, private equity–backed consolidation has the risk of underperforming financially. If this occurs, MSOs may dissolve, causing a reset in the marketplace.

Also, the practice of gastroenterology could become financially challenging with ever-increasing costs, especially those of technology and increased business overhead.

CHAPTER 3

———

BIG BROTHERS

Recently, I was at a private multispecialty facility in a semiurban region. It was less than 100 miles from a major metropolitan area. It had a whiff of industry from good times that had long drifted by.

There was time before my meeting, so I tried to locate a Starbucks. Google Maps spotted one and took me toward the local university campus. As I drove there, I noticed more than a few pain management clinics pop up like Dunkin Donuts.

I was visiting them to understand why they were bleeding money. My curiosity got the better of me, and I went into the center sooner. Once inside, I asked the administrator what the pain clinics were about.

"Oh, this region has all the street drugs," she said almost casually. "Until drug dispensing laws were tightened, some doctors' offices dispensed opioids on demand. For cash."

"What do you mean?" I asked, even though I knew what she meant.

"A doctor got convicted for prescribing excessive amounts of opioids to patients," she continued. "Patients paid cash and got the prescriptions they wanted. People who are addicts are desperate. They'll do anything. Who's to blame?"

As we walked around the facility, I noticed very few patients. She showed me various rooms—X-ray, mammography, MRI, physical therapy. All almost empty. The facility wasn't new, but it had an unused air about it. Physicians had left. New ones had joined. Then they left too—prompting the physician owner to come out of retirement. I wanted to know why, on a regular weekday, there were so few patients.

The administrator gave me a tangential answer. "The nurse tech can't even get enough scans a year to keep up with her license."

"Why?" I persisted.

She finally gave me the whole story. "Well, the two big health systems here bought 95% of the independent practices in the region. So there's no one left to refer patients to private facilities like ours. The health systems mandate that their employees only see doctors within their own system. Doctors in this town are struggling to make ends meet. Whether they're employed or run a private practice, they are stuck. Mostly, we get Medicaid patients, and they don't pay. Then there are patients who come looking for drugs. We don't do that here."

"How's the job market in general?" I was curious to ascertain local market conditions.

"Well, there are a few, but no one's willing to pay. The health systems want to pay minimum wage for someone with my skills. Like $10 to $12 an hour!"

While seeing me off at the door, she said, "I don't know what's going to happen with us in two months. But it was nice to meet you."

It's one thing to read about the surge in hospital-led consolidation but quite another thing to see its effects play out live. When you add declining insurance payments and the competitive gridlock created by dominant players, that's a recipe for despair. Then add the opioid crisis on top of it. One problem feeds off the other, sending an entire ecosystem into a downward spiral.

You have good doctors but no patients. You have needy patients that don't pay. You have patients willing to pay for the wrong reasons. And then you have Big Brothers who are happy to control it all.

To know the future for gastroenterology, you don't really have to travel forward in time. You just need to look around the edges of existing trends, either good or bad. Extreme examples always have an educational tale if we're open to listening.

Health systems aren't the only Big Brothers around. In the next few pages, we'll review the strategies of a few different entities:

- Big insurance companies
- Big health systems
- Big technology companies like Amazon and retailers like Walmart

BIG INSURANCES

Let's examine Big Insurance by taking a look at United-Health Group (UHG). UHG is one of the largest players in the insurance market. Understanding their strategy will give us insight into why big insurance companies are also interested in the provider side of healthcare.

In fact, the fastest growing division inside UHG isn't insurance. It's Optum, the company's provider arm. In 2018, Optum's revenue grew 11.1% to $101.3 billion.

There are several other Optums under the Optum umbrella. Such as OptumRx (pharmacy care), OptumHealth (care delivery and ambulatory care), and OptumInsight (data and analytics).

In 2017, Optum acquired Surgical Care Affiliates (SCA) for $2.3 billion. As I understand it, that acquisition set the base for OptumCare's Specialty Practices division. This division has the charter to acquire or partner with private medical practices. I was recently at a meeting where OptumCare Specialty Practices made a strong pitch to GIs (which we'll discuss more in chapter 12). They offered an alternative to private equity via a partnership buyout. In exchange, they offered GI practices benefits such as payor relationships and growth capital.

By Optum's own words, the division has grown exponentially. Former Optum CEO Larry Renfro said, "OptumCare has grown from a single medical practice serving 350,000 people and one payer to an emerging national ambulatory care delivery platform, focused on high-value care and exceptional consumer satisfaction, serving more than 80 payers and 15 million individuals."

Between OptumHealth and OptumCare, the company has 50,000 employed or affiliated physicians, mostly primary care providers. The company wants to utilize this primary care "distribution network" to refer patients to specialists within its network. It wants to extend itself into other specialties, like gastroenterology. OptumCare plans to partner with physicians through direct employment or independent network affiliation. It also plans to bring them on board at urgent care facilities and ambulatory surgical centers (ASCs). Another plan is to acquire and roll up physician practices.

According to the consulting firm Recon Strategy, Optum has been active in physician practice acquisitions since 2010. Recon Strategy describes Optum's ongoing acquisition model through the following table.

MODEL	DESCRIPTION
Medical group acquisition	Optum acquires full or partial interest in the medical group
Independent physician association (IPA) acquisition	Optum acquires the IPA with contracted network and risk-bearing capabilities
Medical group acquisition followed by IPA build	Acquired practices then have an IPA bolted onto their structure to fuel growth
Greenfield IPA	Optum builds a new network of physicians and supports them with services in an IPA model

Sources: Optum, Recon analysis

Further, Optum is mapping out every step of the journey for patients from diagnosis to cure and even for end-of-life care. They are partnering with hospitals such as John Muir Health to manage nonclinical functions. These include health IT, revenue cycle management, purchasing, and claims processing. Tory Wolff from Recon Strategy suggests that OptumCare can soon reach 70% of the US population. It can become a national integrated delivery network.

And if that's UHG's strategy, why would its competitors stay put? They've taken similar steps as well. Aetna became part of CVS. Humana bought a stake in Kindred Hospitals with $800 million in cash. Cigna bought ExpressScripts in a $67-billion merger.

We don't know yet the outcome of these private closed-loop systems. What would it mean for doctors and their patients? When Big Insurance directly or indirectly controls the entire value chain of healthcare, is that going to mean more good or bad?

In Egyptian mythology, there's a symbol of a dragon eating its own tail. It's called Ouroboros. The Big Insurance strategy reminds me of that mythical creature. The Ouroboros business strategy of Big Insurance seems to be this: *to own what you pay for so you are both the end and the beginning*.

But big insurances aren't the only ones with ambitions of a closed-loop system.

BIG HEALTH SYSTEMS

I met Jeff Griffin, COO of Digestive Disease Specialists, a GI physician group in Oklahoma City. We talked extensively about what the future holds for his group. Like other midsize groups in the country, they have been considering the private equity–funded platforms.

Often, I find it particularly interesting to take the contrary point of view and ask an expert why something would *not* work. So I asked Jeff, "Why would you *not do* a private equity deal?"

He gave me several different reasons, and then finally offered up a big one. He said, "Our relationship with our local hospital and health system."

"How do you mean?" I was curious.

"We would like to explore how to include them in the deal," he replied. "How we position ourselves in this market and continue to serve our patient referral base is connected to our health system. Ultimately, we want to enhance our relationship with the local hospitals."

Hospitals are keen to control their local markets. That might mean acquiring private practices or controlling the flow of patient referrals to private practices. As hospitals consolidate and get bigger, their ability to influence referral flow increases. According to an analysis by Physicians Advocacy Institute, the number of physician practices acquired by hospitals increased by 8,000 from July 2016 to January 2018. And the number of physicians employed by hospitals increased by 14,000 during the same period. To set that number in context, that's possibly more than the count of gastroenterologists who practice in the US.

Practices that choose to remain independent (with or without private equity) will increasingly find themselves in a dance with hospital systems. They need each other but also compete with each other.

This dance is what prompted the formation of US Digestive Health, a private equity–funded platform in Pennsylvania. Dr. Mehul Lalani is one of the drivers behind this initiative (discussed further in chapter 9). When I met with him, I asked, "What's driving rapid consolidation in your region?"

He responded in a heartbeat: "The hospital systems. They are getting bigger. We have three or four health systems in the area. They are organizing themselves rapidly."

Dr. John Allen, who moved from private practice to a health system environment, urges private practices to develop a good negotiating stance. He said, "When healthcare systems become large enough, they can basically internally build what a large group offers. It's important that private practices have a good negotiating stance because even large GI practices can be cut out." (You can read his complete interview in chapter 10.)

It's not that health systems are inherently bad guys, though. Health systems everywhere are dealing with their own problems. Lower reimbursements. Declining inpatient admissions. Higher operating costs, including payroll and technology. They are simply figuring out how to sustain themselves in an evolving value-based care environment.

Value-based care differs from the fee-for-service payment model by tying reimbursements to cost control and quality. It emphasizes on patient outcomes and might require health-care providers to adopt measures outlined by registries such as the GI Quality Improvement Consortium (GIQuIC).

In a keynote lecture at a GI business conference, Dr. Irving

Pike, CMO of John Muir Health, specified five things that health systems are having to do to survive:

1. Major reduction in expenses
2. Mergers and acquisitions, as well as partnerships
3. Brand focus and engagement with consumers
4. Value driven through innovation
5. Financial models adjusted to accommodate an aging population

Hospitals find it economically viable to absorb specialist groups into their fold because it helps them control both professional and facility fees. In their efforts to reduce their own costs, though, they are changing the healthcare landscape surrounding them.

More than 50% of standalone hospitals have consistently lost money from 2012 to 2017. Relatively, about 25% of system-owned hospitals have lost money during the same period. That actually adds a degree of risk to those employed by hospitals. It's not a safe option, either.

Dr. James Leavitt of Gastro Health said, "With a lean organization like a consolidated physician group, we can make a profit on a $300 CAT scan, but a hospital can't make a profit on a $1,000 CAT scan."

The difficulty of making a profit is also prompting hospitals to consolidate and stay viable. The number of hospital mergers or acquisitions every year has nearly doubled over the last decade.

Dr. Narayanachar Murali, a solo practitioner in South Carolina said, "Hospital-based practices can also become very shaky, depending on how reimbursement rules change. I don't think hospitals will have enough money to pay the salaries they pay now. Regardless of employment status, there's no safe option. Even 400-bed hospitals go under." (You can read his complete interview in chapter 7.)

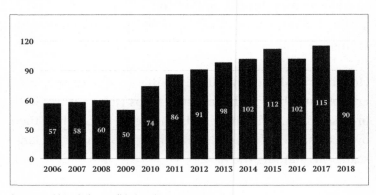

Announced hospital consolidations in recent years

I spoke to Dr. Raffaele Gibilisco, a solo GI practitioner in New Jersey. He was concerned about the increasing dominance of local hospitals. He was possibly referring to Palisades Medical Center in Hudson County and its merger with Hackensack University Health Network.

In 2016, Hackensack University Health Network merged with Meridian Health's system of hospitals. It became New Jersey's second largest health system. A few years later, Hackensack Meridian Health acquired JFK Medical Center in Edison. It then became the largest hospital chain in New Jersey. As of 2019, this health system was a $5.5 billion not-for-profit system and employed 6,500 doctors. By the end of 2019, Hackensack Meridian Health committed another $400 million for a proposed a merger with Englewood Hospital.

Yes, health systems are getting massively bigger. But they are not stopping at providing medical care. With value-based care, they are also coming up with their own tail-eating Ouroboros strategy. As you can imagine, Ouroboros has no end.

Geisinger Health System serves over 45 million patients in Pennsylvania and New Jersey. It now also offers medical insurance. Kurt J. Wrobel, CFO of the Geisinger Health Plan, talked about their strategy. He said, "There's just a connection that hospitals have with their local communities. And extending that to bring in the financing component of the business is a natural next step."

Hospitals will find ways to balance their risk and lower total cost of care. They will continue to seek even more growth options. In doing so, they will step in from the other end of healthcare. A recent CNBC article suggests, "Hospitals could kill the insurance industry."

The Ouroboros business strategy of health systems could then be this: *to own what you get paid for so that you are both the beginning and the end.* While big health systems and big insurances worry about each other, there are still other Big Brothers looming. Technology companies are more interested in healthcare than ever.

BIG TECH AND BIG MARTS

Recently, a story in *The Economist* suggested that pursuing shareholder value was not enough. Big Business, the story suggested, must accept social responsibilities. What can be a bigger social responsibility than healthcare?

Research estimates that 20–25% of healthcare spending is waste. That's the kind of thing that gets the tech industry so excited. They wish to solve big world problems with an engineering mindset. Let's not forget a key element of healthcare that's of primary interest to Tech: *data*. The healthcare industry alone generates a third of the world's data.

In 2018, US investors put $11 billion into healthcare startups. There are new technologies brewing, and the old guards—like Google, Apple, and Amazon—are also busy carving out a space for themselves in healthcare. Even China's tech giants Tencent and Baidu are busy building healthcare verticals. So let's look at the moves that both Big Tech and Big Marts are making in the healthcare industry and then discuss the implications of these developments.

GOOGLE

Alphabet (Google's parent company) has 57 portfolio companies in healthcare alone. Its portfolio includes genomics, clinical research, and insurance companies. Interestingly, Alphabet is an investor in two private insurance startups, Oscar Health and Clover Health. More recently, Google bought Fitbit, the maker of smart devices. They also hired Geisinger Health's CEO David Feinberg to head Google Health. You may recall from the previous section that Geisinger is a health system that offers insurance. Recent announcements indicate that Google Health is bringing better search capabilities to electronic health records (no surprise!). And Alphabet filed 186 health-related patents between 2013 and 2017.

You can say that Google's strategy is driven by data. In their view, the more data they acquire, the better algorithms they can write. The better the algorithm, the better the panacea for healthcare's problems.

APPLE

Apple's foray into healthcare is through its smart devices and its users. Recently, the FDA approved the Apple Watch to monitor EKG and detect irregular heart rhythm. Apple's HealthKit API allows users to share clinical data with developers via trusted third parties. Among other things, apps on the iPhone detect vision and speech problems. An accessibility feature converts AirPods into a hearing aid. In an interview with CNBC, Apple CEO Tim Cook said that the company's greatest contribution to mankind will be about health.

AMAZON

Together, Amazon, Berkshire Hathaway, and JPMorgan Chase created Haven Health. They wish to take care of their employees and disrupt traditional healthcare delivery models. When Haven tried to hire a former UnitedHealth Group executive, Optum vehemently opposed. Amazon is now offering Haven's health plans to its employees in Connecticut, Utah, Washington, and North Carolina. It also began offering virtual care to its employees via smart devices. JPMorgan has indicated a simplified medical plan for its employees. It includes preventative care, no deductibles, and a $15 copay. The plan charges a flat fee for medical services and procedures.

Additionally, Amazon acquired PillPack to deliver drugs

online in all 50 states, and they offer Amazon Web Services (AWS) to healthcare businesses such as Cerner (a health IT company). According to CNBC, Amazon has a stealth lab called 1492 that works on cancer research. Of course, Alexa is already in your home. It will possibly detect your cough soon and get you to try "Prime Health."

MICROSOFT

Microsoft's multibillion-dollar healthcare unit has 168,000 customers. The company has sold its Windows software for many years to health systems. However, they are now interested in extending their cloud-computing platform, Azure, which competes with Amazon Web Services. The company's big bet is, of course, AI. They've created an industry-wide healthcare partnership. It's called Healthcare NExT.

UBER AND LYFT

As you can guess, Uber Health and Lyft are interested in commuters. In particular, their focus is the $3 billion "nonemergency" transportation business. Uber is integrating itself into Cerner's EHR to schedule rides for patients. Earlier, Lyft announced a partnership with Allscripts, a health IT company.

BIG MARTS

Given all these developments, healthcare could become a part of the business strategy for any company that's selling anything at scale to consumers. And say you were a large retailer or technology company. Would you want to watch Amazon's moves into healthcare from the sidelines?

It should come as no surprise then that Microsoft has signed multiyear deals with a variety of retailers. Well-known names like Walmart, Kroger, Albertsons, and Walgreens are now all Microsoft partners. Deals span its cloud platform and other products. Walgreens and Microsoft are in joint partnership to lower the cost of healthcare delivery.

In 2018, there was plenty of media that Walmart would buy Humana, a large insurance company. Aetna (now part of CVS) had tried to buy Humana earlier. However, there have been no recent announcements about Walmart's Humana acquisition.

Toward the end of 2019, Walmart Health launched its first retail clinic in Georgia. The company designed an integrated health experience for its consumers. A one-stop shop. The clinic offers primary care, urgent care, lab tests, X-rays, counseling, dental care, and vision care. Its services are affordable, regardless of insurance coverage.

Promptly, Becker's ASC ran an article titled "Walmart Is Coming to Gastroenterology" after the company made the move. For the benefit of consumers, Walmart partnered with Blue Cross Blue Shield in Arkansas to develop a quality assessment filter. The filter selects gastroenterologists among other specialists. It uses data analytics to narrow doctors based on appropriateness of treatment, effectiveness, and cost.

IMPLICATIONS FOR GASTROENTEROLOGY

As you can see, each Big Brother views healthcare from its own perspective and strategizes toward its own ends. Healthcare is a $3.65 trillion industry and still growing. It's so huge that it's possible to view the industry from any angle and still find large open markets.

1. Big insurers think, "We can make more money if we invest across the entire healthcare spectrum. At least we'll reduce our own cost of payouts."
2. Big hospital systems think, "Let's organize ourselves into large systems. Let's control our local markets. We'll then cut costs, get profitable, and keep competition at bay."
3. Big technology companies think, "The healthcare industry doesn't know how to fix itself. Let's show them how to use technology to get efficient. And by the way, let's capture as much data as we can along the way. With more data, we can write better algorithms that can take on the healthcare burden and reduce waste."
4. Big companies like JPMorgan think, "We spend so much money on healthcare for our employees. Can't we do this ourselves and cut costs? If we succeed, could we not roll it out as a service?"

Of course, everyone says they are doing it for patients and doctors. But are they? Or are they simply in it for themselves for meeting their business objectives?

What I'd like you to take away is this: Big Tech and Big Marts are not small forces. Unlike all other times in healthcare's history, there's strong momentum behind change, and as with exponential technologies, there is a multiplier effect among Big Brothers. One change will trigger other changes, resulting in a domino effect on a global scale. Healthcare will no longer be just local.

Let's look at some examples. Amazon aims to play a variety of vastly different roles. As a retailer, the company plans to deliver drugs. As a technology giant, it's bringing AI to healthcare. As a big company with a huge employee force, it's building a closed-loop healthcare system to reduce costs. Amazon's moves will trigger moves by CVS and Google. Google's moves will prompt the venture capital industry to invest more in health tech. Further, Google and Microsoft have large studies going on at large hospitals in India. The plan must be to learn from that data, build better algorithms, and apply it in the US or elsewhere. With this level of involvement, can we trust Big Tech to not control the flow of healthcare?

Finally, imagine if Walmart oddly decides to bring "everyday low prices" to screening colon cancer. The space of GI will never be the same again.

Maybe patients are already expecting different things from gastroenterology. You'll find out in the next chapter that healthcare isn't just about sickness anymore. It's increasingly about finding ways to make patients feel good, look good, and even live forever.

CHAPTER 4

———

PATIENT BEHAVIOR

In Burlingame, California, a patient gut-hacked his way out of gastrointestinal problems. Josiah Zayner calls himself a "biohacker." In 2016, he decided to change his microbiome by acquiring stool and other samples from a healthy donor.

In a video documentary by *The Atlantic*, you see him burping while speaking on camera. "Gas," he says. Then he proceeds to create poop-pills in his garage out of the healthy stool samples he procured. He checks himself into a hotel and, over a 72-hour period, consumes the pills with the intention that they will rewire his microbiome. In a final scene in the documentary, you see him teary-eyed. He has discovered that his gut microbiome has indeed changed and now resembles that of the donor.

In 2017, Josiah was in the news again when he tried to edit his genome live on stage at a conference.

In Jackson, Mississippi, a HyGIeaCare center at GI Associates attracts a patient all the way from Atlanta, Georgia. As you know, HyGIeaCare addresses a core challenge with colonoscopy—*the prep*. It's an FDA-cleared colon cleansing system. A patient inserts a sterile, disposable nozzle into his rectum. While the patient rests, a gentle stream of water flows into the bowel. This loosens the stool and ultimately cleanses the colon. When I entered the HyGIeaCare center in Mississippi, it looked so nice and clean. There were private rooms with HyGIeaCare stations. It reminded me of a spa.

For some patients, there's a secondary benefit with HyGIeaCare: *a flatter belly*. That secondary benefit is of importance to a patient I learned about. She's a professional model from Atlanta, and a flatter belly is an important factor for her life on the runway. She stopped in Jackson on her way to Los Angeles because it's "nicer" in Jackson.

The Merriam-Webster dictionary defines *healthcare* as: "Efforts made to maintain or restore physical, mental, or emotional well-being especially by trained and licensed professionals." Now, doctors would never say they went to medical school to help patients look good on a fashion runway. Or to watch on the sidelines as patients rewire their microbiome in hotel rooms. But these aren't isolated episodes. They add up to a new movement in which patients demand more from healthcare. They aren't just saying, "Fix me from disease." *They are asking healthcare to make them feel good, look good, and even live forever.*

The problem? Healthcare is not equipped to respond to such needs. Because of that, some of these patients find other ways to get what they want. With or without approval from their doctors.

In this chapter, we'll look at these three patient requests—

feeling good, looking good, and living forever. We'll consider the vehicles by which patients are attempting to achieve these objectives, as well as the implications it has for gastroenterology.

FEEL GOOD

Run your eyes over these services below and take a guess which well-known medical websites offer these.

Acupuncture	Chinese Herbal Therapy
Culinary Medicine	Aromatherapy
Reiki	Tai Chi
Mind-Body Therapy	Music Therapy
Animal Assisted Therapy	Yoga
Massotherapy	Hypnotherapy

No, not an alternative medicine website. No, not Amazon. I found all these services offered on the websites of three large health systems: Cleveland Clinic, Mayo Clinic, and Johns Hopkins.

Of course, they aren't part of mainstream services offered by these and many other health systems. They are simply the add-on, should you need them as a patient. And these health systems are merely following a broader trend—that of patients wanting to feel good.

Calm is a meditation app that, among other things, helps you fall asleep. But that's not why I want you to take note. Recently, Calm became the first meditation app to be valued at one billion dollars. A unicorn. To put that into context, it's valued more than some of the biggest private-equity deals in private practice.

Ask yourself this question. Do you suspect any of your irritable bowel syndrome (IBS) patients are using Calm or another app like it? I bet they do.

Why? Because they might be part of an emerging society that wants to *feel good* by calming down. A friend might have told them that if they are less stressed, they'll feel better. Or they might have read an article that linked neuroscience to meditation. There's enough media dedicated to stress and disease that this is realistically possible.

As the healthcare industry goes about its job, the rest of the world accelerates this trend of self-treatment. People buy apps, subscribe to services, and find ways to *feel good*—with or without the healthcare system.

Apparently, 9 million Americans now meditate. Trendy spaces like MNDFL in New York offer to book you cushions for mindfulness practice. To make you feel good. Between meetings one day, I strolled into their center in Greenwich Village. It was hip. They allowed me to take a breath and sip free tea.

The graph below represents the trending of the search term "mindfulness" on Google over the years. Yes, it's an exponential curve!

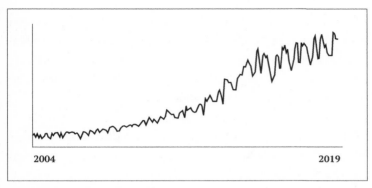

"Mindfulness" search trends on Google

It's clear from this that mindfulness is going mainstream. GI professionals can take advantage of this trend by offering patients what they are seeking elsewhere.

LOOK GOOD

As much as I'd like to think so, the HyGIeaCare story from earlier in this chapter is not an outlier. Of course, not all patients are getting their colon cleansed to look good. But many—I literally mean many—are going all out to upgrade their bodies.

If you've hung out in the Bay Area startup community, you would've surely added some butter into your coffee. A company named Bulletproof triggered the trend. The company's founder Dave Asprey sipped some yak-butter tea while on a trek in Tibet. He then came up with what has since become a sensation.

Forty-five-year-old Dave is the leader of the pack when it comes to upgrading the body. He announced publicly that he aims to live until 180. To do that, he injects his own stem-cells back into his body every six months (including some on his scalp so that he has bountiful hair). He also takes more than 100 supplements every day, bathes in infrared light, and breathes inside hyperbaric oxygen chambers. He's often seen in a T-shirt that says, "Upgraded."

I learned he used to weigh 300 pounds. But now, he's muscular, and his face even shows dimples when he smiles. As an entrepreneur, he converted his personal experiments into business opportunities, including what he named Upgrade Labs. Silicon Valley caught on to his biohacking. His followers take to Bulletproof diets and supplements with names like Unfair Advantage. They pay $15,000 at brain-training retreats to increase their IQ and so on. Other upgrades include nootropics (cognitive enhancers that are colloquially known as "smart drugs") and hormone optimization. The point is people are moving from *sickness* to *health* to a body *upgrade.*

The Bumrungrad International Hospital in Thailand has an exclusive clinic called VitalLife. The hospital partners with international experts of longevity such as Dr. Terry Grossman. VitalLife helps patients analyze where they are. Then they help them use therapies to feel younger, look better, and live longer.

HERE'S WHAT THEY OFFER:

1. Tests: Genetic tests, hormone tests, micronutrient tests, longevity tests
2. Feel younger: Increase energy, sexual health, sleep better, relieve digestive pain
3. Look better: Lose weight, rejuvenate skin, regrow hair

4. Live longer: Remove toxins, boost immune system, regain brain function, early detection of diseases

VitalLife comes across as a repackaged multispecialty clinic. It presents its solutions differently to the market. They aren't just an *obesity treatment*. They combine therapies and say, "Look better."

To understand this trend more deeply, I spoke to Dr. Jeffrey Gladden, an interventional cardiologist turned entrepreneur. He's the founder of a health optimization company called Apex. The company offers strategies to optimize health by deep diving into a client's genetic, physiological, and biochemical makeup and then benchmarking them across various parameters. (You can read his complete interview at the end of this chapter.)

Dr. Gladden had a traditional cardiology practice for 25 years in Texas. In his 50s, when he felt unwell (fatigue, weight gain, etc.), he went to get tests done. The doctors said the reason for all his symptoms was aging. Unwilling to accept that outcome, he went on a hunt to successfully crack the code of aging for himself and turn his health around.

That's when he began asking a different question of both himself and his patients: *How good can you be?* Instead of asking questions like, "Are you having chest pain?" or "Do you have shortness of breath?" He found himself helping clients ask more from their bodies. He began attracting a newer tribe of people who were also asking similar questions. These people were humans who wanted to upgrade their bodies to a higher standard.

Dr. Gladden doesn't accept insurance. His clients pay one

full year in advance before getting started. That includes the costs of tests. They fly into Dallas, Texas, for consultations that can last more than a day. They want to "make it to a 100 and feel like 30 years of age."

This trend of *upgrading* is knocking on the edges of medicine. It'll soon expand into the mainstream. Explore what that might mean to the kinds of patients you'll see in the future. To start with, will they be *patients with a sickness*?

LIVE FOREVER

The goal of upgrading the body is of course to try to live forever. There are many companies (and investors) in pursuit of longevity. There are several approaches in the works to crack the code on longevity. In 2018, investors bet $850 million on longevity companies compared to $324 million in 2017. There's so much momentum in this space. Gerontologist Aubrey de Gray says that the first person to live to 1,000 years of age has already been born. According to him, we are catching up with the "longevity escape velocity."

There are also strange experiments. From 2016 to 2018, a company called Ambrosia conducted young blood transfusions. It's okay if that reminded you of *Dracula*. In fact, in February 2019, the FDA brought the hammer down on the startup.

Alkahest is a clinical-stage biopharmaceutical company. It is targeting neurodegenerative disease with a "deep understanding of the plasma proteome." There are other companies like Baxter, CSL Behring, and Grifols. The human-plasma derived therapeutics market is growing.

Here are a few other approaches:

1. Human Longevity Inc. (HLI)—Develops large-scale computing and machine learning for genomics.
2. Cellularity—Develops cells from placentas against blood cancers.
3. Unity Biotechnology—Works on therapeutics to prevent, halt, or reverse aging.
4. Osiris Therapeutics—Develops stem cell therapies.
5. Insilico Medicine—Applies artificial intelligence to extend human life.

On its website, Human Longevity Inc. (HLI) calls out current healthcare as reactive. Their solution, known as Health Nucleus, is proactive. For $5,500, HLI's core assessment screens for risk factors and optimizes health. The program covers areas of cancer, cardiac disease, metabolic disease, and neurologic disease. Peter Diamandis, one of the founders of HLI, says that everything that HLI measures and tracks today will soon come to consumers on demand through sensors and devices. That's longevity going digital!

Just in case all these approaches don't pan out soon enough, there's cryonics. The idea behind cryonics is to freeze a deceased body in a pristine condition and keep it frozen until medicine discovers a cure for whatever caused death. As of 2014, there were more than 300 frozen bodies in the US and 50 more in Russia awaiting revival. Well, it's a market in waiting.

Longevity is just not for our bodies. What about our brains? Neuralink, a company founded by Elon Musk, plans to upload our brains to the cloud. Human trials of brain-computer interfaces are expected as early as 2020. Then we can plug our brains to the cloud and upload or download whatever we need. Can we call that Enlightenment 2.0?

If exponentials are anything to go by, these trends will accelerate and change what people expect from healthcare. In what ways could GI ride the wave of longevity?

IMPLICATIONS FOR GASTROENTEROLOGY

It's not the scope of this book to talk about the efficacy of these trends. All I want you to take away is this: Patients are beginning to expect different things from healthcare. Surely, they'll expect different things from GI too. Have you considered how you feel about these requests? And are you ready to handle them? These new markets are exploding. Some of these markets could belong to gastroenterology.

1. Patients with stress-related GI conditions are seeking alternative solutions.
2. Big health systems are testing waters. They are responding to patient needs with their own alternative therapy options.
3. Societal aspirations of health are undergoing a shift. Silicon Valley is biohacking. Wealthy entrepreneurs are upgrading their bodies, sometimes without the help of doctors.
4. What's a trend today becomes the norm tomorrow. Years ago, antibiotics were accessible to a select few, but today they're widespread. Today's trend of upgrading will accelerate and take some shape as the norm in the next few years.
5. For gastroenterology, there are many direct and indirect

implications. For example, obesity represents a significant present-day market. The microbiome is a rapidly upcoming market. Genetic editing could be a future market. (You'll get to explore these opportunities further in chapter 12.)

6. Look at the edges of trends. Entrepreneurial doctors are breaking away from health and insurance systems altogether. And their self-pay patient volume is growing.

In his interview with me, Dr. Scott Ketover, president and CEO of MNGI Digestive Health said, "We can't just focus on treating symptoms; we must also keep the entire GI tract in top performance. Whether it's the microbiome or the food we eat, that science belongs to gastroenterology. We must help patients before they become sick." (You can read his complete interview in chapter 8.)

It's true. It's up to gastroenterology to limit its own scope. As for patients, they want more. As a GI professional, you may be reading about these trends in patient behavior or perhaps fielding requests in your practice already. When it comes to these new demands on our industry, you may be wondering how *you* should respond.

With this backdrop, let's look at Huron Gastroenterology's wellness initiative (which I mentioned in chapter 2). The practice is based in Ann Arbor, Michigan. It was started by gastroenterologist Dr. Naresh Gunaratnam. (Yes, you met him and his uncle, Dr. K. Iswara back in chapter 2.)

There are two billion people worldwide who are considered obese. By 2030, 160 million Americans are expected to have a BMI of greater than 30. But less than 1% of medical professionals treat obesity. As of 2015, Americans spent $166 billion in wellness programs.

Dr. Gunaratnam enrolled 250 patients into his wellness program, and 62% of his patients achieved a 10% total body weight loss. Their payment model goes beyond insurance payments and runs on subscriptions. Patients pay an enrollment fee of $500 and ongoing fees of $3,000 per year out of pocket. In return, they get an effective weight-loss solution.

HERE ARE SOME HIGHLIGHTS FROM DR. GUNARATNAM'S PROGRAM:

1. A 12-week, intense meal replacement diet with transition to a plant-based whole food diet with guidance of dietitians.
2. Collaboration with local fitness facilities to target physiological age and not weight.
3. Weekly educational programs tiered to patient experience to teach life habits associated with long-term weight loss and wellness.
4. Patients receive online coaching via smartphones. A centralized team monitors their progress daily, weekly, and monthly.
5. Using AI, the program plans to divide patients into cohorts with high, medium, and low risk.

To start with, the program aims to reverse or improve chronic diseases that include NAFLD, GERD, IBS, diabetes, and hypertension. Dr. Gunaratnam participated in an American Gastroenterological Association (AGA) initiative to develop obesity as a line of service for gastroenterologists. The program is considered a gold standard in obesity management for GI practices. By running a profitable program, Dr. Gunaratnam breaks the norm of the insurance cycle. The initiative is helping patients achieve their weight loss goals. It's no wonder then that people are willing to pay for results. Could you explore a similar initiative in your practice?

In this chapter, we looked at changing patient expectations. Patients are going beyond sickness into the domain of expecting more from their bodies. But present-day healthcare models aren't equipped to meet those expectations. What follows is an interview with Dr. Jeffrey Gladden, who left his cardiology practice to start Apex Health, Human Performance, and Longevity. His patients (or clients) pay him upfront for a full year, including the costs of lab tests. Could his business model offer insights into how future GI practices might *scope forward*?

INTERVIEW WITH DR. JEFFREY GLADDEN, APEX HEALTH, HUMAN PERFORMANCE AND LONGEVITY

Dr. Jeffrey Gladden is the Founder of Apex. Apex Health and Human Performance is a concierge program based in Dallas, Texas. Earlier in his career, Dr. Gladden worked as an interventional cardiologist.

Q: What inspired you to start Apex?

Dr. Jeffrey Gladden: My background is in interventional cardiology. I practiced here in Texas for 25 years. In my early 50s, I fell very sick. I had no energy to get out of bed in the morning. I felt very stressed, depressed. I was losing strength, and I felt like I won't be able to keep up with my kids. I was always very athletic, but I was starting to put weight around the middle. When I got tested, I was told everything was fine and that I was just getting older! That's what really hit the switch for me. I said to myself, "I don't accept this." That's when I switched gears. I explored age-management medicine, functional medicine, and integrative medicine. After two and a half to three years, I actually ended up cracking the code for myself. And once I sorted that out, I really started to feel good again. Then I started to think, "Gosh, if I can feel so good now in my mid-50s, I wonder how good I can be? I want to know how fit, how mentally sharp I can be."

When I was practicing cardiology, I would ask, "Are you having chest pain? Do you have shortness of breath or other complications?" If you said yes to one of those, then I had a tool kit that I was trained in. I'd apply that, and that would be the best I could do for you. It may or may not work, but that's what I would work with. After my switch, I began asking much bigger questions like, "How good can you be?"

The world is changing very quickly. It's difficult to keep up if you are married to the answers you currently have. Because there will be better answers tomorrow. I think it's much more important to be married to the questions that are driving your progress forward.

Q: How did you go about building this business model? Do you take insurance?

Dr. Gladden: I left the insurance model altogether because I realized that medical insurance is not health insurance. It's sick insurance. We don't have healthcare, we have sick care. It's reactive care and not preemptive or preventative. I realized that I was handcuffed to the payors. If payors aren't paying for something, you are not thinking about it. You are not learning about it. You are not talking to your patients about it. And yet, I discovered there's a world full of actionable information out there. That could be very helpful for myself and many other people.

It was difficult in the beginning because I was used to an insurance-based model, where if you saw somebody, you get paid. I tried various iterations, including a hybrid model. Then I figured I wanted to work with people who were asking the same questions that I was. The bigger questions. I took part in different entrepreneurial groups for a year, and my message resonated with people in those groups. I started attracting clients that way, and then it grew from word of mouth. I'm working on a book called *How to Make 100 the New 30*. A podcast I started a couple of years ago called *Living Beyond 120* gained popularity.

Q: How's your business model different from other longevity-focused companies, such as Human Longevity Inc. (HLI)?

Dr. Gladden: It's very different. HLI is really a data play. I've had clients who've gone to HLI before they came to see me. They have their genomes done, scans done, a full-body MRI and some neurocognitive tests. But if things come back a little bit out of whack, they say you need to go see your doctor.

Our approach is that we conduct a lot of tests that they don't. Virtually everything that they do and more. We're really working with people for transformation. So we've evolved to a model where we work with people for a year at a time. They pay us upfront for the entire year—all the tests and everything else that they're going to work with us for. So we have no accounts receivable! We build a program that's customized to their aspirations. It deals with things that they are most concerned about. It's different for each person.

We ask the right question, How good can this person be? We continue to ask as the year goes on. When we are solving one problem, we find other things, and we push things along. We collaborate with people who really want transformation.

Q: Do your patients actually ask you to upgrade them?

Dr. Gladden: In a normal sick-care model, the idea is to get people back to their baseline state, whatever that is. We're really working toward a health-optimization state. In that context, we're looking at ways to help them turn back the clock functionally and psychologically. We want to help them optimize themselves spiritually. We want to minimize the stress in their lives and give them stress-management strategies that really work.

We leave no stone unturned in using technology to augment longevity. There are more technologies in the horizon. If people are interested, then we move forward with those. Clients are wide open to that. They want to live to 120. When they are 100 they want to feel like they are 30. That's why they are working with us.

Q: What do you see happening in the next five to ten years?

Dr. Gladden: We will be able to democratize this information, where more people will have access to it. We are right now at the cusp of being able to stop aging and actually start going backward. The antiaging space is going to gain more and more momentum. On the technology side (from working on telomeres to rejuvenating stem cells), we are going to get people to 30 years and help them stay there. On the implementation side, we are going to scale and reach a lot more people.

Q: How soon do you see results in your patients?

Dr. Gladden: We see progress in three months for some people. If people go all-in with us, we see massive progress in a year. I had a patient in from Nashville, just about a year ago, and she's signing up for another year with us. She's made massive improvements. She was just out hiking in the mountains for five days, five hours per day, and having no trouble with the altitude. She's 60 and there's no way she could've even thought about going on that trip a year ago. She's super happy with the progress. We have lots of stories like that; people write us thank-you notes. They are literally turning back the clock for themselves.

Q: Have you come across any gastroenterologists in this space?

Dr. Gladden: I've come across people in the functionality space that are big on working on the gut. Healing leaky gut and treating for achlorhydria or hypochlorhydria or improving the gut biome. There are a lot of people looking for cancer preemptively. But I don't know any gastroenterologists who are doing that. I think gastroenterologists are married to their current answers, right? "We're trained to scope," so I don't see many of them moving in this direction yet.

Q: Do you think more doctors will shift to this model or a similar model?

Dr. Gladden: I think some will and some won't. There's so much momentum around our current healthcare system—as broken as it is. It's a money-making system for a lot of hospital systems, drug companies, physicians. Even though it's becoming more regulated and controlled, I don't see people suddenly shifting. If somebody's doing something, they are going to stay doing it. Then there are others, like myself, who realize the shortcomings of the system and decide to leave and do something else.

Nobody was trained in functional medicine in medical school; everybody migrated to it. There are more and more people migrating to it. But I don't think it is going to change the established medical community. Quite honestly, who cares whether they do or they don't? All we need to care about is whether we are actually able to help people.

PART 1 TAKEAWAYS: WHAT'S UNLIKELY TO HAPPEN?

In response to a recent article I wrote on disruption in GI, a gastroenterologist asked me to "contain myself." It made me pause and reflect. I realized that doctors are busy with patients and administration, with almost no time to look up. When schedules are full, disruption is the last thing you think will happen. But as you know now, it's happening.

At this point in the book, we may or may not agree on what's likely to happen. So I thought it would be easier to agree on what's *unlikely* to happen. Take a moment to reflect on the *convergence* of the four trends you've examined in the last few chapters. Exponential technologies, consolidation, Big Brothers, and patient behavior.

Let's stir that pot and agree on what's unlikely to happen.

1. It's *unlikely* that insurance reimbursements for GI will significantly go up. Especially for procedures like colonoscopy.
2. It's *unlikely* that DNA testing or AI-based polyp detection will decline in sensitivity.
3. It's *unlikely* that health systems will get less powerful and leave you alone.
4. It's *unlikely* that insurances will make it easier for you to get paid.
5. It's *unlikely* that regulatory burden or administrative costs will reduce.
6. It's *unlikely* that there will be less stringent quality benchmarks. For example, no one's going to lower expectations of adenoma detection rate.
7. It's *unlikely* that you'll spend any less time on computing devices.

8. It's *unlikely* that your patients will have fewer demands as consumers.

So what do you do? Would you ride this wave? Or be disrupted by it?

You can be fearful of these changes and respond by saying, "How do I protect myself from this disruption?" You can choose to be dismissive and wait and watch on the sidelines. You can choose to disbelieve everything. You can think life is unfair. You are meant to be a doctor and this isn't medicine.

That mindset will take you down one path.

Or you can choose to respond differently. You can be excited about what's coming and say, "I'll treat this as an adventure." You'll disrupt instead of waiting to be disrupted. You'll learn what you have to and teach others. When you do that, you'll grow. You'll lead not just your practice but also the industry into a brighter future.

Now, that kind of a mindset takes you down a completely different path.

The former is a *scarcity* mindset. The latter is a mindset of *abundance*. We'll talk about this again later in part 4 of the book.

The next several chapters are for those who wish to go through the path of abundance. It requires taking action—a lot of action. Yes, it requires a spirit of adventure.

Let's scope forward.

PART 2

———

OUTSIDE SCOPE

At the outset, I agree with you that you are a doctor and that much of what I'm about to discuss isn't medicine. You've studied medicine, and you shouldn't have to worry about other skills that run the engine of healthcare. Skills such as technology, business, management, billing, finance, and so on. They are outside scope (pun intended!).

But as we saw in the last section, what if medicine itself shifted gears? What if the definition of "delivering care" or being a "doctor" has moved to its next iteration? Today's gastroenterologist is trained to work with an endoscope. But what if tomorrow's gastroenterologist is expected to work with AI?

Chapter 5 gives you a feel for various nonclinical topics without being exhaustive. These indicate areas that you must pay closer attention to in the coming decade. They are by no means comprehensive.

Chapter 6 on alignment and leadership is crucial for gastroenterology at the present time. Unlike other areas you'll read in part 2 of this book, alignment is an area that you must choose to master. As you will see, the stakes of un-alignment among doctors are too high. If gastroenterologists are aligned, then they will lead the industry into the future. If you are not organized, someone else will come and lead you to a place you may not want to go.

CHAPTER 5

GI BEYOND MEDICINE

Doctors will need to be interested beyond traditional ways of healthcare delivery to thrive in the future. New tools and systems will massively impact what you can do for patient care.

Let's consider AI. You won't have to take a programming course on machine learning, but you will need to know enough to know how to use it. What if it's the new scalpel? To be a doctor, you don't need to know how to make a scalpel, but you need to know how to harness it.

Let's consider money. You don't have to prepare financial statements, but you must know enough to read them. Or you must know someone who can explain it to you in simple terms. Such a skill would help you ask the right questions when your practice contemplates taking private equity.

Let's consider business management. You don't need to know how to run operations using Six Sigma process improvement methodologies. But you need to know what it takes to run efficient operations and what methodical systems look like.

This would help you in choosing the right leaders to administer your group.

Paradoxically, what if becoming proficient in these non-clinical areas actually offers you the freedom to focus on medicine? Because if not executed right, business or technology functions can be a stumbling block in clinical practice.

My goal in this chapter is to provide bite-sized insights to help you *think* in a way that scopes toward the future without getting lost in complexity. What you choose to take on in your practice will be your choice, of course, but all of the topics that follow are worthy thought problems for you to consider.

PURSUIT OF STANDARDIZATION

When you turn the faucet in your kitchen, the water flows. I don't think you imagine the wonders of what goes into it. We use systems without realizing that we do. Well-functioning systems tend to disappear into the background.

A few months ago, I was visiting an endoscopy reseller in upstate New York. He was delayed for the meeting, so I decided to drive around the area and ended up at the Muscoot Reservoir located in the village of Katonah. It's vast and beautiful. The water from Muscoot enters the Croton River to flow into the New Croton Reservoir. From that reservoir, it flows into aqueducts and other reservoirs in the Bronx, Manhattan, and Brooklyn. And it finally ends up in Staten Island.

Along the way, this system makes sure that eight million people get water when they turn on the faucet. Every day, every hour. Rain or shine. Snow or not.

The main reason that healthcare is a mess is because of broken systems or no systems. But let's focus on a single medical practice. It's not hard to spot where, in your practice, you have broken systems. A simple rule of thumb is to identify what bothers you or disrupts your work. Some examples include:

- Staff not showing up to work holds up patients = broken human resources, broken workflow systems
- Mandates that you are rushing to comply with = broken compliance process
- Patients who publicly rate you two or three stars = broken patient engagement

Our goal here is to not solve these problems but to understand them. Understanding systems helps you make progress. You can apply this thinking to any area of your practice: clinical, administrative, or technological.

The key word when we're thinking about systems is *standardization*. Let's take the example of maintaining credentialing status of providers. Many practices have a billing professional who doubles as the credentialing person. Let's call her Hailey. She maintains a spreadsheet or paper files from various insurance companies and hospitals. Possibly, she checks on credentialing status when she remembers toward the end of the month. Sometimes Hailey forgets, so a letter from an insurance company prompts her to act. If she's efficient, she might have entered certain dates into her calendar or set reminders.

There are two questions to ask in this scenario:

- If you add 10 more providers to the group, would Hailey's system scale? Or would she ask you to hire another person?

- If Hailey left the practice next week, could this process be transitioned to a new person?

If you answered no to either or both questions, then it should reveal to you the importance of systems and using technology to standardize tasks. Enormous wastage creeps into healthcare because systems aren't standardized. The greater the standardization, the greater the efficiency. The greater the efficiency, the more reliable your system becomes. There are different tools you can use to track and improve your systems. The simplest tool is a checklist. Dr. Reed Hogan of GI Associates in Mississippi is a big proponent of lists. I saw him use one while performing endoscopies. Atul Gawande's book *The Checklist Manifesto* is a great starting point to explore standardization in your practice. A more sophisticated technique is Six Sigma. Indianapolis Gastroenterology and Hepatology, a GI group in Indiana, embraces Six Sigma to reduce error rates. You could consider implementing the same.

TAKEAWAY

If you desire predictability, like the New York water system, you need to examine every aspect of every function in your practice. Divide the functions into standard and nonstandard tasks. Stitch together a workflow. Develop a system that maximizes efficiency, incorporates automation and technology, and reduces wastage.

ENGAGING PATIENTS—STRATEGY VS. TACTICS

Often practices assume that patient engagement is about

educating them, sometimes through a website or in waiting rooms. Practices advertise for screening colonoscopy on Google or Facebook. They send them birthday cards with colonoscopy recall messages. These are good tactics but not a strategy. When you approach patient engagement as a series of tactics, it appears broken. It's not natural or effortless.

Strangely, I love hanging out in waiting areas in doctors' offices and eating at hospital cafeterias. I get to observe what patients do. I notice signs on glass windows and watch mindless TV along with them. I've even written articles while sitting in the waiting areas of a few well-known hospitals.

When patients are open to a conversation, I chat them up. Many times, patients know more about the practice than the people working there. That's because they live the experience of your practice. Many times, their life depends on it.

Patient engagement is only effective if you immerse yourself in their experience. To that end, here are some elementary questions to ask yourself:

1. Who have been your three best patients? Write them down.
2. How would those three patients introduce you to their family members?
3. What are some of the biggest challenges you've helped patients overcome?
4. What would your patients say you are really good at? List all that comes to mind.
5. If you didn't have to worry about time or money and had two straight hours with a patient, how would you help them?

These questions will help you identify what's already unique about your practice. The problem with most brand engagement tactics is that they are simply the implementation of generic tactics without a unique-to-you overall strategy. They are keywords and catchphrases that won't help your patients find you when you are lost in a maze of other similar-sounding options. Everyone talks about colon cancer screening, everyone displays brochures of various GI conditions, but almost no one taps into the emotion associated with those conditions.

What will give you unique, undivided engagement is to first identify what you mean to your patients and then understand what your patients want to hear from you.

For example, let's say after this exercise you realize that "IBD patients" is a cohort that you attract. Say this group in your region (or beyond) already recognizes you as an expert. Ask yourself, What are the biggest fears that this group deals with?

Then go deeper. Invest additional time with your best IBD patients and understand their burning problems. Understand the emotional angle to inflammatory bowel disease. Going deep will get you to the exact phrases or challenges that your patients have. For example, no one really talks about "urgent bowel movements" or "inflammation of the digestive tract." And yet those are phrases you find on medical websites.

Real people start by talking in the way a ten-year-old might describe the problem. They might say, "I keep going to the bathroom all the time." Or they might say, "I can't remember the last time I went out for dinner without worrying about the toilet." The medical lingo comes much later.

You know this already. That's how patients describe a problem to you. And you know exactly how to approach that problem. So next time your marketing person tells you that it's important to throw a bunch of medical keywords on your website or ad, ask, What's the underlying reason? What's the outcome we want?"

Approach brand building as a more cohesive strategy that truly exemplifies your personal brand. That's when a Facebook ad or Google ad will yield the right kind of results because you'll speak to your potential patient's heart. Donald Miller's videos and David Meerman Scott's books are good takeoff points on this topic. Miller's book is called *Building a StoryBrand: Clarify Your Message So Customers Will Listen*. Scott's latest book is called *Fanocracy: Turning Fans into Customers and Customers into Fans*.

TAKEAWAY

Effective patient engagement requires differentiation. That relies on connecting the dots with their pains and desires. Digital engagement strategies always go inside out. Emotions are at the core of engagement. Social media tactics come last.

EHRS AS BUILDING BLOCKS OF DATA

Much has been said about electronic health records, or EHRs. That they disturb workflow and are badly designed. That they are a necessary evil of medical practice. But there's not much talk about visualizing EHRs as building blocks of data.

Something that your practice's future valuation could depend on. So let's talk about that.

Think of the vital signs that you capture every day, such as BMI. Consider that as one piece of data—a Lego block. When you plot BMI across 10 office visits, you get longitudinal insights on the patient. Think of that information as a handful of Lego blocks shaping into a tower.

Say you plot BMI across all your patients in a certain county. That gives you longitudinal insights into the county's patients on that parameter. Now your Lego farm has a tower, garden, and what not. That farm can have many blocks of valuable data.

Each level has a different level of *abstraction*. Abstraction conceals underlying levels of complexity by providing a higher lens. For example, here are three levels.

- Level 1: BMI on October 1, 2019 is one level.
- Level 2: BMI from 2014 to 2019 is a level higher.
- Level 3: BMI for 10,000 patients in the last five years is an even higher level of abstraction.

Now imagine multiple parameters at play. Lab results, drugs, imaging studies, and diagnosis codes all at the same time. At a Level 1 abstraction, it's what you see every day—one patient's medical notes at a time. But when you go toward higher levels (many notes, many patients), that's when the right technology tools can help you cull insights from complexity.

Such data synthesis has great value. One way is to arm yourself to negotiate better insurance contracts. You might be able to demonstrate to an insurance company that your practice prevented hospitalization. Imagine the leverage you could develop compared to your competition. What if you routinely captured quality information across all your patients and payors?

Let's take this a step further. What if your EHR data is combined with other databases, such as public demographics, environmental databases, or data from health trackers? Data visualization tools can help you view disease conditions as heat maps that you can navigate. Imagine the richness of such data.

This data will have great value in the future. Dr. Michael Byrne (from ai4gi; you met him in chapter 1), when I spoke with him, said, "We'll be able to use a lot of the patient data that right now is hard for humans to interpret. We will be able to put all that data together. Genomic data, patient characteristics, lifestyle, diagnostic and imaging data, and so on. Then we can feed that data into a supercomputer algorithm and come up with current and future prognostic answers."

That's when your EHR begins to help you solve patient problems at scale.

When GI groups roll up and move on to the third or fourth bite of the apple, data will have enormous value. Incoherent data will, of course, have no value. To explore this topic further, study Salim Ismail's work on exponential organizations. His book is called *Exponential Organizations: Why New Organizations Are Ten Times Better, Faster, and Cheaper Than Yours (and What to Do about It)*. You can also follow data strategies of Google and Microsoft. How are they acquiring and applying data? Why do they value data the way they do?

TAKEAWAY

Traditionally, doctors have viewed EHRs as burdensome tools. A template-driven approach to documentation has resulted in a lot of unusable data within EHRs. Instead, if we enrich the data in the EHR by combining it with other types of data (such as demographics or environment), we get deeper insights. When we view data or EHRs in light of its potential value, we will approach EHR documentation differently. Think of data as currency. EHR is a tool that helps you invest in that currency.

OUTSOURCING AS A STRATEGY

For the purposes of this book, when I say "outsourcing," I mean offshoring work to a low-cost region. Most large enterprises outsource one or another piece of their work. Major hospitals outsource accounts receivable, and other areas of revenue cycle management. Some medical practices outsource the entirety of their billing and accounting. Most technology companies distribute their software development efforts across the world. Companies like GE Healthcare use Bengaluru for research and development. Objectives of outsourcing vary from lowering costs to increasing speed of delivery to accessing talent.

My business, NextServices, has had global operations from its first year (2005). As a co-founder, I've experienced both the benefits and travails of operating in the US and India.

Benefits, of course, include cost savings, faster turnaround, and access to raw talent. Challenges pertain to honing talent, retaining staff, and communication. Not to mention the difficulties of dealing with multiple time zones on a daily basis.

With gastroenterology, the industry has yet to fully tap into the advantages of outsourcing. GI practices will need to look for ways to reduce costs and improve earnings before interest, tax, depreciation, and amortization, or EBITDA (more simply stated as profitability). Outsourcing one or more aspects of the revenue cycle will become a crucial lever to do so. For a practice to survive, outsourcing will be inevitable.

As gastroenterology gets bigger, it'll also get more sophisticated. The only way to organize information and simplify operations is a greater reliance on technology. There will be requirements of newer tools, better analysis, more automation. All aspects of software development offer scope for outsourcing.

However, learning how to effectively outsource is unlikely to happen overnight. Developing outsourcing into a competitive advantage will need focus. As with any new business strategy, you are likely to go through a learning curve. But after you reach a state where the outsourced components of your business are consistently delivering, you'll wonder why you didn't do it sooner.

Learning how to effectively outsource will come from executing little experiments first. Next time you face a resource crunch, instead of hiring, ask yourself if you can outsource the task as a project. When a staff member leaves, instead of rehiring, find a way to use a remote resource. During the year, take the time to speak to others who've been through the outsourcing cycle. If you are so inclined, visit an outsourcing destination such as India or the Philippines. During your board meetings, review examples from other industries that outsource. Ask yourself how you might benefit from the same strategy. The book *Reverse Innovation in Health Care: How to Make Value-Based Delivery Work* by Vijay Govindarajan and Ravi Ramamurti takes this a step further. It talks about healthcare innovations from the developing world that have been put to use in the US.

TAKEAWAY

As with business automation, view outsourcing as a tool for growth and competitive leverage. In addition to outsourcing, explore newer on-demand engagement models via Freelancer, Upwork, Kolabtree, or HealthITq. Kolabtree is particularly interesting because it allows you hire scientists and researchers on demand. Next time you have a design task, look up 99designs. You need an article written, find someone on Fiverr. While it may not be the kind of staffing or team building you're used to, it is the way of the future.

GROWTH MINDSET

When I visited GI Associates in Jackson, Mississippi, Dr. Reed Hogan showed me around their facilities (covered in chapter 8). On the top floor, he pointed to a neighboring plot of land from the window. He remarked that it would make a good investment for a parking lot.

Todd Warren, CEO of the group, called Dr. Hogan a marketing genius. It was not surprising to understand why. Dr. Jay

Underwood, the president of the group, talked about the time they considered a unique ancillary opportunity: a laundry service. Dr. Hogan had proposed it, but the board decided to not pursue the business. Later, when I asked Dr. Hogan about it, he smiled casually and said he went on to invest in the opportunity in his personal capacity. I gathered it had a very good investment outcome.

Dr. Hogan and his group have taught themselves to spot opportunities to thrive. They know that growth and profitability are essential for survival. In 2018, they decided to outsource their anesthesia billing. That brought more money into the system. They added $1 million after a year. They are entrepreneurial by nature.

Most successful GI practices are beyond focusing on the baselines of quality, productivity, and patient engagement. They've figured out a method to grow as an organization. They have a *growth mindset*.

There are a few ways you could develop such a mindset. You could start by reading books on business strategy, such as *Blue Ocean Strategy: How to Create Uncontested Market Space and Make Competition Irrelevant*. Attend business conferences or take classes on entrepreneurship in management schools to develop a growth mindset. Taking online courses, such as Ramit Sethi's *Zero to Launch*, can inspire you to borrow ideas from digital industries. Once you are tuned in to a growth mindset, set aside an organizational budget to experiment on business opportunities. Once you see signs of returns, invest more in that direction.

TAKEAWAY

The growth mindset is increasingly crucial for gastroenterology practices, regardless of whether they are independent or private equity-owned. It makes them alert, nimble, and entrepreneurial.

THREE MODELS OF PHYSICIAN COMPENSATION

Many gastroenterologists continue to feel bitter about how they are compensated. Compensation models, when executed well, ensure that money isn't a bone of contention. When executed badly, compensation becomes the main topic of discussion among doctors.

Compensation models also make a critical difference in recruiting new doctors. It also helps in physician governance, lifestyle, and retirement.

Here are three examples of compensation models.

EXAMPLE 1: EAT WHAT YOU KILL

Dr. Louis Wilson's practice in Wichita Falls (covered in chapter 7) uses this model for partnership distribution. The group hasn't changed its structure since its beginning in 2005. Wichita Falls Gastroenterology is a practice of seven gastroenterologists and serves 800 patients every week.

Here are the basic elements of the Eat What You Kill model:

1. Physician pay is determined based on net collections. It equals total collections minus shared overheads and direct expenses.

2. Pathology lab income is part of shared overhead.
3. Endoscopy center income is based on percentage of ownership.
4. Real estate is accounted separately.
5. Nurse practitioner income is divided equally among doctors.
6. Compensation for hospital calls is paid separately.

Shared overheads include rent, staff costs, utilities, supplies, building expenses, EHR and software costs, and other insurance costs. Direct expenses include 401(k) contributions, continuing education, licenses and other dues, personal insurance, and business expenses.

The group also adheres to certain rules so there's clarity among partners.

1. New patients are shared equally.
2. Colon cancer screening revenues are shared equally.
3. Patients are discouraged from flipping physicians.
4. Fired patients are fired from the group.
5. All contracts are group contracts.
6. Group meetings and votes are strictly managed and recorded.
7. All employees are group employees.

EXAMPLE 2: 80% DISTRIBUTION, 20% REWARD

Dr. Scott Ketover broadly shared the elements of the compensation structure at MNGI Digestive Health (covered in chapter 8). Based in Minnesota, MNGI is one of the largest independent groups in the country. Here is how compensation works in their organization:

1. Seventy-five to eighty percent of total compensation is based on shared revenues of the group.
2. The rest of the compensation is based on Relative Value Units (RVUs). By definition, RVUs are factors used by Medicare to determine physician fees for various services.
3. RVU incentives are capped at 120% of total group average to curtail excessive distribution. This indicates earning limits based on a doctor's productivity.
4. Advanced endoscopists are compensated in the same way as the others. These doctors might be more focused on advanced procedures such as ERCPs (endoscopic retrograde cholangiopancreatography).

It's an individual choice on whether someone focuses on advanced or general endoscopy. While one group takes up advanced cases, others compensate by generating volume and RVUs.

EXAMPLE 3: EARN YOUR OWNERSHIP

GI Associates in Jackson, Mississippi (covered in chapter 8), has the following compensation structure.

1. Compensation is based on 50% productivity by units or cases done and 50% collections.
2. Ancillaries, like pathology or anesthesia, are mostly evenly shared.
3. Ownership: All partners get two shares when they start. Each year of work helps them earn two more shares. For example, in the second year, someone would get four shares, and in the third year, ownership would entail six shares. This growth continues up to a maximum of 12 shares.

4. The bylaws mandate a certain maintenance of productivity (for example, performing a certain number of procedures or seeing a certain number of patients).
5. Voting decisions are also made by the number of shares owned by a partner.

TAKEAWAY

Physician compensation is central to all business strategies. The objective of the model must be to remove money as a topic of debate among partners so that everyone aligns toward the growth of the organization.

COLLABORATING WITH HEALTH SYSTEMS

With over 50,000 admissions per year, ChristianaCare plays a powerful role in Delaware's healthcare community. Two of Delaware's largest hospitals, 906-bed Christiana Hospital and 321-bed Wilmington Hospital, are part of the health system. Not only that, they are financially viable and the largest private employer in the state. On the face of it, you could say that if they wanted to build a GI department, they could. But they instead chose to collaborate with local gastroenterologists.

Dr. Jared Hossack, a gastroenterologist at Mid-Atlantic GI Consultants in Delaware, shared the story of their partnership with ChristianaCare with me. Dr. Hossack belongs to a rare, younger lot of gastroenterologists. They are dynamic, friendly, and savvy with technology and business. Plus, they make great clinicians. Leaders like Dr. Hossack seek a different healthcare future. And despite their busy lives, they are willing to invest the time to make that future happen.

The story of ChristianaCare's approach to gastroenterology began when two local GI groups saw an opportunity to build a working relationship with ChristianaCare. The two groups are Mid-Atlantic GI Consultants (MAGIC) and the Delaware Center for Digestive Care (DCDC).

A few years ago, MAGIC was finding it difficult to balance finances and schedules with hospital visits. They decided it wouldn't be feasible to continue seeing patients at ChristianaCare. That's when DCDC stepped in and said that if MAGIC withdrew, it would create an enormous burden for them and the community. The doctors from DCDC would be burdened by all the hospital calls, and patient needs wouldn't be met in time. Something had to be worked out. That's when the three organizations—ChristianaCare, MAGIC, and DCDC—decided to collaborate and find a solution.

The GI groups did some homework and proposed a certain arrangement that would make it economically feasible for the groups to cover the health system. ChristianaCare accepted the proposal and decided to work with the GI groups long term. Interestingly, the success of that collaboration led to a merger of MAGIC and DCDC, leading to an even better economic outcome.

In 2016, ChristianaCare's CEO, Dr. Janice E. Nevin adopted new core values of "love and excellence," conveying their larger goals as a healthcare provider. Seeking "excellence" is common. But naming "love" as a value is unusual. Perhaps that's what is prompting a collaborative environment in that healthcare community.

In most parts of the country, both gastroenterologists and

hospitals are driven by fear. Fear often triggers a fight-or-flight response. Doctors wish to maintain their independence. Hospitals wish to control local markets. But both can't do without each other. There's a strained dynamic. And yet, there are examples of groups that have built a better, collaborative dynamic.

Jerry Tillinger, CEO of US Digestive Health, had this to say about collaborating with hospitals: "Even when there are areas of conflict (for example, on-call coverage or division of services), we collaborate. If there's going to be a change in the market and something's going to have economic impact on one party or other, both sides are willing to sit down and talk those through." (You'll read his interview in chapter 9.)

In fact, it was the influence of local hospitals in the Twin Cities that inspired separate GI groups in Minneapolis to come together to form Minnesota Gastroenterology (now MNGI Digestive Health). More than 20 years ago, a local hospital system wanted to make a move to collaborate with just one of the three main GI groups. But the groups wanted to keep their independence, so they merged together to be stronger. The hospitals didn't respond competitively. Instead, they learned to work with the new, merged group. The group went on to invest in tertiary and quaternary care. More recently, when one of the hospitals lost their endoscopy nurses, MNGI supported them. The group now staffs and manages the hospital's endoscopy unit 24-7. The hospital pays them a contracted rate.

TAKEAWAY

It's crucial to figure out your equation with local hospitals. You can accomplish this by aligning, collaborating, and becoming stronger internally, then opening dialogue externally. Such an approach is driven by a mindset of abundance, not scarcity. Ultimately, it results in better outcomes for patients.

CHAPTER 6

A CALL FOR ALIGNMENT

Alignment among doctors is so important that it determines the future of gastroenterology. But before we can go forward, we need to go back. All the way back to understand the path that doctors have taken.

It occurred to me that people who work closely with doctors would likely have some keen observations about the healthcare landscape, particularly administrators who have successfully managed GI practices for many years. My conversations with Jeff Griffin, COO of Digestive Disease Specialists in Oklahoma, and Todd Warren, CEO of GI Associates & Endoscopy Center in Mississippi, were insightful. After my conversations with them, I took some time to integrate their observations with everything that I've personally observed about the medical profession over the years.

Doctors are one of the most intelligent groups of individuals on the planet. Studying long and hard often entails social isolation. At least, more than the average school-goer. A certain calling to take care of people often inspires them to traverse the long and arduous path of medicine. Once they make it past admissions, it is perhaps the first time doctors engage with others like themselves. They meet *their* tribe.

But they soon realize their tribe is, by nature, competitive. Everyone knows that the person at the bottom of the graduating class is also going to be a doctor. However, no one wants to be that person. They face intense competition for grades. As they approach graduation and gain practical experience, doctors are taught to be decisive, to be sure even when they are not, to take control of a medical situation. Because if they don't, then who will? How will they handle a code blue emergency when the time comes?

Todd Warren, whose father is an internist, told me the story of his best friend who went to medical school. After a few years of study, he started behaving differently—using harsher words and being abrupt. Warren took him aside and asked him what had changed. After reflection, his friend said he was taught to behave this way by his superiors.

This isolated medical tribe moves into medical practices or hospitals. Whatever their path or specialty, they largely lead isolated professional lives. For the most part, it is them and their patients. Them and research. Them and board certifications. When they launch independent practices, they are thrust into the roles of managing a business and staff. In private practice, doctors always know that they are central to its functioning—the world has to revolve around them.

Given that competition almost becomes a survival skill, there has to be something to compete about in private practice. The fee-for-service model allows the competitive mindset to shift from grades to money. How much someone makes in private practice becomes a measure of success. That anchor means that all the hard work and toil from the years in medical school was worth it. With private equity, that comparison and competition extends itself to valuation. Isn't it common to ask in the corners of GI business conferences, "How much X did they get?"—meaning, Was a certain group valued at multiples of five, eight, or ten times? Even though the multiple itself might not mean more money.

The introduction of managed care ensures that the healthcare system pursues volume. Because if you do more procedures, you get paid more. And somewhere along the way, the model diluted the trust that patients have in their doctors. It diluted the trust that doctors have with each other as colleagues. It weakened their relationship with the system. If done wrong, private equity runs the risk of fueling this problem.

The challenge today is that the pursuit of high volume flies in the face of disruptive technology. For example, screening colonoscopy volume could be disrupted by DNA tests. In his interview, Dr. Lawrence Kosinski referred to gastroenterology practices as "colonoscopy factories." And soon, most GI offices might be co-owned by a corporation. Thus, the pursuit of fierce independence flies in the face of disruption led by business consolidation.

More than financial implications, such shifts take an emotional toll. Because it suddenly means that the earlier anchor of success has changed. There's nothing to hold on to. Everything doctors have learned and been immersed in up to this point can no longer be their North Star. So what do healthcare practitioners turn to instead if they want to thrive in the future of healthcare?

THE COMPETITION IS OUT THERE

Social isolation, which helped doctors focus and compete with each other, has become a curse, particularly in the evolving model of consolidated healthcare delivery. Because as Dr. James Leavitt of Gastro Health said, "Hospitals are consolidating. Payors are consolidating. Even unusual partners such as CVS and Aetna are consolidating. We think other physicians are competitors, but we are the solution to each other. The real competition is out there." (Read Dr. Leavitt's interview in chapter 9.)

The problem is doctors don't just compete with other groups. They also compete with each other within the group. Over lunch this past summer, a younger GI doctor shared this anecdote: "Say one doctor made $20K, another made $10K in a certain area. And there's a decision where the first doctor would make $5K more, but the second doctor would make $3K more. The second doctor would vote against the decision or abstain from voting because he can't stand the first doctor making $2K more than him."

In return, I shared with him a story I heard while growing up in India.

There were two neighbors who often competed with each other on everything. One time, both of them undertook deep prayer so that they could be bestowed with special gifts. Finally, God appeared before the first neighbor and asked him to make a wish. But the first neighbor was curious to know what the second neighbor wanted.

God said, "I've not visited him yet. He's next in line."

So the first neighbor wished for twice of anything that the other neighbor was going to wish for.

When God appeared before the second neighbor, he wanted to first know what the first neighbor wanted.

God responded, "He wants twice of what you want."

The second neighbor thought a while and finally wished to go blind in one of his eyes.

Got it?

Board meetings end up being emotionally exhausting because the group isn't aligned toward common goals. There's much bitterness that bubbles below the surface. One doctor owns the building that the group pays rent on. Another has a special hospital status. Senior doctors take fewer hospital calls. Younger doctors feel they do all the work. Senior doctors want private equity. Junior ones feel insecure.

One gastroenterologist I know confessed, "Most of our meetings are shoutfests. They are about who gets to have the final word. We keep talking over each other with emotion until we are tired and it's time to go home. Nothing really gets done."

When administrators intervene, doctors don't like that either.

But while doctors are busy living isolated professional lives on the inside and competing with each other on the outside, healthcare is moving on, with or without them. It's not just CVS-Aetna they're up against. As we saw in the first part of this book, there are many companies that want a piece of healthcare. Consider Amazon, Google, United HealthGroup, Exact Sciences, digital health startups, and local hospital systems. All are keen to control and lead the industry. *Everyone* wants to show doctors how healthcare must be done. Strange, isn't it?

To survive, let alone thrive, in such an environment, doctors need to become their own best friends. If they do, then they can begin to align. If they align, then they can become a powerful, unanimous force. More powerful than the rest of healthcare put together. Mainly because the healthcare ecosystem can exist with or without any actor—*except* doctors.

If gastroenterologists become a singular force, then they will lead the industry and *scope forward*. If they *align*, they will be able to work out their relationships with hospitals. Instead of fearing technology changes such as stool DNA tests, they will shape what's to come and empower their practices to become effective. If they *align*, they will direct the rest of healthcare to act in a way that has patient interests at heart.

As a case in point, alignment within GI is taking shape in the form of the Digestive Health Physicians Association (DHPA). DHPA is a nonprofit trade organization. Dr. Scott Ketover (MNGI), former president of DHPA shared the story.

THE DHPA STORY

For 30 years, there was a group called GI Practice Management Group (GPMG) in existence. Its members shared clinical and administrative best practices. But corporate practice of medicine laws prevented more than two members from the same region to get together. They envisioned a larger trade body to represent the interests of independent GI practices.

That's when Dr. Michael Weinstein and Dr. Scott Ketover got together to start DHPA. They looped in a lawyer, Howard Rubin. Rubin was already involved with an association called LUGPA (Large Urology Group Practice Association), and they figured a similar structure might benefit gastroenterologists. Nine GPMG members met in Washington, DC, in early 2014 and outlined the bylaws. It boiled down to two principle objectives: (1) improve patient care and (2) benefit providers.

That's how DHPA was born. At that time, the association was comprised of 11 groups representing 300 doctors. Six years later, DHPA consists of about 85 groups with more than 2,300 members. Dr. Weinstein is also the former president of the association. Today, DHPA gets together as a powerful voice for gastroenterologists and works with the Senate to update Stark Law and the CRC Screening Act. Previously, they successfully approached Exact Sciences to more appropriately represent Cologuard in their advertisements. They are a shining example of how cooperation and alignment can move us all forward.

WHAT'S POSSIBLE WITH GREATER COLLABORATION IN GI

DHPA has shown what's possible today when gastroenterologists come together, but a lot more can be done. With even greater alignment, DHPA can enable dialogue around the fundamental concerns of GI:

1. What must be the role of GI doctors in shaping future technologies such as AI or DNA testing?

2. How can gastroenterologists stand their ground *and* collaborate with hospital systems?
3. How do you educate the GI community on the pros and cons of private equity? How do you prevent the reoccurrence of the PPM debacle of the 1990s?
4. How do you align gastroenterologists to engage with big insurance platforms?
5. How do you shape GI to address the evolving needs of patients, some of which go beyond the scope of healthcare?

The answers to these questions can all be found in greater alignment within the GI industry. Imagine a future where GI shows the rest of healthcare how to navigate industry changes by owning its problems. That can happen only if

LUGPA

The idea for DHPA germinated from LUGPA, or Large Urology Group Practice Association. LUGPA was formed in 2008 to "enhance communication, promote clinical quality outcomes, and improve legislative and regulatory advocacy." Today, the organization is open to practices of all sizes, not just large. LUGPA supports its members with several resources, including data collection and benchmarking. As of 2017, 150 urology practices representing 2,400 members in 46 states were part of the association. The theme of LUGPA's 2019 annual meeting was, unsurprisingly, the *power of partnership*.

Dr. Neal Shore, past president of LUGPA, spoke on the present and future of LUGPA in January 2018. He had this to say: "You have to have collaboration...we all went to premed, med school, residency, and sort of this lone-wolf mentality. That has to change. It's not sustainable."

gastroenterologists *align* with each other in their groups, in their regions, and nationally.

PART 2 TAKEAWAYS: AN OFFER YOU CAN'T REFUSE

In this section, we explored ideas beyond the realm of clinical medicine, from standardizing operations to collaborating with health systems. More importantly, we delved into why it's more important than ever for physicians to come together as a strong, unanimous force.

Here are takeaways from what we covered:

1. Doctors must choose to be interested in GI beyond medicine. That would not only protect independent practice but also help GI stay physician-led.
2. Doctors wishing to lead GI must develop a strong grasp of business and technology.
3. The lone-wolf mindset of physicians served their interests in an earlier era of medicine, but that world has changed.
4. Doctors are best equipped to lead the industry and protect the interests of patients. That requires them to collaborate more than they compete.
5. With better alignment, GI can serve as a beacon to the rest of healthcare and show what's possible.

Think of the amount of money that the GI industry generates every day, every year. For example, as a collective of more than 2,300 members, DHPA accounts for over one billion dollars a year in insurance reimbursements. Doctors are the principal generators of the healthcare business. And yet doctors are at the pleading end of the payment equation with insurances. Why?

If it were a singular voice, couldn't GI replicate Haven Health's model? Amazon, Berkshire Hathaway, and JPMorgan started Haven as a closed-loop, integrated health system. They are providing better coverage, lowering costs, and modernizing healthcare. For GI, that could mean a GI-first health system that has its own insurance plan. Just as Geisinger Health System brought together healthcare providers and insurance, could we not imagine a DHPA health plan? Like Amazon, could we not imagine a DHPA virtual care model? Like Netflix, could we not imagine streaming advanced endoscopy training orchestrated by DHPA?

With strong alignment and imagination, doctors can create limitless opportunities for the specialty. That's how you *scope forward.*

PART 3

CHOOSE YOUR OWN ADVENTURE

It's time to start asking the right questions and choose your own adventure. During the course of writing this book, I visited a variety of GI practices and met many types of gastroenterologists. Some are based in rural areas. Some in metropolitan areas. Some are building private equity–funded platforms. Some are joining existing private equity–funded platforms. Some never want to get involved with private equity. Some always plan to remain solo. Some are large, independent groups. Some have chosen alternatives to private practice.

In this section, you'll meet all of them, with the intention of helping you determine your best path forward in gastroenterology. These stories will provide a glimpse into how various GI doctors are scoping their way into the future. I will provide takeaways and associated risks at the end of each adventure, as well.

Here are the types of GI practices that we'll explore:

- Solo, small, and midsize practices (chapter 7). Read the story of a seven-doctor group in Texas (Wichita Falls Gastroenterology). Includes interview of Dr. Narayanachar Murali, a solo practitioner in South Carolina.
- Independent groups (chapter 8). Read the story of a large independent group in Mississippi (GI Associates). Includes interview of Dr. Scott Ketover, president and CEO of MNGI Digestive Health.
- Private equity–funded platforms (chapter 9). Read the story of Pennsylvania's US Digestive Health. Includes interviews of Dr. James Leavitt, president and chief clinical officer of Gastro Health, and Jerry Tillinger, CEO of US Digestive Health.
- Alternative models, including the option of choosing scaled alternatives to private practice (chapter 10). Read the stories of Capital Digestive Care and Physicians Endoscopy. Other stories include a multispecialty GI group and an advanced GI practice in Texas. You'll also find an interview with Dr. John Allen, clinical professor of medicine at University of Michigan School of Medicine and chief clinical officer of University of Michigan Medical Group.

What I suggest is that you read about each of these types of practices with an open mind. Without bias toward one approach or another. By the end of your reading, I'm sure you'll know what resonates with you.

CHAPTER 7

CHOOSING SOLO, SMALL, OR MIDSIZE

A SEVEN-DOCTOR GROUP IN TEXAS

After a couple of hours drive from Dallas, Texas, a sign on US 281 announces Wichita Falls with a playful lone star. A tagline in yellow says, "Blue Skies. Golden Opportunities." At the GI Roundtable 2019, Dr. Louis Wilson had participated in a debate on private equity—he chose *against*. He is the managing partner of Wichita Falls Gastroenterology Associates, a group of seven gastroenterologists. I was in Wichita Falls to learn what lessons his group had to offer to others who wished to resist the wave of private equity and still thrive.

Brandon Beshear, director at United Regional Health Care System, and Jeremy Watkins, clinical manager of Wichita Falls Endoscopy Center, walked me through the Wichita Falls Endoscopy Center. It had four rooms with 15 beds. At the front desk of the center, I noticed a kiosk to check patients in. It not only scanned patient IDs but also prompted patients to pay down a prior balance.

United Regional had minority ownership in the center. The rest was owned by physician partners. Co-ownership made it easier to develop a mutually symbiotic relationship. Setting up a collaborative relationship with the hospital was one of the many moves that Dr. Wilson made to safeguard his group's practice.

Another critical move was to renegotiate their insurance contracts on a schedule. Depending on the insurance, the group renegotiated every one to three years. If the insurance declined the group's new offer, they would wait six months and approach the insurance again. The group recently switched from a local insurance negotiation service to a national one called ECG.

What was the impact of this insurance move? On one occasion, the practice wanted to coerce Blue Cross Blue Shield (BCBS) to improve their rates. The group terminated their contract with BCBS by giving a 90-day notice period. But before the termination period ended, BCBS came back with a better contract. Had BCBS accepted the termination, the group planned to restart the contract. A savvy negotiation strategy.

The group's position is bolstered by the fact that Wichita Falls is an independent island of healthcare in Texas. It covers a patient catchment area of 60 to 100 miles in all directions. They are the only gastroenterology group serving 16 counties of North Texas and Southern Oklahoma. If Wichita Falls Gastroenterology terminated contracts with a payor, it would inconvenience the insurance's subscribers. Patients would have to drive two or more hours to Dallas or Oklahoma City to get treated.

Dr. Wilson and his team understood this differentiated positioning in the market. They brought that leverage to the negotiating table with insurances. But they did not rely on geography alone. They strived to stand out through a relentless focus on quality and total cost of care.

Just a few minutes away from the Endoscopy Center are the private offices of Dr. Wilson and his partners. Inside, I noticed quality and accreditation certifications prominently displayed in the patient waiting area. Krista Zimpel, the practice administrator, ensured that the place ran smoothly with a staff of 30 people.

While we moved from room to room, I noticed that some of the doctors used Google Glass while they saw patients. It was part of a "virtual scribe" service called Augmedix that the doctors used to document directly into the EHR. Zimpel said that patients didn't mind the device. Augmedix employs scribes in India who document the medical record in real-time during consultations.

The practice owns a pathology lab to perform the technical component of all specimens from the Endoscopy Center. And they contract with a local pathology group to perform the professional component. "Technical component" refers to the provision of equipment and supplies related to a lab test. "Professional component" refers to the supervision and interpretation service provided by a healthcare professional. As part of the arrangement, Wichita Falls Gastroenterology sells the technical component to the pathology group wholesale. The GI group, therefore, does not have to work on billing or collections for pathology services.

Zimpel walked me to the lab, which was conveniently housed in a separate section of the same office building. Right next door was the group's infusion center that was managed by a partner, Altus Infusion Services. Dr. Wilson mentioned that both pathology and infusion ancillary services gave them substantial benefits.

At the practice, I noticed a staff member hanging a "Happy Birthday" banner by the entrance of the pantry. That's when Dr. Wilson introduced me to Dr. Rick Ho, who has been practicing gastroenterology for 40 years. I learned that Dr. Ho lived through "the decline of PPMs in the 1990s" and had to rebuild his practice.

At the private equity debate, Dr. Wilson had argued, "Nobody wants to be a doctor except the doctor. Payors, hospitals, PE companies don't want to take the meat out of someone's esophagus on Friday night."

He was implying that the risks of providing care must match the rewards. Dr. Wilson made sure that his physician partners were aligned with the same philosophy. They use the "Eat What You Kill" compensation model (described in chapter 6). Removing internal competition helped them stay focused on organizational concerns.

In addition to using Google Glass and Augmedix, the practice proactively used technology to improve efficiency. For example, there was a device to capture patient satisfaction in every consultation room. They also used another tool called Cipher Health that integrated with their EHR. In addition to automated appointment reminders, the group used Cipher for "postencounter care calls." I gathered that using these tools helped the practice stay highly responsive to patient needs.

Driving back to Dallas, I recalled something that Dr. Wilson said at the GI Roundtable panel: "Strategic planning is not about scale. It's about maintaining quality of life and focusing on doctor-patient relationships."

My visit helped me understand what he meant.

WHAT TO CONSIDER ABOUT CHOOSING SOLO, SMALL, OR MIDSIZE AND INDEPENDENT

In my observations of successful businesses, there were certain things in common among smaller independent practices.

1. They were well aware of their strengths in the local market.
2. They proactively safeguarded their practice from competing forces of hospitals and insurances.
3. Quality of life mattered more to them than growth for the sake of it.
4. They proactively procured technology tools to maximize efficiency and engage patients.
5. In a group setting, they had worked out a harmonious equation with other doctors and colleagues.
6. They relied on key staff members for the system to work and nurtured their equation with them.
7. They were entrepreneurial and interested in practice management.
8. They maintained deep-rooted patient-doctor relationships.
9. They strongly believed in the practice of independent medicine. They're strong advocates for it.

10. They relied on external systems of vendors/consultants and nurtured relationships with them.

If you are part of a smaller independent practice and intend to stay that way, focus on the following:

- **Differentiation.** Instead of following the herd, focus on how you are different. You can do this by examining the kind of patients you naturally attract (see chapter 5). Build a strong brand around the themes that make you unique. Constantly analyze data to reinforce your differentiation. It may be with referral networks, hospital systems, and even with insurances. Could you borrow ideas from Dr. Jeffrey Gladden's model on proactive care? (chapter 4)
- **Referral pipeline.** Nourish your referral pipeline consistently. It is the lifeblood of your practice.
- **Hospital collaboration.** They are your biggest, closest threat or ally. Make friends out of them. If it makes sense, offer them some form of ownership so that they are vested in your growth.
- **Less reliance on insurance payments.** Insurance behavior varies from one local area to the next. Develop new ancillary streams of revenue so that you're protected against price compression. For example, Dr. Narayanachar Murali earns from clinical trials (his interview follows). If possible, develop ongoing relationships with payor representatives at a local level.
- **Unified vision with physician partners.** Distracted partners are the last thing you want. Get everyone on the same page.
- **Strong patient engagement.** The doctor whose interview you are about to read, Dr. Murali, sends patients an email with a copy of their electronic medical records. At the

end, he requests them to rate him on physician ranking websites: 97 out of 165 patients rated him an average of 4.8 out of 5 stars on Vitals.com.

- **Take courses in business.** You will need to multitask and be interested in the business of medicine. Constantly learn and develop your management skills.
- **Partner with a group purchasing organization.** In order to stay independent, you can partner with a GPO to build ancillaries such as retail pharmacies, infusion, captive insurances, and so on. See box in chapter 8 on Group Purchasing Organizations.
- **Outsource.** Master the game of outsourcing and on-demand staffing (chapter 5). Run a practice where costs can vary with reimbursements and don't stay fixed. Outsourcing helps you expand or shrink on the fly reducing risk of operations.

RISKS

If you choose to stay small and independent, know your risks.

- **Insurance risk.** Insurances may not be open to negotiating contracts unless you are in a rural or semiurban area. Heavy dependence on certain payors can change the game any time. It's important to consider alternatives if reimbursement pressures continue.
- **Market risk.** If a large private equity–funded group shows up next door, it naturally changes the dynamics of the region. Patients might choose a better branded and furnished group with connected ancillaries.
- **Hospital risk.** Say the hospital in your region gets acquired. And the new, bigger player gridlocks the referral network. That would pose a significant risk.

- **Operational risk.** Costs of operating a medical practice are on the rise. If staff or technology costs cross a threshold, it'll be difficult to stay profitable.

You'll get more insights from Dr. Murali's interview. He runs a solo practice out of South Carolina, and he is an expert when it comes to doctor-patient relationships. Once, Dr. Murali WhatsApped me a photograph of homegrown vegetables that his patients had gifted him. If this is the sort of relationship you envision with your patients, then choosing solo, small, or midsize may be the path for you.

INTERVIEW WITH DR. NARAYANACHAR S. MURALI, GASTROENTEROLOGY ASSOCIATES OF ORANGEBURG

Dr. Narayanachar Murali is a solo GI practitioner based in Orangeburg, South Carolina. His practice, Gastroenterology Associates of Orangeburg was established in 1985. In addition to operating a highly efficient endoscopy center and practice, Dr. Murali also directs several clinical trials.

Q: How do you succeed as a solo GI practice?

Dr. Narayanachar Murali: If you can meet the needs of patients' cost-effectively and establish trust in the community, there's no way a solo practice can't survive. However, you have to constantly fine-tune to what the market wants. You can't expect to have one formula to last year after year.

When there was a trend of declining payments, many doctors moved to hospital-based practices. Reimbursements have been steadily going down. That trend is not going to change. For example, consultation codes were eliminated in one stroke. In my case, I reengineered my practice to include more self-pay patients. I also developed alternative sources of income, including clinical trials. I aggressively renegotiated contracts with insurers.

Although we have AR, we collect copayments up front. You must avoid balance billing. You must collect what you can up front. You need to have staff that's trained to collect these payments. By asking for your money, it must not appear like you are committing some serious crime against humanity.

You also need to retain high-quality staff. That makes or

breaks a practice. More importantly, you have to choose the right place of practice.

Q: Why do you think insurances have been open to negotiating with you?

Dr. Murali: Insurance companies need us. Earlier, insurance companies thought it was better to deal with one monster instead of a hydra of monsters. Instead of dealing with many small practices, they thought it was easier to deal with the hospital. I can't fathom any other reason why anybody would pay twice for outpatient services (in a hospital setting). Insurance companies are realizing the problem now.

Physicians have only two options. One is to knock out insurance companies completely. In that case, many practices may not survive, or patients would get mad. Second, you work with the insurance company, explaining what your leverage is. That's when you negotiate with a position of strength.

Q: What are your views about working with hospitals?

Dr. Murali: Hospitals don't recognize the importance of time as it applies to the physician. They are okay with making you wait for 15 extra minutes between procedures.

The hospital in my area hired a gastroenterologist, but he wasn't the best guy for the job. In my case, there are about 30,000 patients I serve who would rather not go to the hospital as much as possible. Because hospital services aren't cheap. It's a nonstarter for several patients.

Salaries are a bad way of compensating any doctor, unless

it's tied to really good quality assessment of what they are doing: wRVUs (work relative value units) can overestimate or underestimate a doctor's worth many times. I wouldn't buy into wRVUs that hospitals routinely use to compensate doctors.

Hospitals have mandated lunchtime for nurses. That means, in the middle of procedure, a nurse can technically walk out. She could be claiming, "My time is up, I'm going to be back in 30 minutes." She would be replaced by somebody who's not aware of the case. When I do my cases, there's none of that nonsense. But if I say that as an employee of the hospital, they'll fire me. That can never happen in my office. You can do safer work in outpatient settings. If you just look at how patients feel about us, you'll understand.

Q: What's the best thing you love about the way you practice?

Dr. Murali: I work for four or five hours in the office. I see about seven or eight new patients every day when I'm not doing procedures. I just love being independent—both mentally and financially. You earn what you work for. It's predictable. And you can control your time.

Q: What's your advice to someone who wants to go solo?

Dr. Murali: Study the market really well. Understand what you want to do. Know where you are practicing. Have a few trusted staff members who can work with you long term. Hospital-based practices can also become very shaky, depending on how reimbursement rules change. I don't think hospitals will have enough money to pay the salaries they pay now. Even though they are hiring, they are not able to get people who are really committed. Regardless of employment status, there's no safe option. Even 400-bed hospitals go under.

In your own practice, you are answerable to yourself. Accountable to yourself. You need to have a Plan B. Whether you are employed or working solo, you need to know what to do if reimbursement rules change.

Q: Where do you see GI going?

Dr. Murali: There'll always be a need for qualified doctors. That's not going to go away no matter how much someone invades our territory.

The future of GI is excellent. GI problems aren't going to go away. But don't expect to sustain a GI practice by mainly doing colonoscopies or some procedure many times over. You can't overutilize. You have to practice smartly and control costs. A GI business will be a tight ship, regardless of whether it's run by a corporation or the hospital or you.

CHAPTER 8

CHOOSING LARGE

AN INDEPENDENT DAY IN MISSISSIPPI

It was a beautiful sunny afternoon in Jackson, Mississippi. When I entered GI Associates & Endoscopy Center, I was greeted warmly by two ladies. They were greeters who welcomed and directed patients. One of them was Mary Glass. She told me that her role was originally only meant to last for a few days after the building's grand opening. It had been two and a half years since, and her role continued.

Soon, Dr. Reed Hogan greeted me with a big smile, and we walked around the new facilities. Dr. Hogan is a well-regarded physician leader who often lectures at various GI conferences. GI Associates & Endoscopy Center is the home of 29 doctors and serves approximately 450 patients each day. His peers consider his practice to be one of the most operationally efficient in the country. I flew in that morning to find out why.

As we walked around, he helped me understand the design of the center. They had decided that they wanted to house everything in one big building. That included the endoscopy center, consultation rooms, ancillaries, and so on. A lot of thought went into how long it took for a patient to move from one point to the next during a visit, as well as how the doctors would engage them. There were many beautiful photographs on the walls. They covered *all* counties of the state of Mississippi. It helped patients feel a sense of belonging. In just a few minutes, GI Associates gave the vibe of being strongly patient-centric—in thought, design, and action.

We walked in and out of various departments, from the pharmacy to HyGleaCare. Dr. Hogan smiled, greeted, and complimented his staff along the way. Their logo was displayed prominently everywhere. It showed up even on the pharmacy's paper bags.

We completed our tour at one of the endoscopy rooms, where Dr. Hogan explained his procedure. I noticed that he obsessively tracked the quality of his own work on a piece of paper. "Scope in, scope out," among other parameters. That obsession trickled into standardized systems and also a relentless focus on improving quality and efficiency. For better productivity, he and his fellow practitioners liked blocking out the entire day for endoscopy. They didn't prefer distributing a physician's time between consultations and procedures.

Several years ago, I shadowed a CEO of a cardiology hospital. We walked into the physicians' lounge.

Almost immediately, he had quipped, "If doctors relax, we won't be making any money." Simultaneously, he crossed his fingers and shook his head by way of saying, "No, no, no."

The doctors looked up guiltily, like children caught with their hands in a cookie jar. The strangeness of that experience stuck in my head. Those were cardiologists who saved lives. The hospital depended on them for its livelihood, yet they were being told what to do and what not to do.

In contrast, physicians and staff at GI Associates seemed pleasant. They smiled at each other easily. They worked together as a team. They seem to understand their role in keeping the system efficient. *Productivity* wasn't a bad word. It's what made them thrive.

Todd Warren, CEO of the practice, recalled an episode within the first three months of his joining. During a meeting, the senior doctors warned a new doctor that if he wouldn't stop "cussing" at staff, he'd be fired. The fact that the senior doctors took this action and the relaying of stories like these established trust and reinforced culture across the practice's 300 employees. That kind of culture was important to sustain the growth of GI Associates.

The doctors at GI Associates understood from the beginning that an efficient system made money. It made the group focus on growth. For example, physician partners benefited through a real estate investment trust (REIT) that was created to build their new facilities.

Dr. Hogan's son, Dr. Reed Hogan III, also practices at GI Associates. He explained to me the kind of doctor that his father role-modeled for him growing up. "My father always came home in the evenings," he said. "He had time for our school events. And I thought, 'You can have a great life as a gastroenterologist.'"

Back in the endoscopy room, I could hear "Sleep on the Floor" by the Lumineers playing in low volume on Dr. Hogan III's iPhone. Stacey, his nurse, asked the patient a few questions before the procedure began. Soon the doctor worked his way into her cecum.

GI Associates had many options of growth in front of them, including private equity. They were the largest group in Mississippi. The state has about 90 gastroenterologists. It was Dr. Jay Underwood's job as the president to help them make the right decision. Presently, their growth stemmed from three actions:

1. Adding physicians

2. Adding ancillaries
3. Expanding the footprint

The organization designed its physician compensation to ensure that partners committed themselves for the long term (see the discussion about physician compensation in chapter 5). The longer doctors worked with the practice, the more shares they earned. More shares meant more money. And if they wanted better earnings on each share, then the value of the share had to increase. For the value of the share to increase, the entire practice had to grow. The result of this system was that everyone ran by the motto "For the good of the group."

As we've discussed earlier in chapter 6, alignment is critical, especially when there's outside competition. When a local hospital in Jackson tried to hire their doctors, the practice leadership came together to retain them. Clarity on their desired path for growth also allowed them to invest in several technology tools in a variety of areas. Right from recalls to hospital charges to patient access and engagement.

When you distill everything down, GI Associates focuses on two aspects: patients and doctors. I heard Warren and his colleague Lisa Jordan repeatedly say, "We protect our doctors."

WHAT TO CONSIDER WHEN CHOOSING LARGE AND INDEPENDENT

As of this writing, both GI Associates in Mississippi and MNGI Digestive Health in Minnesota are large independent groups. With 85 GI MDs, MNGI is a much bigger organization than the group in Mississippi (29 physicians), but both are dominant players in their local markets. Here are some things they have in common.

1. As leaders of their markets, they don't feel threatened by hospital systems or insurances. They proactively manage both equations well.
2. The organizations are focused on delivering high-quality patient care. They are hyperfocused on patient satisfaction and engagement.
3. They invest in research and reinforce their leadership as innovative GI organizations.
4. They have harmonious physician and staff relationships. Everyone's in it for the long term. More importantly, they are aligned toward growth.
5. They have a great balance between clinical and business objectives.
6. They constantly look for growth opportunities. They're doing this by adding physicians or ancillaries or expanding their footprint. They keep examining costs to improve profitability.
7. They have a predictable meeting rhythm throughout the year, whether that means committee or board meetings.
8. They invest in the best clinical and technological tools. That reinforces their position as leaders.
9. Culture isn't taken for granted, it's consciously nurtured. The leadership uses culture as a medium to keep their system running efficiently.

If you are part of a large, independent group, it's imperative that you achieve the following if you want to scale up:

GROUP PURCHASING ORGANIZATIONS

Group Purchasing Organizations (GPOs) are entities that help healthcare providers realize savings by aggregating purchases. They negotiate bulk discounts for members from manufacturers and other vendors.

As of this writing, Gastrologix is the only GI-specific GPO in the country. The GPO works with its members to lower costs and expand services. They help them stay independent. Four years after starting DHPA, a few of its members created Digestive Health Network (DHN). DHN is a for-profit that aims to create new lines of services for its members and reduce costs. Gastrologix (founded by Chris Metz and Stephen Somers) spun out of DHN.

Here are a few of the programs and ancillary offerings of Gastrologix:

1. **Specialty Infusion Program.** Volume discounts from major pharmaceutical companies for infusions.
2. **Endoscopy Centers.** Bulk discounts for supplies, disposables, capital equipment, scopes, and so on.
3. **Capsule Endoscopy Program.** Exclusive agreements for single and dual camera capsules. No long-term contracts.
4. **Pathology Laboratory Supply and Instrumentation Program.** Setting up in-office pathology labs and enhancing existing lab capabilities.
5. **In-Office Retail Pharmacies.** Developing in-office pharmacies as an ancillary.
6. **Other In-Office Ancillaries.** Include labs, endoscopy center operations, anesthesia, and infusion.
7. **Captive Insurance Program.** A physician-owned captive insurance for Medical Professional Liability.
8. **Data Aggregation, Curation, and Analysis Platform.** Platform aggregates clinical data of participating members to develop population health and value-based contracting opportunities.

1. **Dominance and differentiation.** Create a dominant presence in specific clinical areas or the local region. Or both. Focus on how you can stand out. For example, patients who speak Mandarin, Hindi, or Spanish are niches. Could you build relevant centers of excellence in certain clinical areas such as IBD? As a case in point, Excelsior Medical IPA in New York brought together 300 physicians to meet the needs of 100,000 ethnically diverse patients in the five boroughs.

2. **Efficiency.** Achieve economies of scale in your operations (sometimes achieved by outsourcing). It will help you to minimize costs and keep EBITDA (profits) healthy. It's always good to keep your accounting in shape for private equity, even if you don't need them.

3. **Management.** Acquire either part-time or full-time talent to address business objectives. Use consultants to support other needs. GI Associates in Jackson uses Ask Mueller Consulting to conduct regular coding audits.

4. **Ancillaries.** Partner with a GPO or independently expand on ancillaries, such as pharma retail, clinical trials, anesthesia, infusion, and so on.

5. **Technology.** Invest in technology with the objective of improving efficiency and profitability. Use analytics to demonstrate to insurances that you are saving them money, for example, by reducing readmissions.

6. **Innovation.** Every six months, pick an area of business that can get better with process or technological innovation. Look at this area of the business and then ask, What could you do differently? What would you rather not do?

7. **Patient engagement.** Protect your customers, and they will protect you. High-quality patient experience is a baseline for practices that are considered leaders.

8. **Collaboration with hospitals.** Work out your equation

with various hospitals so that they don't feel the need to compete with you. (See chapter 5 on collaborating with health systems.)

Each of these areas are critical to maintain your independence. But more importantly, constantly ask yourself, How do you grow from here? What must happen to elevate your practice to the next level? To grow, explore strategic investments in smaller companies as Cambia Health did (coming up in chapter 12). It's time to think as a GI business rather than a GI practice.

RISKS

If you are choosing to be large and independent for the long term, know your risks. As a larger independent practice, you likely already de-risked yourself from local hospitals and major insurances. However, market conditions can change over time. Risks can resurface in other forms.

1. **Insurance risk.** Even large groups in metropolitan areas are finding it difficult to get insurances to negotiate. It's important to develop a system to consistently prove your value to insurances. For example, your data analysis must show how you reduce total cost of care compared to hospitals. (Read how MNGI Digestive Health negotiates in Dr. Ketover's interview at the end of this chapter.)
2. **Hospital risk.** Market dynamics in a region can suddenly change as hospitals organize themselves. You must know your action steps if a certain risk surfaces. For example, your local hospital may be acquired by a larger health system. (We saw the example of Hackensack Meridian in New Jersey in chapter 3.)

3. **Competition from private equity platforms.** Are you comfortable being on an independent GI island surrounded by private equity–fueled groups? If they get even bigger, spend even more, and get much better contracts, how would that impact your group?

4. **Operational risk.** Say insurance reimbursements stay flat or decline, and you've already maximized on ancillary revenues. That's when profitability can dip. The only way out would be to reduce costs. Such operational risk can limit your ability to invest in growth. Save more money than you need.

5. **Technological risk.** If significant technological changes play out in GI, then it can put your sustenance at risk. Embrace disruptive technology and create newer revenue streams.

6. **Strategic risk.** As the industry moves toward Gastroenterology 2.0 platforms (coming up in part 4), your present business model risks becoming less relevant. You must constantly evaluate if the industry you identify yourself with is aging or growing. Then you must evaluate if *your business* is aging or growing within that industry.

If these sorts of challenges and opportunities sound like your practice or the ideal you have for your future practice, then the following interview with Dr. Scott Ketover, president and CEO of MNGI Digestive Health, will be of great insight to you. Over an afternoon at his beautiful office in Minneapolis, Dr. Ketover spoke to me at length on a variety of topics: How MNGI began and where it's going. Present and future challenges. Advice he has for midcareerists and those new to the field of GI. And why medicine is different from other professions. Read on.

INTERVIEW WITH DR. SCOTT R. KETOVER, MNGI

Dr. Scott Ketover is the President and CEO of MNGI Digestive Health (formerly known as Minnesota Gastroenterology). MNGI has 250,000 patient visits annually with 85 gastroenterologists. Dr. Ketover also serves as the President of the Digestive Health Network (DHN). Previously, he was President of the Digestive Health Physicians Association (DHPA).

Q: How did MNGI form?

Dr. Scott Ketover: In the past, there were three main GI groups in Minneapolis. Two in St. Paul and my group in Minneapolis. More than 20 years ago, one of the hospitals in St. Paul wanted to hire one of these three GI groups. But that group wanted to retain control and independence.

So we merged and created a group of 30 GIs. We realized that scale in your market is important. With scale, you have a better negotiating stance with payors. It's also important to keep independence.

When we merged, we used to have an east and west division. About five to seven years later, we merged that too and created a central board for greater efficiencies.

The merger resulted in tremendous strength in the market. We built more surgery centers. We built a reputation for the highest quality.

Q: How did the practice grow?

Dr. Ketover: In the early 1990s, we had one endoscopy center with two rooms. At that time, we had a small distribution to partners—significant but small. We were performing the majority of our outpatient procedures at hospitals. I did a back-of-the-napkin calculation and figured that if we moved half of these patients to our endoscopy center, our distribution would go up tenfold. Such a strategy would lower the total cost of care and be much more profitable for physicians. The board asked me to show the calculation three times before agreeing. Our investment paid off within 12 months.

Then we built a second endoscopy center. We centralized our expenses and improved our throughput. We ran smooth operations.

We always differentiated ourselves in our use of quality. With the help of Dr. John Allen (he's now at University of Michigan School of Medicine; read his interview in chapter 10), we built our Quality Improvement Program. We began measuring adenoma detection rate (ADR) back in 2004. We implemented pay-for-performance before everyone else did it.

We looked around for underserved regions to seek growth. We've had many firsts here. For example, we introduced Spy-Glass, double balloons, fecal transplants in our market. Our philosophy has always been to be academically minded in a private practice environment.

We moved to our present location about one and a half years ago. We now have seven surgery centers and eight clinical locations.

All our growth was organic. We hired physicians and expanded.

Q: Where does the growth story go from here?

Dr. Ketover: Over the years, we added various ancillaries—pathology, infusion, subspecialties—and created centers of excellence.

As we approach saturation in metropolitan Minneapolis and St. Paul, the questions we ask now are, do we expand our footprint across the state? What do potential changes mean for our culture? How do we orchestrate change?

About one and a half years ago, we educated ourselves on private equity (PE). We hired Deloitte and lawyers to brief us. We evaluated if we should go down the private equity investor route and grow outside Minnesota. We have a national reputation. We were innovating here before academic centers were doing it. Doctors were happy. We asked ourselves if PE was really necessary for us.

There are two reasons to seek private equity: (1) Financial—To help physicians convert their illiquid assets into liquid assets and (2) Growth plan—When it's difficult to execute a growth plan without capital and business expertise.

Here's the downside of PE. They are particularly interested in the medical services organization (MSO). The entity buys the majority interest in the MSO—you still own the medical practice. You give up some governance control. Physician groups don't get to choose what happens in the second turn.

For private equity, their goals are mainly financial. They are tuned to produce a significant ROI for their investors.

We provide a lot of care that's undercompensated. For example, we are poorly reimbursed for manometry studies of the esophagus. We still do it when clinically necessary. Some of our doctors produce fewer wRVUs, but the procedures and ancillaries subsidize the underreimbursed activities.

In the end, we think that if you already have high-quality care and are growing, then it is a difficult decision whether or not you engage a private equity partner.

Q: How are decisions made in the organization?

Dr. Ketover: Our overarching concept is that we are physician-led. Physicians have a final say in decision-making.

When I wanted to perform push enteroscopy, we needed a special scope in practice, and we simply procured it. I was the first one to perform capsule endoscopies in Upper Midwest.

If doctors wish to focus on certain advanced areas, we ask if there's a clinical need, a patient need, and if yes, then we ask if it's financially viable.

If administration has certain business objectives, we go back and ask, Does this have a compelling clinical objective? If not, then why are we doing it? There has to be a compelling clinical reason for doing something.

Our focus has always been clinical.

Q: Does MNGI have enough leverage with insurance companies? How do you negotiate with payors?

Dr. Ketover: In one AGA meeting, I asked everyone to stand up. They all did. Then I asked, sit down if you don't think you deliver GI care at the highest level possible. No one sat down. Obviously, everyone thinks they are all performing at the 95th plus percentile. But that's not possible. That's not how the payors see it. So you can't just say that you are doing highest quality. You have to demonstrate quality with data.

We have leverage because we have better data. Because we've been using an EHR for 20 years now, we can demonstrate quality and long-term outcomes. We use surrogates for quality, such as ADRs or appropriate follow-up intervals. We demonstrate value from centers of excellence and ancillaries by showing that we don't waste time moving patients around.

Insurance relationships are often going to be market specific and region specific. A payor has the opportunity in some regions to force you into accepting their terms. But you must talk to them and propose contracts.

If a payor is unwilling to negotiate, we would write them a letter, copying several senior executives. The letter would explain what we plan to do in the next 30 days, leading up to potentially canceling the contract with them. We would also notify the state insurance commission, citing that the insurance company isn't negotiating in good faith.

If a payor looks at colonoscopy as a commodity, then they'll pay like we pay for gas. When we don't consider quality, don't we pay the least amount possible?

On another note, the payor mix is shifting more to the government side as the population ages. There are more Medicare

Advantage plans that are run by commercial insurances for an operating fee.

As the pendulum swings more toward government payors, the commercial payors have a different role to play. They make a margin on Medicare Advantage plans to stay in existence.

Finally, the challenge for everybody is moving toward value-based care. Big hospitals are trying to figure that out. Gastroenterology practices will need to figure that out.

Q: What are the near-term and long-term challenges facing GI?

Dr. Ketover: A first big challenge is surrounding reimbursements. If Medicare goes through a reevaluation process of its procedure codes, that's a big risk. Second is if the rate of rise in expenses becomes greater than the rate of rise in revenues.

Answers to our challenges will come from entrepreneurship. We must figure out new ways to deliver care.

We've created a system of healthcare delivery where we chop the body systems into silos. There's no interdisciplinary care to coordinate across many specialties. Question for GI is to ask, How do we deliver more comprehensive care without more revenue sources? For example, irritable bowel syndrome [IBS] may be caused by trauma, insomnia, and goes beyond GI. While we might be focused on the GI tract, we may need psychologists, social workers, or sleep medicine doctors to assist in coordinated care.

Yet another factor to consider is the evolution of subspecialties—such as colorectal surgery, ENT, pulmonary medicine, neurology—into the GI domain.

Gastroenterologists need to look beyond colonoscopy as the revenue source of the future. We should lead, create, and manage programs for the entire GI tract. If you put something in your mouth and swallow it—it is in the domain of GI. For example, for nutrition and dietary services, our margins aren't high, but we still do it. We keep asking, Will it help patients?

Q: What's the future of gastroenterology?

Dr. Ketover: Demand for GI is going to grow even if that need is satisfied by new and possibly nonhuman technology. As we develop more non-face-to-face means to see patients, the role of gastroenterologists will evolve.

The highest level of skill that gastroenterologists can offer is not endoscopy—it's our cognitive skills. Many non-GI physicians can learn the technique of endoscopy, but if you don't know what you are screening for and what you are seeing, then you can't solve the underlying clinical need.

We can't just focus on treating symptoms; we must also keep the entire GI tract in top performance. Whether it's the microbiome or the food we eat, that science belongs to gastroenterology. We must help patients before they become sick.

Businesswise, scale will continue to be important. Hospitals and payors will continue to grow.

Q: What advice do you have for people entering the specialty and midcareerists?

Dr. Ketover: For new entrants to GI, I'd say give three to five years to be a generalist GI, as much as you can. Then you can decide to become a superspecialist. Take practice management and business courses.

For midcareerists in smaller practices, ask, "How long can your group of five survive?" Because if you are not willing to scale, you'll continue practicing until the economics force you to walk away from your practice. Ask, What would you do when you are compelled to perform fewer colonoscopies? Because that day is coming. These gastroenterologists should attend practice management meetings, like the GI Roundtable and the ASGE GO Course to become aware of changes before they occur. Also, see what the big groups are doing and ask how you could participate in that. Stimulate your knowledge; otherwise, you'll become a cork in the ocean instead of a speedboat.

Q: Why's the healthcare industry in the state that it's in?

Dr. Ketover: We are in this state because of the fee-for-service system. It brought us to the point of producing volume and getting compensated for that instead of focusing on quality.

The thing that's different about medicine compared to other professions is that it's a higher calling. You are almost like a religious leader. You must want to help people. But the system can beat you up. You must retrain and find joy in the practice of medicine.

Patient care is very rewarding when you look for the joy in the interactions. There's a trend in hospitals to ask retired physicians to volunteer to just talk to patients and help them navigate options. Doctors find that activity very fulfilling.

Whenever I feel sorry for myself for staying up all night at the hospital, I reset my perspective. I tell myself, "I'm not the patient lying on that bed." That's important.

CHAPTER 9

CHOOSING PRIVATE EQUITY

A $130 MILLION PE AND GI WEDDING IN PENNSYLVANIA

"It's like a wedding, so we checked their cultural fit too," said Dr. Mehul Lalani. (You met him earlier in chapter 2.) He was telling me the story of US Digestive Health. Regional GI, and two other groups in Pennsylvania partnered with Amulet Capital to make the merger happen. The deal resulted in the fourth private equity–funded platform in gastroenterology. According to PE Hub, the transaction was valued at $130 million. Dr. Lalani also serves as the treasurer of Digestive Health Physicians Association.

Leading up to 2017, two competing groups in Lancaster, Pennsylvania, merged. Lancaster Gastroenterology and Regional Gastroenterology Associates of Lancaster created a new group. The new group became known as Regional GI, and it was a 23 doctor practice. Their consolidation took 18–24 months and required a substantial amount of time and financial commitments from all parties.

Meanwhile, health systems in Pennsylvania were organizing themselves and becoming larger. To stay independent and competitive, Dr. Lalani and his colleagues had to grow bigger, faster. That's when they created a subcommittee to scope the possibility of private equity. Then they called their lawyer, an accountant, and an investment banker.

The team studied consolidation opportunities in Pennsylvania. There was a lot of fragmentation. They invited private equity funds to pitch for their business. After shortlisting the funds to a final three, they finally chose to work with Amulet Capital, a Connecticut-based PE fund. The entire process took 18 months.

A typical path to private equity funding requires creating an investment playbook that outlines financial information, ownership structures, and other details. If a practice hires an investment bank, as Dr. Lalani's group did, they invite bids from funds. In other cases, a fund or practice might approach each other directly. Subsequently, interested funds extend offers and conduct due diligence. After negotiations, the parties conclude the transaction with suitable terms.

There are many aspects that need to fall into place before a deal materializes. More than a year ago, I introduced a healthcare-focused fund to one of my GI clients. They liked each other and proceeded on to due diligence. However, the fund faced an unexpected bottleneck with one of its portfolio companies (unrelated to the GI transaction). When they backed out, another PE fund showed interest in putting together a deal in the region. Even while conversations were proceeding, the dynamics of the region changed. A neighboring GI group joined a larger organization. Yet another contemplated a multispecialty merger. Simultaneously, local hospitals merged and became more powerful. As of this writing, my clients are evaluating multiple offers to decide the way forward. As they say, *it's never a done deal until it's a done deal.*

Dr. Lalani remarked, "We liked all three but chose to go with Amulet. Trust had a pivotal role to play. Clinical governance and autonomy was important to us."

Once the doctors had decided to go the private equity route, it took six months to double in size (growing from 23 doctors to 60). Three groups came together as the deal took shape. They were Regional GI, Digestive Disease Associates, and Main Line Gastroenterology Associates. Amulet brought on board a nonphysician management team, including a new CEO, Jerry Tillinger. He was particularly experienced in working with physicians.

One of the first steps that Tillinger and Amulet took after coming on board was to bolster the management team of the Management Services Organization (MSO). A stronger leadership team would help them take on future growth.

With PE, the pace of operations has changed. Tillinger said, "If you go on vacation for a week, you will surely miss something." Talking about future challenges for the MSO, he remarked, "I can't predict every curveball is going to come my way, but I know that I need to be preparing my organization to swing it at the pitch and hit it successfully." (Read Jerry Tillinger's complete interview at the end of this chapter.)

"Everyone's in a similar situation—dermatology, radiology,

everyone. But GI will consolidate faster. This is a logarithmic change," Dr. Lalani said.

Expect more weddings.

WHAT TO CONSIDER ABOUT CHOOSING PRIVATE EQUITY-FUNDED PLATFORMS

While there are significant differences across various PE-funded platforms, there are also many things in common. Many of the commonalities are based in private equity's focus on seeing a return on their financial investment within defined timelines.

1. **Technology.** There's a strong reliance on technology. For example, Gastro Health invested in building dashboards to track growth. One of the first moves of US Digestive Health was to invest in data warehousing. Data warehousing involves analyzing data across disparate IT systems. This reliance on technology ensures PE's ability to track and increase the likelihood of seeing a return.
2. **Speed.** Private equity deals in any industry typically range from three to seven years because they expect a return by the end of that term. That makes them accelerate the pace of any industry that they step into. As of 2020, gastroenterology is entering its fourth year with PE.
3. **Management makeover.** PE funds are quick to hire or replace management teams until they get it right. For example, Gastro Health in Florida has had several changes in its leadership since it took investment.
4. **Debt.** While not often discussed publicly, most PE deals are leveraged with significant debt. PE deals use debt because it's financially efficient. Think of it as taking a

loan from the bank for your house because of attractive interest rates, even though you may technically not need the loan.

5. **Physician-led.** Most PE funds realize that it's beneficial to have physician leaders be at the forefront of their health platforms. This visibility helps in recruiting other doctors into the platform. Depending on the arrangement, these physician leaders may or may not make business decisions.

6. **Build-and-buy strategy.** Refers to a practice management platform that acquires other practices and grows. Once acquired, the practice management company will increase EBITDA through a variety of strategies, such as streamlining systems or renegotiating insurance contracts.

7. **Valuations.** Share price of certain platforms is often determined once a year by executing a build-and-buy strategy. Many practices join a PE platform within specified time periods to avail the benefits of a valuation increase.

RISKS

Plan for the following risks if you join a PE-funded platform or become one:

1. **Reimbursement risk.** In my knowledge, most deals are not considering a Plan B or Plan C if expected insurance payouts don't occur. Business models expect physician productivity and reimbursements to continue as they have in the last five years. If for any reason, there are significant reimbursement cuts, there will be huge pressure to meet ROI goals.

2. **Market and debt risk.** If a recession hits, interest rates

could increase. Money gets pulled out of the system (there's no lending). As mentioned earlier, most PE deals are leveraged. If this risk surfaces, a fund's ability to invest as planned might be compromised.

3. **Clinical autonomy risk.** There's significant interest among PE funds to create management teams on the business side. However, not all funds are driven to mandate clinical governance. Strong clinical governance protects the organization from risk. Dr. Kosinski's interview in chapter 2 discussed this risk in depth.

4. **ROI risk.** In a rush to consolidate the industry, PE funds tend to offer higher multiples for companies, which results in higher valuation. The funds will expect ROI from their investments. They themselves are held accountable by limited partners at the end of the fund period. If the platform struggles to deliver on its plan, a higher valuation would pose a bigger hurdle because a higher valuation would mean a higher dollar expectation of return.

If you are a GI professional who is considering PE investments, I've written a complete book on the topic. It's called *Private Equity in Gastroenterology: Navigating the Next Wave.* I also recommend *The Private Equity Playbook* by Adam Coffey—it's an easy-to-read primer on how private equity firms think and operate. In summary, here are your options in private equity:

1. **PE-funded platforms.** Explore the option of joining one of the existing platforms. Initially, everyone expected PE-funded platforms to develop regionally. But there have been cross-regional deals. Gastro Health in Florida brought home a group from the state of Washington. GI Alliance in Texas acquired a large group in Illinois.

Outside of financials, cultural fit is driving acquisition decisions.

2. **Shortlisting PE funds via an investment bank.** Most large groups hire an investment bank. The bank helps you understand options and develop a playbook. Then they have funds pitch and compete. They help you shortlist, negotiate, renegotiate, and finally arrive at closure. For example, Provident Healthcare Partners and Nexus Health Capital are active investment banks in GI. It's the most methodical approach, but it requires significant investment of time and money. Large groups create subcommittees of three or six physicians who undertake this responsibility. Dr. Kosinski's interview in chapter 2 spells out the approach that Illinois Gastroenterology Group took.

3. **Working directly with PE funds.** Several PE funds are keen to enter gastroenterology. Many of them prefer not to work with investment bankers. Often consultants who are plugged into the PE network will facilitate introductions. They make the deals happen. In this case, a PE fund directly engages with practices and works toward a roll-up strategy.

You can also keep reading right now and learn directly from successful professionals who chose the route of private equity—one is a doctor and the other a CEO. You've met both Dr. James Leavitt and Jerry Tillinger earlier in the book. Together, their thoughts will give you a fuller picture of the private equity experience.

INTERVIEW WITH DR. JAMES LEAVITT, GASTRO HEALTH

Dr. James Leavitt is the President and Chief Clinical Officer of Gastro Health in Florida. Audax Private Equity invested in Gastro Health in 2016.

Q: Why's gastroenterology consolidating?

Dr. James Leavitt: Physician groups will continue to consolidate. Physicians must lead healthcare reform. We are the best advocates for patients. That's our obligation to healthcare. In order to do that, we are going to need to consolidate. Hospitals are consolidating. Payors are consolidating. Even unusual partners such as CVS and Aetna are consolidating.

There are many things that hold us back. We think other physicians are competitors, but we are the solution to each other. The real competition is out there.

The main goal for healthcare reform is to achieve the Triple Aim. That's

1. Improving patient experience of care
2. Improving the health of populations
3. Reducing the per capita cost of healthcare

At the same time, by consolidating and improving services, maybe we can stop physician burnout. That can be a side-benefit.

In order to lead healthcare into the future, there's a whole bunch of infrastructure we'll need around data analytics and AI. It's going to cost a significant amount money to develop that infrastructure. By consolidating, you can amortize that cost over many, many doctors. A smaller group, even 20 or 30 doctors, can't really afford it. With hundreds of doctors, it's a more scalable thing to do. Without that type of infrastructure, it'll be hard to meet the Triple Aim.

Hospitals aren't going to be good leaders of healthcare reform and driving down costs because their infrastructure involves more administration, more bricks and mortar. With a lean organization like a consolidated physician group, we can make a profit on a $300 CAT scan, but a hospital can't make a profit on a $1,000 CAT scan. There's no way that they are going to be able to compete in meeting the Triple Aim and cost.

The whole idea of consolidation is also to build a platform that delivers all aspects of gastrointestinal outpatient care, including radiology and pathology. That's what we want to build in order to meet the needs of healthcare reform.

Q: How much are insurances influencing changes on the provider side? Will we continue to rely on insurance reimbursements?

Dr. Leavitt: There will be new models. I don't know what those models will be. All I know is that whoever can provide great care with great customer satisfaction at the right price will have access to those patients. If you can do that, then you'll be competitive in the marketplace regardless of the type of insurance.

We can't predict how payor behavior will change. Tactics may be different, but principles will be the same.

Q: What would make PE deals fail?

Dr. Leavitt: If there's a significant rise in interest rates, access to capital would be more difficult. Because a lot of these investments are leveraged buyouts. Multiples would go down. It would be economically more difficult to consolidate because borrowing would get more difficult.

When a PE platform just stacks EBITDA, adds doctors, adds groups, without trying to build a better company, that could cause a problem in the future because they don't have the infrastructure to support the doctors and the mission of the doctors. When that happens, doctors become unhappy. You can't become competitive in the marketplace. You don't develop the capability to build a great company. Not just to grow fast. If you outgrow your infrastructure capabilities, that could be a problem.

Q: When talking about risks of PE, people bring up Physician Practice Management companies (PPMs) of the 1990s. What are your views?

Dr. Leavitt: PPMs in 1990s were different. At that time, the PPMs were buying groups randomly. They didn't have the types of platforms and technologies that we have today that could consolidate the back-end office. They didn't have EHRs. They didn't have sophisticated cloud-based practice management and revenue cycle systems. They couldn't really get economies of scale. They weren't really consolidating in a way that consolidation really means—*building something better*. Not just putting things together, but to get better. That's why you can't compare what's happening now with what was happening then.

Q: What are the biggest challenges you face today?

Dr. Leavitt: It's culture. As you grow, to continue to build and maintain a culture of excellence is challenging. Culture eats everything. If you don't get culture right, it'll eat everything else away. How do you build the best culture? That's our biggest challenge.

How do you build the best clinical pathways? How do you influence doctors to change behavior in a way that can drive better outcomes? How do you compensate doctors who are used to getting fee-for-service in a non-fee-for-service, value-based paying system? These are some of the challenges that we are working on.

INTERVIEW WITH JERRY TILLINGER, US DIGESTIVE HEALTH

Jerry Tillinger is the CEO of US Digestive Health. The organization is a single-specialty MSO formed by gastroenterology practices in Pennsylvania. It's funded by Amulet Capital, a private equity fund.

Q: How did you come on board US Digestive Health?

Jerry Tillinger: I was recruited by the chairman of our board, Scott Hayworth, MD. Scott and I have known each other for almost 20 years. He is the CEO of CareMount and is actively involved in our management now. Scott has led management retreats for our MSO team. He visits with our M&A groups so they see first-hand the level of physician leadership. He is one of five physicians on our board of directors, so there is a strong physician presence at the highest levels of the company.

Amulet has tremendous experience in finance and healthcare and wanted to expand its footprint in medical group management. They were looking for a CEO who could take that on. My expertise is in working with physicians and helping medical groups perform at their absolute best. So far, it has been a very good match.

Q: As CEO, what were your priorities in the first 90 days?

Tillinger: The initial 90 days were spent in assessing what we already have and what blanks we needed to fill organizationally. We had an impressive leadership team from the founding practices, but we needed a management structure designed for the growth of the Management Services Organization (MSO). Status quo was not the mission. As we saw the growth opportunity of coming together, we had to build a team of people necessary for the group to thrive.

We immediately started recruiting a chief financial officer, a director of revenue cycle, a compliance office and an HR leader. Those roles were folded into other jobs at the founding practices, so we needed to look outside.

Q: Did you separate the clinical board and the business board? Are there overlaps?

Tillinger: They are two separate groups with a lot of cross-pollination. There's a physician committee that's in charge of clinical leadership and decision-making. This is physicians leading physicians in every aspect of clinical decision-making, such as, "Are we going to set a protocol for the way we do specific aspects of gastroenterology?" or "Are we going to consider new technology?" As CEO, I am a nonvoting member of this committee, but management is an advisor-only on this part of the company.

Operations, compliance, HR, and finance is entirely under the MSO, but we have three Chief Medical Officers who I work with on a continual basis. They are involved in management meetings. We get their feedback on the management decisions we're making on a real-time basis.

There's a pretty good dynamic between those two sides for decision-making. On the business side, we try to involve them as much as possible so that they're aware what we're doing and understand why. The physicians are always key decision makers and partners. It's all one team.

Q: One of the things that came up in my conversation with Dr. Mehul Lalani was the importance of physician autonomy. Is that playing out like the physicians wanted?

Tillinger: I think that's a process still in motion. I've met with almost all of the physician leadership. In fact, Dr. Lalani and I had this very discussion. About how we would make certain decisions and communicate them. For the most part, decisions are very consensus-driven. Once you get the information on the table, the answer is usually obvious to everyone involved.

We listen very closely to physician concerns and incorporate that into the decisions that ultimately come under me. The bigger challenge for doctors is that decision-making isn't happening in the clinical hallways. Organic communication is harder because of our geography, so we are leaning more heavily on formal management structures. As we become a much larger organization, organic communication simply won't suffice.

I try to get out to clinics as much as possible, but not every day of the week. The president and chief medical officer from each division are at my MSO office multiple times a month. I talk to them every week.

As we move down this pathway, I suspect some of the doctors would tell you that it feels more different than they anticipated. Much of that has to do with the pace of change. We've had to do a lot of things to get the consolidation of MSO operations to happen in a short period of time. If you go on vacation for a week, you will surely miss something. As the pace of change settles down and day-to-day operations become more stable, the sense of connection will restore itself. There's no question that there is a level of disruption that happens. It's impossible to prepare yourself for that if you haven't done that before.

Q: And what kind of role does Amulet (the PE fund) play in the MSO?

Tillinger: Amulet is involved with us in a very active way. Not micromanagement, but in a very engaged and supportive way, particularly on our M&A work—preparing valuation and structuring practice acquisitions in a win-win model. They are actively involved in the way we organize our business. They help us set priorities. We need our board of directors and our capital partners to be involved in the discussion so there is no daylight between them and the MSO team. We all understand what's going on. We're able to manage resources and expectations in a collaborative way. My experience with Amulet has been extremely positive.

Q: Are physician leaders taking out time from clinical practice? Are they doing more administrative or leadership activities? Do you see a change?

Tillinger: Absolutely. To keep that dynamic of physician engagement, it is imperative that there are physician representatives involved. We have three CMOs working in different areas of the company. We also have a robust physician subcommittee structure that provides us with formal venues for physician communication and leadership.

Q: Now that the groups are bigger and together, is there a

difference in how you are coming across to health systems in the region?

Tillinger: That's an evolving topic. We've been doing this for six months or so. Our communication with health systems has been almost universally positive. At a strategic level, our mission is to support our local medical centers with our local physicians.

We may not agree with the hospitals on every issue, but we are finding ways in every market to be collaborative with them. Even when there are areas of conflict (for example, on call coverage or division of services), we collaborate. If there's going to be a change in the market and something's going to have economic impact on one party or other, both sides are willing to sit down and talk those through. There's no question that being larger makes it easier for us to treat them as equals. But we have yet to find an issue that we haven't been able to solve with the hospitals.

The business of healthcare never stops. Even before the PE partnership, the physicians had negotiations going on with the hospital about different aspects of the practice. So when I got here, I started engaging with them on those items. Things that have been lingering were brought to resolution more quickly. Now that we are getting ourselves organized and are able to articulate our broader strategic mission, we are starting to talk with the senior levels of the health system leadership.

I don't expect them to like everything we do, but I anticipate our discussions will have openness and honesty. We are all part of the patient care continuum, so we will always work with them to improve access and quality. That's going to create a healthy paradigm with our medical centers.

Q: Most of the PE platforms initially wanted to expand regionally. But during the course of the year, we started seeing interstate deals. How are you differentiated in your strategy compared to other PE platforms?

Tillinger: Our focus at this point of time is strongly in the Pennsylvania region where we have our footprint. We're obviously the youngest of the groups in terms of the GI PE roll-ups. There's no shortage of legwork to do here in Pennsylvania. However, Amulet's expertise isn't limited to just the state of Pennsylvania. They are experienced with healthcare on a national level. There's an enormous amount of green space within GI at a national level. We will always look around to see if expansion outside our region adds value for our physician partners, our investors, and our patients. We see all of this as a huge potential. This industry in itself is very much in its infancy. It's hard to predict how those movements will look six months to two years down the road.

Q: As a bigger group, what has been your experience with insurance negotiation?

Tillinger: It's too early to answer that question for US Digestive Health. We haven't had any engagement with the payors other than simply enrolling the doctors together onto a single Tax ID. We haven't had any contracts come up for renewal.

At a strategic level, we see our size giving us the ability to work on value contracts. Small groups often have ideas on savings that should appeal to their insurance partners but almost never get traction because their size is too limiting.

As we grow, we can implement value programs on a scale that makes it worthwhile for the payors to engage. That's the conversation that we will need to have.

I don't think it's the lack of willingness on behalf of insurance companies. In fact, it's quite the opposite. Insurance companies are struggling to find ways to do exactly that. But they have to be able to do it in an efficient way. We see ourselves as a vehicle to bring that efficiency to the table.

Q: But how much bigger is bigger? Even if GI groups were to consolidate into the many 100s, it may not add up to make a big dent for the big insurance companies. I'm wondering how this game might turn out in the end.

Tillinger: Every insurer is going to have a different strategic approach. The Blues carrier tends to be more local or regional. They are going to be more engaged than some of the national players who've got 50 states to worry about. Whether a payor will negotiate is an impossible thing to predict until you sit with each one of them and have that conversation. I can say that GI spend is one of their top priorities in 2020. They see a group like US Digestive Health as a potential vehicle to bend that cost curve. Their conversation with us would be an attempt to begin the journey. Payors are looking for a roadmap that they can turn around and bring to our peers around the country.

Q: What are your big priorities for 2020?

Tillinger: 2020 is going to be the continued evolution of

the group in terms of mergers and acquisitions. Every gastroenterologist in America is wondering whether this PE partnership that's evolving in GI is right for them. And for this area, we are that PE company. We are very busy out on the road talking to our peers, showing them what it means to be in US Digestive Health.

The other side is improvement of our own operations. We need to make sure that we are taking the best possible care of patients' health. We'd like to cross-pollinate ideas and develop our own understanding of what best practices look like for GI.

Q: What short- and long-term challenges do you see coming your way?

Tillinger: Short term is going to be the management of growth and integration of the groups. Every time a group joins the MSO, there's a lot of communication that has to happen. There's a lot of fresh learning that occurs. We must stay sensitive to what this means to a group to make this kind of change. Every group that joins us—whether they have two doctors or 20 doctors or 60 doctors—it's going to be the same level of change for each of them.

The broader challenge for us as we get into 2020 and 2021 is the level of sophistication we will need to develop to operate and grow in this market environment. We have to be nimble as we go forward so that we can adapt to what the market brings. I can't predict every curveball that's going to come my way, but I know that I need to be preparing my organization to swing it at the pitch and hit it successfully. That's our long-term challenge. The status quo isn't going to last very long for us because we will have a new status quo every couple of months.

Q: Let's assume that stool DNA testing steadily moves into the domain of screening colonoscopy. If such technologies disrupt your plans, what do you plan to do?

Tillinger: We are already envisioning those changes in the market and are preparing for whatever they might turn out to be. One of the truisms of healthcare is that technology doesn't sit still for anyone.

If you don't think testing is going to change the way we do colon cancer screening, you're behind the times. The question that remains is what it will impact on the procedure side of colorectal screening or if its growth will be driven by further penetration of the noncompliant colorectal screening population. We expect DNA tests will continue to improve, but we also expect colonoscopies to improve through the application of artificial intelligence and other emerging technologies. With both of these tools in our arsenal to help improve screening of colorectal cancer patients, we believe we will dramatically improve screening percentages in our communities. Identifying and treating these patients before they develop colorectal cancer is our number one mission.

In the end, we see ourselves as the champions of colorectal screening in our communities. But the GI community as a whole needs to find the right way to engage with DNA testing. We see too many patients today that have had inappropriate DNA-based testing. We need to be supporting our PCPs as partners in the CRC screening challenge, and proper use of DNA testing is a serious concern.

Q: From your perspective, what's the future of gastroenterology?

Tillinger: When you look ahead, you'll see that the gastroenterology community is going to continue to embrace PE partnership because it fills in some of the gaps in the industry. Medical practices have always been a cottage industry with a small group of doctors who view the world with the same lens. They practice together in the same building. They share calls at the same hospital. And they share a common philosophy of clinical care and business. When such a practice becomes a larger single-specialty or multispecialty entity, the doctors get further away from each other in those shared elements. It's harder for them to understand why they are in partnership. That drives a wedge between doctors. Groups like that struggle to stay together through tough times.

PE builds a business model that helps overcome that barrier. It's a value-creation vehicle that helps bring doctors together economically in a way that those personalities and personal philosophy issues don't necessarily drive the business, at least not in the same way as it used to. So I see this model having legs. I see more and more doctors joining this kind of structure for the duration of their careers.

As that happens, you will see the business of gastroenterology evolving just as quickly as the clinical side. If we want to take on the champion role for gastrointestinal care of our communities, size and scope are going to be critical. That may not be immediately apparent. Initially, PE comes in as an economic and management tool. But as the physicians find themselves practicing together in larger and larger organizations, they will find synergy at a clinical level.

CHAPTER 10

―――

CHOOSING ALTERNATIVE MODELS

In earlier chapters, we discussed the options of staying independent and choosing private equity. However, you are not limited to those options alone. The purpose of this chapter is to explore other alternative adventures. You will learn about strategic partnerships, advanced GI practices, and multispecialty GI groups, among others.

A STRATEGIC MSO: CDC AND PHYSICIANS ENDOSCOPY

When I met Barry Tanner, Physicians Endoscopy was about to launch its GI practice services division in partnership with Capital Digestive Care (CDC). Tanner is the chairman of Physicians Endoscopy, a company based in Jameson, Pennsylvania. Physicians Endoscopy specializes in developing and managing endoscopic ambulatory surgical centers (ASCs).

Tanner said that he had known the leadership team at CDC for many years. At the time of our meeting, he was also busy with sign-offs for one of their partnered ASCs. The ASC's affiliated GI practice was joining a private equity platform. It was indeed a time of rapid change.

With 68 physicians, CDC is the largest independent GI group in the Mid-Atlantic and Northeast. About 18 months before partnering with Physicians Endoscopy, Dr. Michael Weinstein and Kevin Harlen led an internal strategic planning exercise. Dr. Weinstein is the president and CEO of CDC. (You met him earlier in chapter 6.) Until recently, he served as the president of the Digestive Health Physicians Association. Harlen was then the COO of CDC. They began by asking the question, "Where do we want to be 10 years from now?"

Along with the rest of the GI world, CDC was dealing with several concerns: a competitive labor market, disruptive technology, an ever more challenging reimbursement environment, opportunities and threats associated with GI ancillaries, and ongoing pressure from hospitals seeking to hire GI physicians.

CDC realized that even at its current size as a GI group, it wasn't big enough to ensure ongoing success. They had to get bigger and better. As a result, they considered the following options:

1. Invest their own money in additional expertise, technology, and infrastructure and grow.
2. Sell to a large health system or ask them to invest as more of a defensive strategy.
3. Do a traditional private equity deal and surrender significant autonomy.
4. Find a strategic partner to stay one step ahead of the

rapidly changing GI landscape. In this option, CDC would combine its resources, operational expertise, and GI-specific knowledge with an industry partner and grow.

As indicated at the beginning of this story, CDC chose option 4. They partnered with Physicians Endoscopy.

Meanwhile, given its interest in starting GI practice services, PE was interested in learning more about CDC's operations. CDC had a central business office that provided a comprehensive suite of services to its affiliated practices. These included finance, revenue cycle management, HR, accounts payable, IT, marketing, quality, and so on.

Both organizations wondered if the current environment offered an opportunity to combine strengths and create an alternative to private equity.

"Private equity is like rocket fuel," Tanner remarked to me. "It can be everything that you need to supercharge the growth of your organization. However, because it is highly combustible, it needs to be handled with extreme care and only in a controlled environment." He should know. Physicians Endoscopy has benefited from many successful private equity partnerships over the years. Kelso, Physicians Endoscopy's current partner, bought the company from Pamlico Capital. Pamlico bought the company from Silver Oak Services Partners in 2013.

In August 2019, Physicians Endoscopy and CDC announced their new MSO, PE Practice Solutions. Harlen became the president of the MSO. This platform capitalized on the core strengths of each organization. It created an alternative option for gastroenterologists. They could now stay independent *and* access the benefits of a larger organization.

Tanner said in our meeting, "We bring to the table the business expertise required to scale. And physicians will guide us with improvement of care quality, clinical pathways, and data analysis."

In some ways, Physicians Endoscopy is reapplying its philosophy from its ambulatory surgery center experience. Since its inception, the company has been a minority owner in most of its partnered GI ASCs. Similarly, in its partnership with CDC, the arrangement involves a minority interest in the practice. Importantly, PE Practice Solutions allows CDC to lead. It also utilizes the infrastructure of the practice. It continues to provide services to CDC as it did in the past at the same cost.

The MSO, as a jointly owned investment vehicle, ensures alignment of everyone involved. When CDC improves efficiency or adds new services or technology, the MSO benefits. Physicians who are part of the MSO benefit. As CDC grows, the MSO also grows and increases the value for all its shareholders.

In a newsletter, David Young, the new president of the company, explained the engagement model. "In addition to acquiring a majority of the MSO, PE is also purchasing 15% of CDC's practice net income. Of that 15%, half will be rolled into equity ownership in the MSO." According to the article, Physicians Endoscopy would buy 15% of the doctor's income and essentially take 7.5% as a multiple in cash off the table. The way the company (the MSO) acquires income is through a management fee. Young continues in the article, "It is effectively like buying an ownership stake, but we do not own the practice. The physicians maintain full control and continue to make all clinical and operational decisions."

In most instances, there's no effective buying or selling of the practice. Physician practices would primarily be joining forces with CDC. You would utilize its services and central infrastructure. For smaller GI groups, this MSO also offers an opportunity to tap into ancillary services, such as pathology and infusion.

The MSO benefits from fees that practices pay for managed services and CDC membership. Think of it like the ASC-partnership model but on the private practice side. When you hook your wagon to CDC, you become part of the CDC Tax ID and access associated benefits. When it comes to other independent GI groups, CDC is open to strategic mergers. They told me they would explore shared ownership in the MSO to invite larger practices.

Dr. Weinstein reflected on how physicians typically view autonomy. He said, "As doctors, we want control over the speed of seeing patients and the number of patients we see. We want to manage our vacation days and weekly off days. We need control over hospital calls, clinical staff, and medicines we prescribe. That's, in essence, a general sense of control over our immediate environment."

He contrasted this scenario with an example of a friend involved with private equity. He said, "A doctor friend I know is part of a 1,500-doctor group that's funded by investors. They grew from 150 doctors a few years ago. Recently, the friend said, 'I have 98 days left for vesting.' He's just waiting to exit."

While seeing me off, Tanner said, "My vision is for physicians coming out of GI fellowship to choose our platform as their most desirable option. I want them to know that our platform will allow them to fulfill their goals and aspirations as physicians. Whether those goals are focused on clinical care, leadership, or research. If we can achieve that, then we will know that what we've done for GI has been deemed successful."

As of this writing, the MSO's plan was to build super GI platforms in four regions. Those were Washington, DC/Virginia/Maryland, Pennsylvania, New Jersey, and New York. For GI professionals seeking an alternative to private equity, this MSO might be something to consider. It offers the opportunity to stay independent by aligning with a larger, established organization that's also growing.

OTHER ALTERNATIVES

The options for your business and career path as a GI professional don't end there either. Without attempting to be exhaustive, let's take a peek into a few other alternative adventures.

OPTUMCARE SPECIALTY PRACTICES

At a GI meeting in the fall of 2019, OptumCare Specialty Practices (OSP) made a strong pitch to gastroenterologists. They presented a partnership model as an alternative option to hospital employment and private equity.

OSP recognizes the environment of declining fee-for-service models and rising costs. It's challenging for small practices to invest in infrastructure and new ancillaries. They need management talent and will need to gear up for value-based arrangements. To address this need, the OSP partnership offers a joint venture that's equally owned and governed.

OSP offers gastroenterologists support in the following areas:

1. **Clinical integration.** OSP offers contracting capabilities needed in a value-based care environment.
2. **Growth capital.** For the purposes of expanding service lines, OSP offers strategic capital.
3. **Practice management.** OSP offers benchmarks and analytics dashboards to help OSP partner with practices in collaborative decision-making.
4. **Network participation.** OptumCare is building the country's largest ambulatory healthcare delivery system. They also have a referral network of 50,000 primary care providers. OSP plans to offer the strengths of an integrated network to specialist physicians.

In exchange for practice co-ownership, OSP aims to reduce the burden of management and growth for physicians.

ADVANCED ENDOSCOPY PRACTICE

Dr. James Burdick is an interventional gastroenterologist who performs over 500 ERCPs in a year. ERCP (endoscopic retrograde cholangiopancreatography) is a diagnostic procedure that combines colonoscopy and fluoroscopy. After working at Baylor University Medical Center for several years, Dr. Burdick branched off on his own in 2017. Now based in

Dallas, he has created a niche, independent practice called Advanced Endoscopy Consultants.

One of the reasons he performs his procedures at a hospital is because they have the equipment needed for what he does. While he bills for his physician services, the hospital bills for the rest. He usually deals with high-risk cases, such as refractory bleeders, endoscopic coiling of varices, double-balloon enteroscopy, or pancreatic necrosectomy. Consulting only half a day a week, Dr. Burdick spends most of his time doing "high-end inpatient" work.

I'm sure, people outside medicine can't fathom what it must take to remove a dead pancreas surgically with minimal incisions, but Dr. Burdick handles that complexity and risk with ease every week. No wonder he received the American Gastroenterological Association (AGA) Distinguished Clinician Award in 2017. However, there's a challenge he still has to overcome. Just like the rest of the GI industry, even renowned endoscopists like Dr. Burdick have to overcome bureaucratic systems to simply do what they love every day.

For Dr. Burdick, his relationship with the hospital enables him to maintain his independence while still accessing the necessary equipment and infrastructure for his work. Dr. Burdick shared with me that he wants to partner with other "heavy hitters" and expand the reach of his advanced endoscopy practice. After covering a certain city, the model could be expanded to other geographies in need of advanced GI practitioners.

MULTISPECIALTY GI GROUP

In keeping with the interviewee's request, the following story has been de-identified. The Multispecialty GI Group (referring henceforth as MGG) has over 80 participating providers, including 30 MDs. The group offers services in gastroenterology, nephrology, and internal medicine. The group soon plans to bring on board cardiologists to clip "referral leaks."

In fact, it was a threat to their referral base that prompted the lead doctors of the three original groups to merge. The regional hospitals kept buying up private practices, making it challenging for independent specialists to simply stay put. Not only that, the hospitals in the region heavily competed with each other, creating greater uncertainty for private practices.

When MGG created their MSO, each partner purchased shares into the newly formed organization. Payments were distributed from profits after taking out costs. Each group might have different cost requirements. For example, GI might need to utilize more billing resources on prior authorizations than internal medicine, but that was balanced out by the safety net that specialists provided, for example, by the pathology work that GI doctors generated. In the beginning, the MSO also subsidized the cost of billing to stabilize the entire group. The success of MGG relies on the symbiotic relationships among various specialties that form the group.

As per one of the leaders of the group, the MSO helped clean up the billing practices of others who came on board. My interviewee said, "We are walking the talk by helping other specialties be successful in a challenging environment." The doctor I interviewed also serves on national-level leadership committees. That gives a broader view of the changes occurring in gastroenterology.

I was curious to know what the holy grail was for the MSO in this kind of an arrangement.

The doctor responded, "Right now, our priority is to maintain autonomy and secure our positions."

As with other GI groups in the country, MGG has received proposals to join hospitals in the area. Maintaining their independence allows the group to offer cost-effective outpatient care to patients. A multispecialty setting allows them to control patient referral flow in the region. At the same time, the group is evaluating the best way forward by balancing their relationships with local hospitals.

SCALED ALTERNATIVES TO PRIVATE PRACTICE

Many doctors today are choosing alternatives to private practice. Instead of making an impact one patient at a time, some doctors are choosing to impact patients at scale. Here are some highly successful examples.

Dr. Ashish Atreja wears many hats. While serving as the Chief Innovation Officer at the Icahn School of Medicine at Mount Sinai, he spun off a start-up called Rx.Health. It's an EHR-connected platform that doctors use to prescribe apps and digital therapeutics. Dr. Atreja also happens to be a gastroenterologist who trained at Cleveland Clinic and was recognized among Top 40 Healthcare Transformers of 2017 by *MM&M*, a medical media publication.

Dr. Dan Murrey completed his MD from Harvard Medical School. He was an orthopedic surgeon for 18 years. Under his leadership, OrthoCarolina grew from 75 to 160 physicians. Today, he's the chief medical officer for Specialty Practices at OptumCare.

Alvin Rajkomar is a doctor of medicine from Columbia University. He's an artificial intelligence researcher at Google Brain, the company's deep learning team. In a recent Google Health video, Rajkomar explains how the company is empowering doctors to be "the best versions" of themselves. Google Health is headed by Dr. David Feinberg, the former president and CEO of Geisinger Health.

Earlier in the book, you met others who are also choosing different career paths. Dr. Jeffrey Gladden runs Apex, a concierge practice (chapter 4). Dr. Michael Byrne runs an artificial intelligence startup, Satisfai (chapter 1). Dr. Lawrence Kosinski was previously a managing partner of Illinois Gastroenterology Group (chapter 2). Today, he works at SonarMD, the startup he founded.

In 2017, *Scientific American* ran an article in their wellness section titled "In 'Drop Out Club' Doctors Counsel One Another on Quitting the Field." The article featured Dr. Mary Schultheis, a colorectal surgeon who left clinical practice. She "balances part-time consulting and health insurance industry roles."

In 2019, Beth Kutscher, a senior news editor at LinkedIn, wrote an article titled "Silicon Valley wants to hire doctors. But how do you know whether it's the right fit?" Kutscher wrote about Dr. Melynda Barnes, who has a passion for "design thinking." Dr. Barnes works at Ro, a telehealth company in New York.

LinkedIn surveyed more than 500 physicians and pharmacists in the US who completed degrees in the last five years. Close to 50% were interested in working in Tech. I asked Ira Bahr, chief commercial officer of AliveCor, a medical device company in Silicon Valley, about his views.

He said, "Working in MedTech might give a physician the opportunity to work on technology that could benefit larger groups of patients. The answer lies in the hearts and minds of an individual practitioner."

Several clinicians are stepping out of consultation rooms to choose a different adventure. They are doing so by anchoring themselves to other fields connected to technology and management. Perhaps they believe that healthcare will continue to rely more and more on technology and business processes to deliver care.

WHAT TO CONSIDER ABOUT CHOOSING ALTERNATIVE MODELS

Each of these alternative models are fundamentally different from each other. Each has a different strategy. But all of these models are going against the grain of dominant themes in GI today. If you are considering an alternative model, consider these takeaways and risks.

1. **Strategic partnerships.** Picture business relationships like those of Physicians Endoscopy and CDC. To get bigger, Capital Digestive Care created an MSO with an industry

partner, Physicians Endoscopy. In such partnerships, there's no financial merger, at least not in the beginning. But arrangements are mutually, strategically beneficial. Practices joining the MSO get to maintain independence and yet benefit from CDC's robust infrastructure. The risk for strategic partnerships is to generate enough engagement as they roll up, especially in an environment that's hyperfueled by private equity. Another challenge for the MSO is to differentiate itself if other companies come up with similar offerings.

2. **Going niche.** Dr. Burdick's advanced practice builds on the niche of tackling higher risk cases in gastroenterology. It has the potential to offer itself as an advanced service to other generalist GI practices. The risks for such a model are getting reimbursed accurately for complex procedures and working out an interdependent arrangement with hospitals.

3. **Going multispecialty.** MGG takes a broader approach. They integrate other specialties into their fold. Their strategy would be to expand as a multispecialty outpatient clinic. The risks of a broad-based strategy are being able to differentiate itself enough to keep hospitals at bay. And being able to invest in the resources required to build centers of excellence in GI care.

4. **Strategic partnerships.** OptumCare Specialty Practices (OSP) has an offer that capitalizes on its existing platform. The risk for such a partnership is to clarify what the endgame looks like in a closed-loop network. Say OptumCare (part of UnitedHealth Group) was to control gastroenterology end to end in several markets. Ask, How would market dynamics change?

5. **Scaled alternatives.** Choosing a scaled alternative career path for a physician is a difficult choice. However, the

question to ask is whether you wish to make an impact at scale or one patient at a time. The risks for such a path would be a sense of disconnectedness with the human aspect of medicine. It's less likely that a patient you impact would look you in the eye, hold your hand, and say thank you.

Finally, joining an academic medical environment has worked out well for some gastroenterologists, such as Dr. John Allen from the University of Michigan School of Medicine. Earlier in his life, he worked in private practice, Minnesota Gastroenterology (now MNGI Digestive Health). Talking about academic medicine, he said, "You are less pressured by productivity goals. There's still time allotted to think, teach, and conduct research." That has allowed him to contribute to the field of gastroenterology in a number of ways. Read Dr. Allen's insightful interview to learn about his transition to academic medicine and why he's excited about consolidation in gastroenterology.

INTERVIEW WITH DR. JOHN ALLEN, UNIVERSITY OF MICHIGAN SCHOOL OF MEDICINE

Dr. John Allen is Clinical Professor of Medicine at University of Michigan School of Medicine and Chief Clinical Officer at University of Michigan Medical Group. Previously, he worked at MNGI Digestive Health and has been the President of AGA Institute. In 2019, AGA awarded him the Julius Friedenwald Medal for his lifelong contributions to the field of gastroenterology.

Q: What are some advantages of consolidation in GI?

Dr. John Allen: The great potential is the collection of a large enough patient population within a very granular electronic medical record or databases so that we can actually do population health studies. And for practices that are large enough or for academic centers, to be able to present payors and patients real outcomes that are more than process metrics by having to say we're following guidelines.

The pediatric inflammatory bowel disease registry is the most compelling case that I have seen. It's called ImproveCareNow, a collection of 14–20 pediatric inflammatory bowel disease centers that now feed data into a single database. It's really driven by parents wanting their child to be part of this. What it allows them to do is analyze things like how many days at the school, outcomes that are really important to patients.

Megapractices can build a large enough database. Not only can you change your practice internally and improve quality, but also use that data for payor negotiations. I really see that as a huge advantage.

If I was the head of quality of a 500–1,000 provider group, you know, I'd really take on big questions about incident colon cancers, inflammatory bowel disease, IBS, and so on. And really start parsing out true outcome metrics that are important for patients and start analyzing that internally. For the first time, we really would have large enough patient population within a single database to be able to do that effectively.

Q: What are the cons of consolidation?

Dr. Allen: The biggest con I've seen is the influence of dark money solely to enhance reimbursement rates. I don't think this has happened in GI but certainly has happened in anesthesia and other areas. You consolidate and get PE backing with the intention of going out of network and then charge astronomical prices to patients, I am so against that. It's just so unethical in my mind. The group that came together to block the legislation around surprise billing, I think, is one of the most unethical things I've seen in a long time. Once that gets out in the open, doctors are going to lose respect and credibility. It's going to be just terrible. I have not heard of that in GI. But that would be the downside.

The second downside is, What if the second exit fails? What if this becomes a repeat of the nineties, when the practice management companies couldn't quite translate consolidation into a viable business model. You end up selling off assets with little left for the remaining physicians. I think that would be the second potential downside.

Third downside is coming in as a graduating fellow. I don't know what kind of contracts will exist at the entry-level. If you've already sold out to PE and there's been a distribution of assets, then you're locked into basically a discounted payment model/income model. I think that hasn't played out yet. I get a lot of questions from fellows. They ask, "But if I sign onto a group that's already sold to PE, what does that mean for me?"

Those are the three areas where there are still a lot of questions.

Q: How do you see payor models develop with the use of better data?

Dr. Allen: Let me give you an anecdotal experience. I'm on the board of Allina Health in Twin Cities. So I went to them and said, "You know, we have a couple of tools in inflammatory bowel disease that could help in payor negotiations or a model that could become a bundled or episode payment."

Their response to me was, "That's great! But we have about 20 different payors and to have enough IBD for each payor will be virtually impossible."

They weren't interested. But once you start wrapping that up to a regional or national practice, then all of a sudden, that becomes a pretty powerful negotiating technique. Not only for payors but also to attract patients. That can turn into enhanced negotiation within a fee-for-service model or an episode payment.

When I was at Minnesota Gastroenterology [now MNGI Digestive Health] we were large enough even back then that we could negotiate annual payment increases based on proven quality outcomes. We had a sophisticated quality department and could prove good outcomes that helped in payor negotiation. If consolidation of practices is really pointed toward proving quality and patient outcomes, then that's a really positive step. You simply can't do that with even wield sufficient negotiating clout if you are in a smaller practice. You really need a huge database to pull enough number of patients into the model. That's a really exciting next step in GI.

Q: How did you start and fund quality improvement programs in Minnesota Gastroenterology [now MNGI Digestive Health]?

Dr. Allen: There were two specific things. Very early on—in our EHR—we built in a structure where we could measure adenoma detection rates very accurately because we had a pathology module. In 2010, we ran our 2009 data for 42 gastroenterologists, and we found a sevenfold difference in ADR, which was completely unacceptable, right? Because, we were saying that if patients come to us, they'd come to Minnesota GI and not to a specific doctor. One-third of our doctors had rates that fell below national standards. At a partner meeting, I put up a graph where every single partner's adenoma rate was illustrated in a blinded manner so they could see the difference in ADR amongst them. That really got their attention. Internally it spurred us to do a lot of quality work because, you know, we were proud of who we are.

The second thing was when we went to payors, we basically asked for a raise in reimbursement rates by demonstrating quality. So those are the two motivations internally and externally that I used in 2009 to move this forward.

Q: You were in private practice, and then you moved to academic medicine. Why would a physician choose one versus the other? What advice do you have for someone who's coming into GI?

Dr. Allen: Both options present exciting opportunities. I see consolidation in GI moving further and further. If you go into private practice, you still have to be comfortable with being an employee of someone. It is now rare that a physician goes out and builds their own, independent practice like we used to. You're going to be an employee of someone. If independence is important to you, look for an area where you can have as much autonomy as possible. I still see that as possible in some private practices. I see going into private practice, now, with these consolidating groups as a huge opportunity for people to study and demonstrate population health and quality in ways that just has never been done before. With the amount of support and infrastructure now, the field is really exciting.

If you're going to go into academic medicine, I think you'll always feel asset constrained because academic medicine is struggling to meet margins at the moment. Academic health systems are, by nature, less efficient than private practices, and subsidies for their massive infrastructure—24/7 availability, complex care—are becoming more difficult to sustain. However, in academia, you are less pressured by productivity goals. In academic medicine, there's still time allotted to think, teach, and conduct research. But to do that, you have to sacrifice your income by probably 50% of your private practice income potential. Those are the trade-offs.

Q: What prompted you to go back to academic medicine from private practice?

Dr. Allen: When I was in Minnesota Gastroenterology [now MNGI], I had never wanted to only perform colonoscopies. I always wanted to do something more. It didn't take me very long to go part-time just to get into GI leadership and participate in national cooperative studies that I was involved in. About 10 years ago, when I was still in practice, I was a visiting professor at the University of Miami, and the chair of medicine offered me an academic position. It got me thinking that it was possible to go from practice to academic medicine, especially if I brought a business sense to the university. I didn't end up going to Miami, but shortly thereafter, I was recruited to Yale to be clinical chief of GI. Academics has always felt to be my home. Ironically, each time I moved, I took a pay cut, which, you know, most people don't want to do that! But it was really from a personal motivation standpoint.

Q: What do you see as the future of academic GI medicine?

Dr. Allen: Academics systems will change to be more like other large integrated healthcare systems. That's what we're trying to do here in Michigan. The traditional models—such as chair-centric departments are changing. Operating margins of academic centers are thin. So I think that recruitment packages are not going to be nearly as flush as they were before.

Academics will fall into several categories. Some will be heavily research-focused and will receive substantial NIH support: Michigan, Harvard, Hopkins, Penn, and so on. Many will emphasize teaching, and clinical care will become kind of apprentice shops to train clinicians where research is secondary. Successful academic centers clearly are going to an integrated healthcare system model. Successful models will pull operations out of individual clinical departments into a more integrated practice plan.

Q: In the current environment, even large groups are finding it difficult to get the attention of the insurance companies. They are not negotiating like they used to in the past. How would using quality indicators play out now or in the future?

Dr. Allen: Well, insurance companies are consolidating as well. The way we used it at Minnesota Gastroenterology [now MNGI] was to just talk to patients when they came to see us about quality. We also positioned ourselves as an indispensable partner that delivered high-quality services. Now, I think, gastroenterology is almost becoming a commodity practice. There are fewer niches in gastroenterology that you can actually use that thinking to such a degree. Still, it's important to lead with proven quality. But I agree with you. I think its effectiveness now—in light of changing reimbursement rates and payor consolidation—is less.

Q: Do you see GI practices making money outside of the traditional insurance cycle?

Dr. Allen: That's a really interesting question. Most large practices have already done the usual stuff, like pathology, imaging, anesthesia, and so on. Outside of those traditional venues, I think that there are going to be very few that can do innovative stuff, whether it's information management, predictive analysis, population health, or remote patient monitoring. These are areas where I see a lot of potential.

Q: Can GI practices start thinking like digital health platforms and solve specific GI problems? Could that be an angle people could take if they wish to create alternative revenue streams?

Dr. Allen: That's a really good point. To think of a GI problem that has a big enough base that translates for practice. I think we've kind of lost the obesity space. And there are really not many others. Colon cancer prevention has almost been commoditized, and more naturally, it sits at a health system level. IBD, IBS management, and liver disease still have potential for practices to create valuable service lines. As I stated before, people have tried to approach IBD, and it hasn't really been successful because they didn't have a large base. That's potentially changing. I do think that's a really good idea. Chronic disease management will move out of a traditional one-on-one encounter and into a more structured service line approach. We are seeing that already, but it will move even further.

Q: I'm curious if the University of Michigan Health System has its own insurance plan.

Dr. Allen: We just acquired Physicians Health Plan. It has 20,000 members. It's a foot in the door to develop a payor program. We're in the process of hiring a population health executive leader to look into that. I don't see how, as a health system, you can survive without either a payor partner or an integrated payor system.

Q: Is this a strategic initiative or an economic one for Michigan?

Dr. Allen: Strategic. It's not going to pay off for a while. But it will allow us to develop all the things that you need for population management, such as marrying claims data to clinical data, adjudicating claims, and so on. But then also be able to use that information to negotiate financial risk contracts and hopefully increase market share.

The country has gone through horizontal integration in healthcare delivery, and we will see increasing vertical integration. This trend is going to accelerate. It'll be really interesting to see who will bring in the most critical expertise to make it work. Is it going to be a company like Amazon? Or is it going to be a provider-based organization? Or is it going to be a payor-based? And I agree with you completely that all three are trying to do this.

Q: When this trend actually plays out at scale—when big insurance companies and health systems get more powerful—how would it impact private practice GI?

Dr. Allen: A lot of it depends on how much of a narrow network is developed within a region. And you know the Department of Justice still hasn't really weighed in on a lot of this consolidation. Within a region, payors or employer groups are narrowing provider networks. That could stress private practices. That's been one of the main motivations of this tremendous consolidation. Mega regional groups or nationally consolidated groups can bring in the kind of expertise that might counter those narrow networks. The small groups in GI are really going to be under tremendous stress in terms of maintaining network availability without cutting their prices to the bone.

Q: When I go to business of GI meetings, the same people show up. They and their practices are largely aligned. But when you hit the ground, most GI practices are not aligned.

Getting alignment is critical to move the industry forward. What must happen to create better alignment?

Dr. Allen: Really interesting question. I completely agree that when you go to these meetings, it's the same people that show up. Their groups have come together because of pretty dynamic and forward-thinking individuals. The next transition has to be around a core focus on quality or core focus on making this better for patients. Unless that's there, I don't see this making a real transition into a long-term sustainable model. Unless you transition this from a person-centric, leader-centric model to a model that's based on a good concept, we might stumble.

If I were the head of one of these groups, I would start writing, publishing, talking about the benefits of a single electronic database that can pull out patient populations and measure outcomes that are important for patients. I'd really change the conversation to a consumer and a patient-centric model. Because that will attract providers, patients, and payors much more so than saying, I've got a huge group, so you need me in your network. I would also develop an internal education program and internal practice algorithms based on national guidelines but more pertinent to that practice. I would build within the practice, many things that our specialty societies now provide, such as educational offerings, guideline development, and outcome measurement. Academic centers must focus on making healthcare and healthcare delivery better. Increasing the value of healthcare, that's where the alignment really needs to go.

Q: What are some short- and long-term challenges and opportunities for GI?

Dr. Allen: A huge challenge for private practice GI is the continued increase in regulations combined with a relentless increase in labor and supply costs. The regulatory environment is challenging for groups that don't outsource some key backroom processes, such as HR and payroll. As always, we will see continued reimbursement challenges.

I would like to point out that Medicare for All will only work if our reimbursement rates go from commercial to Medicare rates, which would be devastating for academic centers, practices, and hospitals. The demographic shift of the country from a commercial population to a state- or government-based payment population is going to be very challenging. Reliance on colonoscopy, whether it continues to be discounted or replaced, is a huge threat for gastroenterology. Because that's the basis of our income. Those are some of the biggest challenges.

Opportunity is to get into a private equity-backed or some sort of capital-backed situation. Gastroenterology is a very attractive specialty right now because of the demographic need. There's an opportunity to take a really good group that's well-led and translate that into an asset-backed infrastructure. Long term, we have to get into population health and develop the ability to do real outcomes work. At Yale, we looked into the EHR and identified every single unique individual that hit the Yale health system and who had some type of liver disease. We were able to divide the total population into seven types of liver disease. From there, we looked at our two thousand patients with decompensated cirrhosis and found 70 patients that accounted for the majority of readmissions. We were able to pretty rapidly identify what the reasons were for their readmission and develop interventions that could mitigate that risk. That kind of large database utilization would be so helpful.

Q: What are some of the key skills outside of medicine that GI doctors need in the coming decade?

Dr. Allen: Understanding drivers of health economics and health finances are absolutely critical. That's really going to be important. The ability to use large databases and do analytic work. We need leaders who truly understand the potential of large databases. I tell fellows those are the things that make them valuable.

Q: Was there anything else that I could have asked you but didn't?

Dr. Allen: Allina Health tried to partner with Minnesota Oncology, a large consolidated oncology practice. A number of years ago, this group had been purchased by US Oncology and then McKesson. Because of their asset-backed practice structure, Allina couldn't bring them into the health system in a manner that met Allina's needs. So we basically stopped negotiation, and now, we are in the process of building Allina's own oncology structure. This should be a warning to GI practices that move into a PE-backed structure that careful negotiation and partnership with large health systems will be important. There will remain a potential to be cut out of networks, like what is happening to Minnesota Oncology.

I see that as a bit of a danger. When healthcare systems become large enough, they can basically internally build what a large group offers. It's important that private practices have a good negotiating stance because even large GI practices can be cut out.

PART 3 TAKEAWAYS: CHOOSING AN ADVENTURE THAT MATTERS

There you have it—when it comes to choosing your own adventure in the world of gastroenterology, your options are plenty. In brief, your choices are:

- Stay small (solo, small, or midsize)
- Stay or get larger independently
- Join an existing private equity–funded MSO
- Form an MSO by raising money from private equity
- Join a strategic MSO
- Join (or start) an advanced GI practice
- Join a hospital or academic center
- Join a technology company or industry partner as a consultant
- Choose another alternative adventure either unlisted or yet undiscovered

What did you choose? Or what would you like to choose moving forward?

Now here's the interesting thing: in each of these adventures, the tale of gastroenterology will have its heroes. There'll be gastroenterologists who'll choose solo and figure out a way to survive. There'll be groups that roll themselves up into private equity platforms and create positive impact for their patients. There'll be strategic partnerships that'll shine. We'll find hospitalists who innovate and lead the industry into the future. We'll find clinicians who join tech startups and make a dent that way.

Choosing your own adventure has less to do with other people's adventures. There's a reason certain aspects of your career feel right for you today. It might be because of how you engage with your patients or how you make life-impacting clinical decisions. It feels right because you've had the courage to choose many meaningful adventures that led up to this one.

Regardless of the adventure, know that people could end up on the right or wrong side of disruption. Some don't see what's coming. (You can't really say that if you are reading this book.) Some choose to do nothing even after knowing what's coming. Without the right mindset and strategy, any of the above options can put you at risk.

Finally, there are others who choose to take big action and lead in the face of disruption. Time after time, when disruption occurs, there are some players who end up winning. Not all. But definitely some.

- Music was disrupted. Apple thrived.
- Phones were disrupted. Samsung thrived.
- Brick-and-mortar retailers were disrupted. Amazon thrived.
- Hotels were disrupted. Airbnb thrived.
- Movie rentals were disrupted. Netflix thrived.
- Basic education was disrupted. Coursera thrived.
- Taxis were disrupted. Uber thrived.

You may be thinking, "There aren't any traditional companies on that list above." Okay, think of Disney, a company founded in 1923. The company transformed its traditional park experience through the *My Disney Experience* app. Guests now use a smartphone to manage and pay for their entire park experience.

That said, in less than a decade, Uber's ride-sharing model itself is getting disrupted. The company may still survive if its self-driving investments take off, or someone else may step up to replace them in an entirely unexpected way.

But the point is that someone is always winning. Why can't it be you? The entire healthcare industry is getting disrupted. But surely, something will thrive. That thriving part of medicine might as well be within gastroenterology. Choose the industry path that inspires you, and find a way to the future. How? The final part will offer you plenty of ideas to *scope forward.*

GASTROENTEROLOGY 2.0

Lake Minnetonka in Minnesota freezes with over a foot thick of ice during winters. Life on the surface appears to come to a standstill. Nature is locked in stillness. Growth and expansion come to a halt. But in the early spring, everything begins to melt. As spring progresses, the green buds reappear. By summer, nature is well into her expansion plan. Many years ago, my buddies and I lost and found our way while boating on that lake. It was so much fun—an adventure.

Right now, gastroenterology is a bit like that lake in the early spring. The winter rules of how everything works cease to apply. But new rules are still in formation. The old practice models—like relying on screening colonoscopy reimbursements—are melting. Newer models—like integrating AI into everyday GI—are not yet fully formed.

This time in the GI industry is a time rife with possibilities, yet doctors are not at the forefront of this new spring. That's not because there's not enough demand for medical care. The anomaly is that doctors are short in supply. And without doctors and their patients, no healthcare system can function.

That means for those of you who are doctors, it's a great time to make your voice heard in the industry. *If you want to and if you have a vision for the future.*

Doctors who have a vision for the next evolution of GI care will be the ones that emerge from the industry's winter. Remember that while winter is the time of scarcity, spring and summer are the times of abundance. As such, we need to have an *abundance mindset*. And demographical changes indicate a huge, unmet demand for GI care.

Dr. Scott Ketover (MNGI) said, "Demand for GI is going to grow. Even if that need is satisfied by new and possibly nonhuman technology. As we develop more non-face-to-face means to see patients, the role of gastroenterologists will evolve." He added, "The highest level of skill that gastroenterologists can offer is not endoscopy—it's our cognitive skills."

Old models of healthcare delivery are already obsolete. It's time to rethink healthcare delivery models and build Gastroenterology 2.0.

But where do we come up with this vision? Consider the stories of disruption from other industries. What messages can we find there? And what can they tell us about how gastroenterology might evolve? What do we, as GI professionals, want the landscape to be? Here are three examples of industry-wide disruption that we can look to for inspiration.

CHAPTER 11

———

THREE STORIES OF DISRUPTION

Disruption is not something that happens out of the ordinary. In fact, *disruption is the norm.* Industries begin and end. They transform themselves into newer forms. What's different today is that industries are disrupting themselves faster than they ever have and in unexpected ways. That's heaving up chaos and opportunities at the same time. What we glean from the disruption is up to the perspective we choose to take.

Let me tell you three stories of disruption, starting from the past and working up to the present.

TOILET PAPERS TO TELECOM: DISRUPTION ISN'T A ONE-TIME EVENT

In 1865, a mining engineer named Fredrik Idestam founded a pulp mill in Finland. His friend and partner, Leo Michelin, wanted to expand to electricity generation. But Fredrik opposed it. After the founder's retirement, Leo went ahead and expanded the company into both electricity and rubber. You could say that Leo disrupted the preconceived notions of what a pulp mill company could do.

A hundred years later, the company was still evolving into forestry, cable, rubber, and electronics. It ventured into networking and radio. A division even made military equipment and gas masks. By the 1980s, this Finnish company began acquiring other companies in areas of television, computer systems, and mobile telephony. Like Leo, the company did not rest on its achievements in any single area but continued to look for areas of growth and possibility.

Now a giant, the parent company expanded to 11 different entities. Eventually, the leaders disrupted that model too. They sold what they considered as unstrategic. These included the divisions of rubber tires and computers. In 1992, Jorma Ollila, the head of the company's mobile phone business took over as the chairman. He decided to focus on telecom. By 1998, the company became a world leader in mobile phones.

You must've guessed that this Finnish company is Nokia. Most of us think of Nokia as a maker of the mobile phones that disappeared from our memory ever since we bought our first iPhone or Android device. But Fredrik Idestam's company didn't really disappear. Just in the last few years, Nokia went through a failed merger with Microsoft. It unsuccessfully bought and sold Withings, a health devices company. It also acquired the legendary Bell Labs in 2016. The company that once made toilet paper now develops network equipment and software. It's still a story in the making because it insists on being disruptive in good and bad times. Nokia today calls itself a technology maker that "connects the world."

Nokia's story reinforces that one-time industry leadership does not guarantee survival. It's both an example of what to do and what not to. At one time, Nokia disrupted itself and the industry to dominate the mobile space. But it lost that position of dominance by failing to change itself soon enough. That's why industry forces disrupted Nokia.

To survive, you must be willing to disrupt yourself even when life's good. That's what Netflix did.

NETFLIX VS. NETFLIX: DISRUPTION WHEN LIFE'S GOOD

In 2004, Blockbuster was at its peak with more than 9,000 video rental stores and 84,300 employees. I recently learned that there's only one Blockbuster store left on the planet in Bend, Oregon. As you likely know, the video rental industry got *Netflixed*.

Starting as a mail-order business for DVDs in 1997, Netflix revamped itself many times. By mid-2000s, internet speeds were good enough that people began watching movies online. To provide some context, Google bought YouTube around that time (in 2006). By 2007, Netflix had delivered one billion DVDs via its mail-order business, but the world was moving on to video streaming. So that same year, the company chose to disrupt its own DVD business. Netflix launched video on demand over the internet. Then the company expanded the model globally.

In 2009, the company offered a million-dollar prize. The goal of the competition was to improve Netflix's recommendation algorithm by 10%. People and companies competed heavily. A team called BellKor Pragmatic Chaos won. It's another matter that after paying $1 million for the algorithm, Netflix never really used it. It was disruptive of the company to go beyond its walls to find ways to be even more useful to its customers.

By 2012, the company found yet another way to disrupt another industry. They started producing their own original programming, and their production methods flew in the face of both the television and film industries. As of today, there are 150 million Netflix subscribers, and the company occupies the number five slot on Fortune's list of fastest-growing companies.

Netflix's disruption story was not just about video rentals, film, or television. It was mainly about disrupting itself. The company is a disruption machine that's constantly reinventing its business model and being ahead of itself.

There's yet another company that has made a business model out of disruption. Disrupting many industries every time it makes a move. Just an announcement that Amazon is entering a certain industry makes industry insiders shudder.

CLOUD TO HAVEN: DISRUPTION INSIDE-OUT

Many companies like Netflix run their platform on Amazon Web Services (AWS). AWS is Amazon's cloud service that offers companies computing infrastructure, database storage, and other functions. It generates over $25 billion of revenue. But AWS itself was an accidental business.

Amazon found itself spending too much time on computing infrastructure problems. This was especially accentuated when demand peaked at different times of the year. To solve this problem, they worked to standardize their infrastructure and automate it as best as they could. Soon the company realized that they weren't alone in experiencing this pain. Other companies also needed scalable servers and data storage services, often on demand. Amazon asked itself, "Can we offer our internal computing infrastructure to others?" That's how the AWS cloud service was born. AWS began offering computing power over the internet. It disrupted the notion that you had to host your software on computer servers you bought. Companies no longer needed to buy servers. They could simply host their applications on Amazon's servers via the cloud.

More recently, Amazon began solving another internal problem. That of shipping and logistics. In the beginning, Amazon relied on others like USPS for shipping. But by 2019, the company delivered 26% of its own orders directly. The Amazon Air division ordered 20,000 vans and 50 planes to expand their delivery power. Amazon started testing sidewalk robots to reimagine package delivery. And not surprisingly, Amazon is now solving the problem for others—they are testing a FedEx-like service that delivers packages for other companies in Los Angeles and London—and continuing to disrupt the delivery industry in the process.

It's a pattern. The company solves the problem for itself, then shapes it as a service for everybody else. In the process, it disrupts industries.

In 2018, the company began solving yet another internal problem. Amazon was spending too much on healthcare. That prompted them to make the unexpected choice to partner with Berkshire Hathaway and JPMorgan Chase. They called the partnership Haven Healthcare and appointed Dr. Atul Gawande, a well-known writer, to lead the effort. In some ways, the plan is an internal healthcare system for employees. But what do you think Amazon will do next after it solves the problem for itself?

Yes, they will sell the system to you.

WHAT WE CAN LEARN FROM STORIES OF INDUSTRY DISRUPTION

These stories of disruption form the basis of what's to follow in the rest of part 4 of this book. Here's what you should keep in mind as we continue to talk about the possible world of Gastroenterology 2.0.

TAKEAWAYS

1. Disruption is an ongoing chapter in industry growth. It's not a one-time event. With exponential technologies, industry cycles are getting faster than ever.
2. Disruption is an inside-out process. Before you disrupt others, you must be willing to disrupt yourself.
3. It's safer to disrupt yourself when the going is good than to wait for disruption to happen to you.
4. Disruption is a pattern. It's about solving problems, sometimes starting with yourself or your clients, and then for the rest of the world.
5. Disruption is also about collaboration beyond the walls of your industry.

CHAPTER 12

CONVERGENCE

Regardless of the adventure you choose as a GI professional, the keyword to look for is *convergence*. The future of gastroenterology will rely on you mastering convergence of three areas: *clinical, business,* and *technological.*

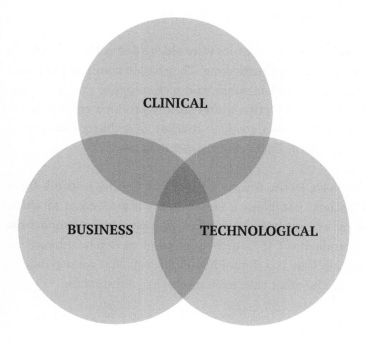

Until now, doctors have vastly been focused on the clinical aspects of medicine. The fee-for-service model ensured that our system pursued reimbursement-based medicine. While GI doctors have been busy with patients, other forces have been hard at work to change what a visit to the doctor will look like in the future. Technology (in the form of DNA testing or AI) is ready to displace what are bread-and-butter procedures for most doctors. Businesses are coming in and changing how hospitals and clinics are managed. The commonality? External forces are organizing medicine for doctors.

And isn't that what disruptive companies do? Apple wasn't a music company, but they organized music via iTunes. Netflix was essentially a subscription shipping company, but it reshaped entertainment. Amazon sold books; now it's organized computing infrastructure via the internet.

None of these companies were able to disrupt based on their original core services alone. They had to combine their core knowledge with business and technology to create change. For example, Netflix didn't simply produce great content. They figured out a way to market, distribute, and service that content. That's *convergence* in action.

To thrive in the future, GI must be willing to think fresh like these companies. The industry must look at all three areas of convergence: *clinical, business,* and *technological.* To understand this further, let's look at two healthcare 2.0 stories. One is a digital health startup that went public in 2019. The other calls itself a 100-year-old startup.

HEALTHCARE 2.0 STARTUPS—FIVE TO 100 YEARS OLD

A few years ago, serial investor Glen Tullman came on board with a company that was primarily a pharmacy benefit manager (PBM). One of his first moves was to sell the PBM. He refocused the company's energies on computerizing medical information. Over the next two years, the organization transformed itself into an electronic business. In 1999, Glen took the company public. That company was Allscripts. You now know them as a vendor of electronic health records (EHRs).

But this story is not about Allscripts. It's about what Glen Tullman did after stepping away from Allscripts. He focused on diabetes. In 2014, he founded a digital health company called Livongo. The company redefines the experience of patients with diabetes and other chronic conditions. As of this writing, more than 200,000 people had enrolled with Livongo for Diabetes.

Even though Livongo is based in Silicon Valley, its focus is not on developing technology. The success of Livongo's model depends on solving people's healthcare problems through its platform. Technology simply enables the platform. For example, Livongo's members use a mobile-connected blood glucose meter. They receive personalized "health nudges" based on their blood glucose levels. The platform uses Amazon's voice AI to make it easy for members to simply *ask* Alexa about their test results. A peer-reviewed study in the *Journal of Medical Economics* showed that Livongo's members reduced medical spending by 21.9%.

Livongo has also acquired other digital health companies to expand their offerings. These include Diabeto for diabetes, Retrofit for weight loss, and myStrength for behavioral health. It made $169 million in revenue in 2019, exponentially up from $2 million in 2015. It expects to make nearly $300 million in 2020. The payment model succeeds because Livongo doesn't completely rely on consumers or insurances. Livongo's clients are self-insured employers, health plans, and government and labor unions.

The number of patients impacted by diabetes is projected to grow to 629 million in the next 25 years. Digital health is estimated to reach $500 billion by 2025. Livongo has set itself up on an exponential wave. Diabetes is a big, growing problem. Clinical solutions accelerated by technology and business innovation can solve that problem.

You might think it's easy for Livongo to be exponential as a new startup with no historical baggage and good timing. So let's talk about one of its strategic investors, Cambia Health, that calls itself "a 100-year-old startup." Before 2013, Cambia was known as the Regence Group, short for "regional alliance." Over 100 years ago, a group of timber workers pooled their wages and founded the company. It served as insurance for the workers.

When you visit Cambia's website today, it hardly comes across as a traditional insurance company. In fact, it appears to be a diversified technology investor in patient-centric solutions such as Livongo.

Cambia took two approaches to transform its legacy business. First, they acquired and invested in companies that were capitalizing on exponential technologies. For example, Genome Medical, a company in its portfolio, brings genomic-based medicine to patients. Another company they invested in, TytoCare, provides on-demand medical exams. Second, Cambia created a multidisciplinary team called Innovation Force back in 2011. The team accelerated innovation from inside out. They reshaped the company's culture around innovation. Those moves slowly transformed the company from an aging giant to a growing 100-year-old startup.

To signal its way forward, Cambia recently hired Faraz Shafiq. He's the former global head of data science at Verizon. His new title? Chief *artificial intelligence* officer. That alone shows you that Cambia is invested in the convergence of the clinical, business, and technological. It's willing to disrupt itself inside out.

WHAT WE HAVE TO LEARN FROM EXAMPLES OF CONVERGENCE
TAKEAWAYS

For the future, you will need to develop platform thinking into your business model. If you think about it, Livongo provides an alternative to doctors who offer diabetes care. With weight loss, it provides an alternative to doctors who offer obesity treatments. Do you see the possibility of a platform for Crohn's disease or IBS?

Here's how the convergence of clinical, business, and technological advancements can inform our vision of the future:

1. Cambia invested its way to capitalize on exponential technologies. Livongo made acquisitions to build on its success. Acquisitions and investments can speed a company toward exponential growth. Strategic investments

can guide the direction of the company, especially when you see that the existing model is about to plateau.

2. Future-focused organizations have a strong, well-defined purpose. Livongo empowers people with chronic conditions to live better and healthier lives. Cambia serves as a catalyst to transform healthcare. Without a strong purpose, Livongo or Cambia would not be able to attract the talent they need.

3. Livongo behaves and thinks as a complete platform that solves specific problems. Platform-thinking makes them plug gaps in their business model through acquisitions or other means.

4. Technology integrates into the platform to the point of becoming invisible. These companies aren't asking consumers to buy a product with a manual. They aren't selling piecemeal services. They are filling a gap by solving a burning problem.

5. Platforms take advantage of assets that customers already own. For example, Livongo relies on the smartphones or AI devices of its members.

6. These companies are quick to embrace exponential technologies to improve user experience. For example, Livongo uses Amazon Alexa.

7. In a platform strategy, everyone is part of a well-knitted solution. These could mean medical providers, algorithms, dietitians, payors, scientists, and medical devices. Clinical, business, and technological areas *converge*. There are no individual actors or products. Everything is part of one seamless solution.

8. Data plays an integral role in making the platform consistently better.

9. Cambia didn't ask itself how to safeguard from AI. They asked themselves, "How do we disrupt ourselves so we stay relevant for the next 100 years?"

Even though Livongo is riding an exponential curve at present, the company knows it can't sit still. There's plenty of competition in digital health. According to the *Financial Times*, there were over 500 investors in the space in 2018. Compare that to a little over 100 in 2011. But that could mean a great thing for the rest of us with our own unique ideas on how to shape the healthcare of the future.

CONVERGENCE IN GASTROENTEROLOGY

You may be wondering how you think from a convergence mindset. It may feel overwhelming to not only have to come up with clinical ideas but also to now have innovative thoughts on business and technology. To help you with this, ask these four questions about convergence in gastroenterology:

1. What does clinical convergence look like?
2. What does business convergence look like?
3. What does technological convergence look like?
4. When these three areas intersect, what do we see emerge?

To put it in another way, we must probe these questions:

- What's Netflix for GI?
- What's iTunes for GI?
- What's Airbnb for GI?
- What's Amazon for GI?

Don't worry about arriving at the right answers. This is brainstorming. The right questions will help you discover the answers. Don't get caught up in trying to figure out how you implement an idea, either. Focus on the *what*. Not the *how*.

Clinical convergence refers to various clinical aspects that are blending into each other. For example, you might ask yourself questions like these:

1. How do you bring in microbiome analysis to your clinical practice?
2. What subspecialties or niches are underserved in your area (e.g., IBD, pancreatic procedures, liver disease)?
3. What's the next evolution of ancillaries like pathology or infusion? How do you roll those in?
4. What will happen when DNA testing improves in sensitivity and drops in cost? How could you take advantage of that?
5. If you were to "own" the GI tract, what subspecialties could you use in your clinical practice?

Technological convergence is about using technology to speed up gastroenterology to the future. Ask these kind of questions:

1. What aspects of your technology must you move to the cloud?
2. When and how can you incorporate AI into your endoscopy room?
3. How can you automate repeated transactions in your revenue cycle?
4. Which areas of your practice could belong to a virtual clinic?
5. How do you capitalize on the devices your patients already own? (For example, can you prescribe an app?)

Business convergence spurs you to think about making the business of healthcare happen. Ask questions like these:

1. How can you access talent from outside your organization? What could you outsource versus keeping in-house?
2. What kind of data must you collect to negotiate better with insurance companies?
3. For what problems will patients readily sign up for a subscription model?
4. How do you develop covenants with local hospitals so they don't become a threat?
5. If GI could be digitized and global, then what services could you offer to patients regardless of location?

Convergence means that clinical, technological, and business aspects overlap. To get at this, you can ask even more focused questions:

1. How do you create a subscription model that results in 10–30% decline in weight for obese patients?
2. What parameters must show up on a dashboard that will make top insurances negotiate?
3. What if you experimented with free FIT tests to a certain segment of your patients in the next quarter?
4. Which specific functions must you standardize to ensure fail-proof automation or outsourcing?
5. How can patient communities help you reduce Crohn's disease in your region by 20%?

You get the idea. Let a question about each area inspire you. Go deeper within each area and then mix it up, iterate, and come up with fresher questions. When you ask questions like these, you move steadily in the direction of convergence. If you let yourself think freely, these questions disrupt the status quo. But it bears repeating that you must not focus on finding solutions right now. Focus on arriving at the right questions. Here's why.

Asking empowering questions like the ones I've presented to you throughout this section sets you in the direction *you* want to go. When you keep moving in the right direction, you'll discover answers along the way. In this context, Dr. Jeffrey Gladden of Apex said, "The world is changing very quickly. It's difficult to keep up if you are married to the answers you currently have because there will be better answers tomorrow."

For example, you may not have the answers for applying AI for inflammatory bowel disease. But if that question becomes your focus and if you make that focus known, then you'll discover the answers in the years to come. There might be other companies or startups who want to partner with you. There could be devices that are in the works. But if you drop your questions, then you'll never encounter those solutions. If you continue to freely question everything around you, then you will discover, learn, contextualize, experiment, fail, relearn, and ultimately find the answers you seek—even if your very first question is, "What does convergence have to do with me?"

EVOLVING DIGITAL HEALTH MODELS

- Vivante Health: Digital health for chronic digestive conditions. Offers an all-in-one gut health program called GIThrive. Raised $19.3 million.
- Oshi Health: Digital health for GI care. Startup aims to reinvent GI care through a virtual clinic model combining human and data-driven care.
- ModifyHealth: Food as medicine startup. Delivers Low-FODMAP meals nationwide to patients of IBS and other conditions. Offers support through GI trained dietitians.
- Ro: Digital health clinic for men (Ro) and women (Rory). Plus, a digital clinic for smoking cessation (Zero). Raised $176.1 million.
- Vida: Digital coaching for chronic disease. Raised $78 million.
- Talkspace: Online therapy. Offers online therapy via thousands of licensed therapists. Raised $106.7 million.
- Nurx: Digital health for women. Raised $93.4 million.

CHAPTER 13

———

NEXT STEPS

We put off decision-making because of fear or uncertainty about what an option might lead to. It's natural. People typically do one of three things when they don't or can't decide. They act out of fear, distract themselves, or go where other people wish to take them. They might react without thinking through various options.

For example, think of these two scenarios:

1. Practices who might take on private equity without knowing what it entails.
2. Practices ignoring private equity out of fear of disaster.

Both could be wrong options if those choices are not made from a position of strength.

Wouldn't it be better to play an active role in shaping the future? Isn't it a better option to *design* Gastroenterology 2.0 on your terms instead of constantly reacting to industry forces?

In part 1 of the book, we looked at the future based on four trends:

1. Exponential technologies such as DNA testing or AI
2. Business consolidation spreading across healthcare
3. Ongoing pressure of Big Brothers like hospitals and insurances
4. Changing patient expectations of healthcare

In part 2, we delved into certain nonclinical business concepts. These are especially important if you wish to lead GI and the business of healthcare. We talked about the importance of alignment in the industry. For the GI industry to not only survive but make a difference, more professionals need to come together as a unified, powerful voice.

In part 3, we explored a few career and business options that are in front of you. Staying small. Staying large and independent. Taking private equity. Choosing several alternate options. We saw examples for each adventure.

Finally, here in part 4, we noted that industrial disruption isn't unusual. Stories from Netflix to Amazon show us that disruption is, in fact, the norm. Disruption is the basis of growth and the formation of new industries. We also learned about new and old startups such as Livongo and Cambia. These companies are not only benefitting from convergence in healthcare but foreseeing it. Their success leaves us an idea of what Gastroenterology 2.0 could be about.

Now, it's time to take stock of your situation. Use the worksheets below. Think of it as a health marker for the success of your future practice. Don't worry about getting it right, but focus on developing your own point of view. Don't skip this. You can download and print these worksheets at Scope-Forward.com/worksheets. I recommend you repeat this exercise and measure yourself every few months. Because whatever area you measure, you make progress.

WORKSHEET 1: PHASE OF LIFE

Name the industry that you think you belong to: _____

Below, mark or identify whatever phase your industry is in at this time.

Birth   Growth   Prime   Aging   Death

Here's a general guideline, but you don't have to be accurate.

- Birth is marked by uncertainty and high risk. For example, the field of 3D printing of human tissue is somewhere in this phase.
- Growth is marked by an upcoming market that has no clear leaders. The area of self-driving cars is an upcoming market, but there are no leaders yet. But you know that there's going to be high demand soon.
- Prime is marked by maturity and established industry leaders. Mobile technology is in its prime with established leaders and marked territories. Also, this phase tends to have less dramatic innovation.
- Aging is marked by a sense of hanging on followed by entropy. Consider taxi cabs in London or Mumbai. There's heightened competition and a constant talk of unfairness.

- Death is marked when most companies in the space aren't able to sustain themselves. Think of the industry that Kodak thought it belonged to.

Now identify where your company (or practice) is on a similar timeline. In what phase of life are you in?

Birth   Growth   Prime   Aging   Death

For organizations,

- Birth is marked by the startup phase. There's a high degree of uncertainty. A founder is often a one-person army trying to figure it all out.
- Growth is marked by lack of systems. There's a lot of focus on top line or revenues and less focus on sustaining profits.
- Prime is signified by profit maximization. You are on top of your game. There's total certainty of your position in the marketplace.
- Aging signals that if you don't innovate, you are going to die. You feel that things are unfair. You hold on to the old ways because there's comfort in it.
- Death is when the business is no longer sustainable. Usually, chaos and inability to pay bills or sustain the company's position in the market leads to it.

Now name the industry you could belong to in the future:

_____

WORKSHEET 2: TAKING STOCK BEFORE SCOPING FORWARD

Type of disruption	Will it impact your practice in the next 5 years? Score on a scale of 1 (low) - 10 (high)	Why do you say that? If your score is high, how will it impact your practice? If your score is low, what would change that?	What must you DO or NOT DO in the next 12 months?	What are the consequences of action or inaction?
BUSINESS CONSOLIDATION				
Competition taking on private equity				
Impact of PE-funded platforms in your region				
Formation of large, independent groups				

Type of disruption	Will it impact your practice in the next 5 years? Score on a scale of 1 (low) - 10 (high)	Why do you say that? If your score is high, how will it impact your practice? If your score is low, what would change that?	What must you DO or NOT DO in the next 12 months?	What are the consequences of action or inaction?
CHANGES IN PATIENT BEHAVIOR				
Patients seek solutions outside of healthcare (e.g. apps, biohacking, alternative therapies and so on)				
Patients have newer expectations				

Leadership: What SKILLS (e.g. business, technology, operations, etc.) must you develop in the next five years that go beyond clinical practice?

Leadership: What could YOU do differently for better ALIGNMENT in gastroenterology?

CHOOSE YOUR OWN ADVENTURE

Adventure	Pros	Cons	Notes
Stay small to mid-size			
Large and independent			
PE funded group			
Alternative 1 (name it)			
Alternative 2 (name it)			

Type of disruption	Will it impact your practice in the next 5 years? Score on a scale of 1 (low) - 10 (high)	Why do you say that? If your score is high, how will it impact your practice? If your score is low, what would change that?	What must you DO or NOT DO in the next 12 months?	What are the consequences of action or inaction?
	EXPONENTIAL TECHNOLOGIES			
DNA Testing				
Artificial Intelligence				
Microbiome				
Telehealth				
Other Exponential Technologies				

Based on your choice of adventure, consider a SWOT (strengths, weaknesses, opportunities, threats) analysis as outlined below.

WORKSHEET 3: SWOT ANALYSIS

STRENGTHS (S)	WEAKNESSES (W)
What are the advantages of this option over others?	What are the disadvantages of this option relative to other options?

OPPORTUNITIES (O)	THREATS (T)
What external factors could help you exploit this option?	What external factors could cause trouble if you choose this option?

Now that you've taken the time to take stock of where you are and have a clearer vision of your future, here are the next steps.

- Step 1: Educate yourself and your colleagues. Identify areas you need to know more about. Dive deep into resources, such as those mentioned at the end of this book.
- Step 2: Develop your point of view. After understanding where the future of GI is going, develop your own perspective. Ask, What does it mean for you to scope forward? What does GI 2.0 mean for you?
- Step 3: Decide what outcomes you want and why. Know what outcomes you are after. Why are those specific results important to you? More on this in a moment.
- Step 4: Form a group of like-minded colleagues beyond the walls of your current practice. It can be a simple WhatsApp group or a cohort at a GI or healthcare conference or beyond. Share resources with each other (such as this book). Explore ideas. Make it fun!
- Step 5: Decide the duration of your research and analysis. Is it the next 30 days? Or would you be spending the next 12 months analyzing but not taking action?

- Step 6: Plant your flag. Draw the emotional energy to make a decision and plant your flag. Make that decision the right one. Once you've thoroughly evaluated and made a decision, have the resolve to follow through with it. Make it an adventure to remember.

Before you set off on your adventure, there are two important questions to answer. Discover that in the final chapter.

CHAPTER 14

DISRUPTION IS A MINDSET

While writing this book, I gave a talk at a meeting on the future of gastroenterology. Through the next day, doctors and other attendees came up to chat.

One of them asked, "But Praveen, you kept asking what do we really want and why. While that made me think, don't we all want the same things?"

I waited for him to continue.

"We don't want to lose our independence. We don't want to join hospitals. We don't want to lose our referrals or patients."

After he finished speaking, I said, "Doctor, do you realize you just told me all the things you *don't* want. What do you really *want*?" I paused before continuing. "What would you do with your independence? What do you want for your patients? What do you want from gastroenterology as a whole? How would you like to lead GI?"

That's been the entire premise of this book. I wrote it to

bring our focus to what we want from the future of gastroenterology. If all that you want by staying independent is to stand still, it's unlikely that you'll stay that way for very long. You'll get swept away by the tides of change. It's inevitable.

I do understand the doctor's statements, though. In a disruptive environment, what leaps out to us more easily is what we wish to avoid. We want to avoid pains and fears. We want to avoid financial disruption, job loss, and the embarrassment of being wrong. We worry about the industry leaving us behind. But guess what? If these are the things you'll focus on, if those are the things you put your energy into, then your fears will play out.

We must bring our focus to a different question: *What do we really want?* Now, we begin to look at disruption differently. Not as something to worry about but as something that we can use as a tool for change and growth. We stop running from our fears and instead move toward creation.

For example, if you ask yourself, *How can I protect my practice from disruption?* the answers to that question take you down one path. But if you ask yourself, *How can I lead GI to the future?* the answers to that question will take you down a completely different path. The first question revolves around a mindset of scarcity—there's not enough of this industry for all of us. The second is all about abundance—there's more than enough business, money, and technology for all of us to create our ideal.

Having absolute clarity in *what you want* and *why* shifts your energies. Scarcity changes into abundance. Fear becomes excitement and adventure. Where would you rather be coming from? Scarcity or abundance?

Close your eyes and see what visions come to you when you think of gastroenterology in the year 2030. Make that vision brighter and bigger. Isn't it more empowering to lead yourself into *that* future?

Go back to the original reason *why* you pursued healthcare. Your *why* was strong enough back then. That's why you put in the hard work to get to where you are. In truth, you are at that intersection again today. If you know *why* you want that future you just envisioned, you'll do whatever it takes to make it happen. Your decisions will impact not just you, but countless others who depend on you and healthcare. The answers to these two questions—*what* and *why*—are going to change your trajectory. And that will change not just your path but that of our entire industry.

More than market forces, *disruption is a mindset*. It's our response to the future. We can either wait for the future to happen *to* us or we can choose to shape that future on our own terms. That second option allows us to channel disruption in the right direction. It'll transform our industry into a force for good. What we do about such a choice reminds me of an old story.

Once upon a time, a wise monk was teaching his students under a banyan tree. One of his students hatched a plan to discredit the teacher. His idea was to capture a butterfly in his hand and ask the monk whether the butterfly would live or die. If the monk said the butterfly would live, he planned to kill the butterfly. If the monk said the butterfly would die, the student planned to let the butterfly escape. Either way, he would prove his teacher wrong.

After the student finally managed to catch a butterfly. He stood up and asked his teacher, "Sir, if you are really wise, tell me if the butterfly in my hand will live or die?"

The monk calmly responded, "Son, whether the butterfly lives or dies is *entirely in your hands.*"

AFTERWORD

COVID—THE ACCELERATION OF DISRUPTION

After reading an ebook I wrote on the impact of COVID-19, a GI doctor wrote to me. He said the current times reminded him of what King Théoden said in *The Lord of the Rings*. At the darkest point in the story, Théoden wonders, "How did it come to this?"

That's a question many of us in healthcare will ask time and again during this period. There's much in our healthcare system that's broken. Appalling finances. Inequity in care. Wasteful tests and procedures. Soul-sucking paperwork. Burdensome technology. Mind-numbing regulations. Hyper-litigation. For many years, we've pushed this dust under the rug and chugged on. COVID-19 shredded that rug and brought our problems to the surface.

As of this writing, the US leads the world in COVID deaths (100,000) and infections (1.5 million). To put that into context, that's nearly twice the number of Americans who died over 20 years during the Vietnam War. Physician practices have been pushed to the brink. After sitting tight on a quagmire of telemedicine rules for years, the government was forced to deregulate the field almost overnight.

Scope Forward has been an invitation to make disruption into a positive outcome for gastroenterology. When I wrote the earlier chapters, I didn't see a pandemic coming. I only saw disruption coming. But COVID-19 has become the mother of all disruptions. It has shaken the very foundations of our healthcare system. COVID-19 will accelerate everything you've read in *Scope Forward*. It'll change medicine as we know it.

Welcome to the acceleration of disruption.

THE BIG PICTURE

Let's first understand the big picture of this pandemic. The COVID-19 period can be divided into two phases: during and after. The first phase (let's call it "During COVID") deals with a long period of uncertainty until we've reliably solved the coronavirus problem. The second phase (After COVID) deals with the period that follows, when the world would've been permanently altered.

The During COVID period will continue until we've invented, manufactured, and administered a vaccine. Most experts suggest that it will take one and a half years or longer before that happens. A daily preventative pill or a convalescent serum might be other solutions that may show up sooner. Coronavirus is expected to wax and wane during this period. Its effects will change season to season and region to region. It'll depend on demographics, social distancing, contact tracing, and other factors. Expectedly, we will see widespread economic uncertainty. Businesses will shut down. There will be sustained job losses in the millions. Some of those jobs will never come back. Many people will be out of health insurance coverage.

Let's consider the impact of this phase on gastroenterology practices.

Historian Eva Schlotheuber referred to coronavirus as a "pandemic of the mind." Even if GI practices open doors to sanitized offices and surgery centers equipped with protective equipment, many patients would be too spooked to enter a healthcare facility. They would constantly weigh the risks of elective procedures versus infection.

Patient behavior will also be influenced by economic conditions in local regions. Business losses usually translate to unemployment, which leads to loss of health insurance. When health insurance coverage is squeezed, we would see a corresponding drop in elective procedures.

The other challenge that GI practices are dealing with during this period is the uncertainty associated with their staff. How willing would people be to work in risk-prone healthcare environments and return to their families every night?

Even after GI practices and surgery centers are fully operational, a second wave in the region or an infection would mean a replay of locking down facilities. It'll entail contact tracing, quarantining, and sanitizing facilities. That's yet another unknown that we have to deal with.

The complexities created by social distancing will increase the time required to see a patient in person or perform a procedure. Consider other needs of testing, monitoring, wearing and removing personal protective equipment, sanitizing rooms, and adhering to COVID-19 guidelines set forth by GI societies. This puts a great strain on the productivity of GI offices and surgery centers. Even if patients show up at the door, the ability to deliver services at a pre-COVID pace will be challenged.

Relief funds from the Coronavirus Aid, Relief, and Economic Security Act (CARES Act) temporarily buffered the financial impact of COVID-19 on medical practices. It remains to be seen to what extent private practices will be able to sustain themselves after these funds run out. Balancing new cost pressures against suppressed patient volumes will stretch practices in multiple directions.

For practical guidance on actions you could take in the During COVID period, refer to my ebook, *COVID-19—The Way Forward for Gastroenterology Practices*.

What follows this long phase will be the After COVID period. We will be safe from the coronavirus, but by then, we will be living in an altered world. New regulations (surveillance). New norms (virtual meetings). New customs (no handshakes). New technology (robots). New ways of delivering care (remote). New needs (veggie washes).

Before we imagine further on what After COVID entails, let's consider a few reflections.

EXPONENTIAL TECHNOLOGIES

We began the *Scope Forward* journey by delving into exponential technologies. By all means, exponential technologies will accelerate during the COVID period. To understand why, let's consider one area that's closest to disrupting gastroenterology: stool DNA testing for cancer screening.

In the During COVID period, the number of patients visiting a medical facility for elective procedures will go down. But patients will continue to be worried about cancer risks. DNA testing companies will market themselves as safer, home-based alternatives. As we saw in chapter 1, DNA testing and liquid biopsy companies will not be sitting still. With more data, they will aim for greater sensitivity and specificity.

It should be no surprise that Exact Sciences (the parent of Cologuard) pivoted to telemedicine. This move allows patients to request Cologuard online through a provider. Here's what Kevin Conroy, CEO of Exact Sciences, had to say on the company's post-COVID-19 outlook: "COVID-19 will change the way people interact with their healthcare providers. And with these investments, Cologuard fits seamlessly into, we believe, a permanently changed healthcare environment."

Meanwhile, artificial intelligence has been at the cornerstone of COVID-19-related developments. AI is stepping up to meet the needs of screening, social control and monitoring, and drug repurposing. Online triage tools are identifying infected patients. Chatbots are answering basic clinical questions. Infrared sensors are scanning for body temperature. AI is interpreting lung scans and detecting COVID symptoms.

Researchers are deploying AI to screen nearly every known drug against coronavirus drug targets.

There's a new urgency to use technology during this period. This urgency will accelerate the use of AI across the board for other purposes, such as endoscopy. Dr. Michael Byrne (whom you met in chapter 1) wrote an editorial in *Techniques and Innovations in Gastrointestinal Endoscopy*'s April 2020 edition. The cover story was on AI in GI. Dr. Byrne opines that we've now passed the "first true inflection point" for artificial intelligence in GI. He writes, "To adapt a phrase used by leaders in medical AI, it is unlikely that AI will replace endoscopists, but perhaps endoscopists who use AI will replace those who do not."

Since the beginning of the pandemic, there's one category of medicine that's doing better than the S&P 500: digital health. These include public companies like Teladoc (remote healthcare), Livongo (chronic care management), and One Medical (in-person and virtual visits). Meanwhile, other privately held companies such as American Well (telemedicine), Omada Health (chronic care), Mindstrong (mental health), LifeStance (mental health) raised hundreds of millions of dollars.

After wrapping telemedicine up in myriad rules for years, the Centers for Medicare and Medicaid (CMS) suddenly cleared the way. They began paying for televisits across states. Seema Verma, the administrator for CMS, had this to say in an interview with the *Wall Street Journal*: "I think the genie's out of the bottle on this one." She added, "I think it's fair to say that the advent of telehealth has been just completely accelerated, that it's taken this crisis to push us to a new frontier, but there's absolutely no going back."

The underlying theme here is that the world is rethinking what it means to "see" a patient. Telemedicine points to the low-hanging fruit of digital transformation of healthcare. What'll start by "seeing" patients remotely will eventually transform into more sophisticated remote healthcare delivery. Other exponential technologies will plug into telemedicine bandwagon and multiply its effects. It'll become a pathway to digitize healthcare. And yes, there wouldn't be any going back.

CONSOLIDATION

COVID-19 disrupted most businesses, but it didn't really take away capital (or "dry powder" in industry speak) from private equity (PE) investors. The pandemic has left much of private equity in a bind. Private equity investors make money only when they invest on behalf of limited partners (management fees). But if they invest in deals that go south, then they still don't make money (performance-based compensation).

As of this writing, most of the PE industry is waiting and watching. Funds that have investments in medical practices have been quick to trim costs of their portfolio companies. They want to ensure that their investments can withstand this financial downturn. There are other funds who are on the hunt for bargain deals. These funds plan to make offers to struggling practices and roll them up into larger entities.

In April 2020, a private equity fund Webster Equity Partners invested $22 million in Gastro One in Memphis, Tennessee. The new platform is called One GI. The organizations were in the midst of the transaction when COVID-19 hit, and they didn't see any reason to stop. When I spoke to Dr. Michael

Dragutsky, Chairman of One GI, after the deal, he referred to the pandemic as a "blip on the road" and felt that "private equity deals may actually accelerate." He said, "A lot of physicians see the benefits of banding together." You met Dr. Dragutsky earlier in chapter 2, "Business Consolidation."

Earlier in the book, we talked about risks of leveraged deals in the face of unexpected disruption. Well, we are in the middle of disruption now. To remind you, leverage refers to using debt during a financial transaction. During the pandemic, a fund's portfolio company may find it difficult to pay what it owes to lenders (busting covenants). Normally, such delays result in lenders pursuing punitive restructuring. Given the unusual circumstances of the present time, lenders might be willing to look the other way temporarily. But if the situation presses on, companies might be forced to file for bankruptcy. Companies like J.C. Penney and Hertz filed for bankruptcy in the second quarter of 2020. By May 2020, US hospitals were losing more than a billion dollars per day. It shouldn't surprise us if hospitals or debt-heavy medical practices file for bankruptcy during this period.

Valuations are likely to go down during the pandemic. Alternatively, valuations may be pegged to 2019 productivity levels but with riders. For example, a PE fund might offer a portion of the payout at closing with a promise to pay the balance when the practice matches productivity of pre-COVID levels. Therefore, the component of cash payouts during transaction closures may also undergo a change.

If gastroenterology practices don't make money in the long-term, then private equity will take its money elsewhere. They will no longer be interested in private practices such as gastroenterology. For example, investor money is chasing telemedicine or digital healthcare deals during the COVID period.

BIG BROTHERS

Most hospitals in the country are facing extreme financial pressure, especially after canceling elective procedures. It's possible that there might emerge a scenario where there will be more sellers than buyers. A few hospitals with stronger financials will acquire and consolidate, especially in their local regions. As described in chapter 3, health systems—if they can—will buy private practices in their respective regions to lockup the referral network.

Even as physician practices shrank down operations, retailers like Walmart Health doubled up. Google, Microsoft, and the rest of Big Tech are eager to step up their role in healthcare even as the industry hastens its technology adoption. By responding quickly and offering support, Big Tech is also changing public perception toward the industry. Meanwhile, there have been high-profile exits from Haven, the healthcare venture of Amazon; Berkshire Hathaway; and JPMorgan Chase. The media was quick to point out that Haven has failed to disrupt. But knowing Amazon's tenacity, the company will iterate until it gets it right.

If you must remember only one thing from this chapter, let it be this. By the time we get to the After COVID-19 period, gastroenterology will be altered by a variety of forces.

TWO BUSINESSES TO OPERATE

Many gastroenterologists I speak to nowadays wonder when they can get back to their pre-COVID days. That's unlikely to happen.

Once patients have experienced the ease of seeing doctors from home, they'll only want more of it. The industry has to be responsive or risk losing their business to a myriad of digital health apps. Businesses that successfully pivoted to a more digital, cost-efficient business model will not roll back the clock. There will be newer jobs surely. But the majority of the older, displaced manual jobs will not come back.

As a leader in gastroenterology, you must accept now that you have *two businesses* to run henceforth: (1) the business that you are *currently* in that's bringing all the cash flow: the *During COVID business* and (2) the business you will need to *become*: the *After COVID business*.

Based on everything we've discussed so far, you already have the insight and tools needed to *scope forward* toward your After COVID business. It's time to accelerate your efforts to be relevant in the future.

What if the healthcare industry was unwilling to change itself? Wouldn't there be a perverse acceleration of problems instead of technology or business? Consider the scenarios that follow.

SCENARIO: A DYSTOPIAN DAY IN THE FUTURE

Hundreds of thousands of people died in the pandemic, including a few clinicians you knew. Your former practice is no longer in existence. You tried to do whatever you could. But in the end, you got tired of managing COVID infections, cash flow, staff issues, and intolerable regulations. You and your partners could never agree on anything—from cutting costs to investing in technology. The government's treasury eventually ran out of funds to support healthcare businesses. Finally, you were compelled to accept the offer from a [fill in the blank] who kept approaching troubled practices. A few of your colleagues joined big hospitals to seek safety in numbers. But some of those hospitals went belly-up. It put those doctors out of jobs. They scrambled to jumpstart their careers.

Practicing gastroenterology has become a chore. You are paid far lower than what you used to make pre-COVID. Demand for elective GI procedures declined rapidly during the COVID era and never went back up. It was hard to keep up with the many technologies that steadily disrupted medicine. It's strange that once upon a time, we even thought of medicine as recession-proof.

It's Orwell's 1984. You constantly get the feeling that you are under Big Brother's watch. Not one but many. Every morning, your administrator sends you productivity emails you detest. Insurance companies squeeze every dollar. Regulators have become all too powerful. You are forced to adhere to countless guidelines and near continuous surveillance. If that wasn't enough, Big Tech companies have encroached deep into medicine. Walmart now offers GI care. You seem to have to compete every day with some strange, new technology or everyday low prices. It doesn't even sound right. Your own patients seem to have lost the regard for what you do. They behave like demanding customers instructing you on what they want done. A part of you wants to say, "We asked for this, didn't we?"

Why not play the game of acceleration differently now? By multiplying the trends that are underway. Consider this fantastic scenario.

SCENARIO: A FANTASTIC DAY IN THE FUTURE

Who would've thought medicine would change so quickly. You see many of your chronic patients remotely. Your team monitors a dashboard that plots patients based on risk. It helps you take care of them proactively. New technology in the form of portable ultrasounds, electrical devices for digestive activity, and force sensors expanded the scope of virtual physical exams. Walgreens and CVS now routinely deliver prescriptions via drones. Patients love this new convenience. They also love interacting with your avatar that looks and talks like you. What started as a chatbot is now available to answer basic questions any time of the day. Your practice recently began using a service that brings healthcare inside self-driving cars.

Meanwhile, your practice and surgery center have transformed into touch-free zones. What started with Amazon Go stores eventually spread to most healthcare environments—people simply walk in and out and are checked in. Your practice also offers curbside service. Your remote team interacts with patients via telepresence robots that buzz around the surgery center.

The scope of what constitutes GI care massively expanded in the past few years. DNA tests are now the standard treatment of care not just for colon cancer but for fifteen types of cancers. Testing and manipulating the microbiome is a routine part of care. Who would've thought mental health professionals, dietitians, data scientists, and AI would become an integral part of your team. Advancements in AI, sensors, robotics, and imaging, allowed endoscopic surgery to progress rapidly. Many inpatient procedures became part of outpatient care. It shifted patient volume from hospitals to surgery centers. Patients find surgery centers much safer. You are busier than ever.

Artificial intelligence is so pervasive in the endoscopy room and beyond. Insurances started to pay based on adenoma detection rate and that prompted everyone to go for AI-assisted scopes that auto classified polyps. If all these changes weren't enough, some of your IBD patients 'visit' with you from Europe and Asia. Maybe the COVID disruption was needed to wake us up from the drudgery of the old healthcare system to this vibrant new reality.

Both these scenarios—dystopian and fantastic—exist today. There's nothing in these narrations that aren't already happening in some form. Walgreens is experimenting with drones. Singapore is using robot dogs to facilitate social distancing. What actually ends up as a dominant reality has more to do with one *final* scenario.

A MORAL IMPERATIVE

On one of my trips to Ann Arbor, Michigan, I booked an Airbnb. To my surprise, my host was a real-life Indiana Jones. As a paleontologist and researcher at the University of Michigan, he taught sometimes and took off on surreal adventures some other times. Among the fossils he discovered, there was a particularly curious one: a snake about to eat a baby dinosaur from Western India. On his recommendation, I went to see the model at Michigan's Museum of Natural History.

What I saw was primordial. The egg of a baby dinosaur had just hatched, amongst other eggs the size of American footballs. A primitive form of snake called Sanajeh was about to pounce and eat the hatchling. Unexpectedly, an avalanche or mudslide inundated the setting, fossilizing that moment for 67 million years—until an Indian dinosaur egg expert and my Michigan-based Airbnb host figured out what the fossil was about.

I'm not exactly sure why this anecdote comes to mind now. Perhaps it's fascinating to experience frozen moments of time. And even more fascinating to unravel stories from those moments.

I wonder how it would be if our healthcare system was somehow frozen in time, in the middle of the COVID-19 pandemic. And say a researcher of the future discovers our frozen relic.

To begin with, the researcher finds many, many dead people. Curious, she pores over records of some of their dying words. One said, "Who's going to pay for it?" She wonders, didn't they have resources to take care of the sick? But she discovers nice facilities, big hospitals, fantastic gizmos everywhere.

Puzzled, she digs further and discovers a system full of dichotomies. Doctors looked for patients, even while millions of patients needed doctors. They performed countless tests and procedures out of fear of litigation. Disjointed and complex, this system had many medical streams that were missing in a cohesive whole. It was mired in bureaucracy and paperwork. Everyone seemed like a pawn in a massive game influenced by hidden economic forces. A system so broken that it drove some doctors to commit suicide.

She finds, among the dead, poor people who were surprisingly obese. The socioeconomic factors were downright confusing. Wealthy corporations but massive unemployment. A debt-trapped society living paycheck to paycheck. Plenty of committees and organizations but no coordinated agenda. Couldn't they have figured out a way to help each other? The researcher is baffled. How could they be so rich and so poor at the same time?

Getting back to post-COVID, a real day in the future will possibly land somewhere in between the dystopian and fantastic scenarios.

But a more absurd post-COVID day would be Groundhog Day, a day that repeats itself ad nauseam. Imagine the healthcare industry goes back to whatever it was pre-COVID. A pandemic comes and goes, ravaging life as we know it, grinding the entire world to a halt. It brings us face-to-face with all the brokenness of our healthcare system. And yet if all that we do post-COVID is crawl back in time, we would waste this opportunity. Such a Groundhog Day would be truly sad. If we fail to change healthcare *for* good (I intend the pun), then we have no one else to blame but ourselves.

What day we finally end up living depends on choices we make now. Our actions (or inactions) will leave behind a story for the future of healthcare. Choosing wisely is but a moral imperative.

THRIVE, NOT JUST SURVIVE

Thank you for allowing me to take you on this journey. What's next?

If you think you are ready to make progress, I'm here to help. All momentum begins because of a first step. A step—even a small step—in the direction that you want to go. The problem of not acting on what we want is that it creates feelings of conflict. And those feelings never really go away. They remain monkeys on our backs.

Along with my team, I help healthcare organizations develop the right business strategy and get to the next level. On their terms. My work delves into exponential technologies, business consolidation, and other concepts covered in *Scope Forward*. To book a free 30-minute strategy call, go to Scope-Forward.com/consult. I'd say that's the way to *scope forward*.

ACKNOWLEDGMENTS

Scope Forward is the synthesis of many conversations. A great number of people contributed to the book by offering their wisdom.

First, I'd like to thank my family for their love and support through my various projects leading up to this one. You rejuvenate me in a way that helps me give myself to work that matters. A big thank-you to Dr. Naresh Gunaratnam, who saw the potential of *Scope Forward* even before I wrote it. Your help brought in wide-ranging perspectives to the book. I wish to thank Digestive Health Physicians Association for its tremendous support of this project.

The following individuals generously offered their time and views: Dr. Latha Alaparthi, Dr. John Allen, Dr. Ashish Atreja, Ira Bahr, Dr. Pradeep Bekal, Brandon Beshear, Abe M'Bodj, Dr. James Burdick, Dr. Michael Byrne, Dr. Michael Dragutsky, Dr. Raffaele Gibilisco, Dr. Jeffery Gladden, Jeff Griffin, Kevin Harlen, Dr. Reed Hogan, Dr. Reed Hogan III, Dr. Jared Hossack, Dr. Kadirawelpillai Iswara, Lisa Jordan, Dr. Scott Ketover, Dr. Lawrence Kosinski, Professor M.S. Krishnan,

Dr. Mehul Lalani, Dr. James Leavitt, Dr. Paul Limburg, Dr. Narayanachar S. Murali, Prabhu Raghavan, Sid Sahni, Mark Stenhouse, Barry Tanner, Jerry Tillinger, Dr. Jay Underwood, Todd Warren, Jeremy Watkins, Dr. Michael Weinstein, Dr. Louis Wilson, and Krista Zimpel. Thank you so much.

I want to give a shout-out to Dr. Nathan Merriman for suggesting that I write a choose-your-own-adventure book for gastroenterology.

Special thanks to my wonderful team at NextServices for creating the space and time I needed to focus on *Scope Forward*. In particular, I'd like to thank Harshal Chaudhari and Vaishnavi Murali for helping me with research and editing. Thank you, Dr. Erik De Jonghe, Dr. Mitchell Spinnell, and James Turner for reading early drafts of the book and providing feedback. And thank you, Tucker Max, Hal Clifford, and the team at Scribe Media and Lioncrest for your guidance.

Finally, I wish to thank my clients. The journey of *Scope Forward* began because you shared your concerns and asked me questions. Listening to you has made the biggest difference to my professional life.

NOTES

CHAPTER 1

Ramirez, V. B. "The 6 Ds of Tech Disruption: A Guide to the Digital Economy." Singularity Hub, November 22, 2016. https://singularityhub.com/2016/11/22/the-6-ds-of-tech-disruption-a-guide-to-the-digital-economy/.

McAlone, N. "This Man Invented the Digital Camera in 1975—and His Bosses at Kodak Never Let It See the Light of Day." *Business Insider*, August 17, 2015. https://www.businessinsider.in/This-man-invented-the-digital-camera-in-1975-and-his-bosses-at-Kodak-never-let-it-see-the-light-of-day/articleshow/48520882.cms.

"Waymo." Waymo. Accessed November 22, 2019. https://waymo.com/.

Korosec, K. "Waymo to Customers: 'Completely Driverless Waymo Cars Are on the Way.'" *TechCrunch*, October 9, 2019. https://techcrunch.com/2019/10/09/waymo-to-customers-completely-driverless-waymo-cars-are-on-the-way/.

Davies, A. "This Lidar Is So Cheap It Could Make Self-Driving a Reality." *Wired*, July 11, 2019. https://www.wired.com/story/lidar-cheap-make-self-driving-reality/.

Burns, M. "'Anyone Relying on Lidar Is Doomed,' Elon Musk Says." *TechCrunch*, April 22, 2019. https://techcrunch.com/2019/04/22/anyone-relying-on-lidar-is-doomed-elon-musk-says/.

"Exact Sciences Corp (EXAS) Q4 2019 Earnings Call Transcript." The Motley Fool, February 11, 2020. https://www.fool.com/earnings/call-transcripts/2020/02/12/exact-sciences-corp-exas-q4-2019-earnings-call-tra.aspx.

"Colorectal Cancer Screening Tests." American Cancer Society. Accessed November 25, 2019. https://www.cancer.org/cancer/colon-rectal-cancer/detection-diagnosis-staging/screening-tests-used.html.

"Cologuard Plans to Capture 40% Market Share: 21 Takeaways from Exact Sciences Q3 Earnings Call." NextServices, November 18, 2019. http://www.nextservices.com/cologuard-plans-to-capture-40-market-share-21-takeaways-from-exact-sciences-q3-earnings-call/.

"Premarket Approval (PMA)." accessdata.fda.gov. Last Accessed November 25, 2019. https://www.accessdata.fda.gov/scripts/cdrh/cfdocs/cfpma/pma.cfm?id=P130017.

"Premarket Approval (PMA)." accessdata.fda.gov. Last Accessed November 25, 2019. https://www.accessdata.fda.gov/scripts/cdrh/cfdocs/cfpma/pma.cfm?id=P130017S029.

Newman, J. "Exact Sciences Stock Swells on Revised Guidelines for Colorectal Cancer Screening." *Wisconsin State Journal*, June 1, 2018. https://madison.com/wsj/business/exact-sciences-stock-swells-on-revised-guidelines-for-colorectal-cancer/article_c1a813b2-c56c-57c8-b822-8c95d8422e1a.html.

Naber S. K., Knudsen A. B., Zauber A. G., Rutter C. M., Fischer S. E., Pabiniak C. J., et al. (2019) "Cost-effectiveness of a Multitarget Stool DNA Test for Colorectal Cancer Screening of Medicare Beneficiaries." *PLoS* ONE 14(9): e0220234. https://doi.org/10.1371/journal.pone.0220234.

"Cologuard Helps More People Get Screened in a Cost-Effective Way." Exact Sciences Corporation, September 10, 2019. http://investor.exactsciences.com/investor-relations/press-releases/press-release-details/2019/Cologuard-Helps-More-People-Get-Screened-In-A-Cost-Effective-Way/default.aspx.

"Cologuard Plans to Capture 40% Market Share. 21 Takeaways from Exact Sciences Q3 Earnings Call." NextServices, November 18, 2019. http://www.nextservices.com/cologuard-plans-to-capture-40-market-share-21-takeaways-from-exact-sciences-q3-earnings-call/.

"Cologuard Expects to Make Over $1 Billion in 2020. 17 Takeaways You Must Know from Exact Sciences Q4 2019 Earnings Call." NextServices, February 20, 2020. http://www.nextservices.com/cologuard-expects-to-make-over-1-billion-in-2020-17-takeaways-you-must-know-from-exact-sciences-q4-2019-earnings-call/.

"Blood Sample Collection to Evaluate Biomarkers in Subjects with Untreated Solid Tumors—Full Text View."—ClinicalTrials.gov, September 7, 2018. https://clinicaltrials.gov/ct2/show/NCT03662204.

Newman, J. "Exact Sciences, Mayo Clinic Say They've Developed Blood Test for Liver Cancer." *Wisconsin State Journal*, June 6, 2018. https://madison.com/wsj/business/exact-sciences-mayo-clinic-say-they-ve-developed-blood-test/article_77c92674-02d7-56b7-ad7b-afba44eae4c3.html.

Castellino, A M. "CancerSEEK: Blood Test That Detects Eight Common Cancers." *Medscape*, January 18, 2018. https://www.medscape.com/viewarticle/891491.

"Liquid Biopsy with Emphasis on Cancer: Global Markets Forecast to 2023 with 175 Company Profiles." PR Newswire, October 10, 2019. https://www.prnewswire.com/news-releases/liquid-biopsy-with-emphasis-on-cancer-global-markets-forecast-to-2023-with-175-company-profiles-300936573.html.

"ESMO Congress 2019: Seven Liquid Biopsy Companies at ESMO Conference 2019 Spain." Verdict Medical Devices, September 27, 2019. https://www.medicaldevice-network.com/features/esmo-2019-liquid-biopsy-companies/.

Joseph, S. "Diagnostic Company Exact Sciences to Buy Genomic Health in $2.8 Billion Deal." *Reuters*, July 29, 2019. https://in.reuters.com/article/us-genomic-health-m-a-exact-sci/diagnostic-company-exact-sciences-to-buy-genomic-health-in-2-8-billion-deal-idINKCN1UO1AK.

Taylor, N. P. "Triple-Digit Liquid Biopsy Growth Powers Guardant to Beat-and-Raise Quarter." MedTech Dive, November 8, 2019. https://www.medtechdive.com/news/triple-digit-liquid-biopsy-growth-powers-guardant-to-beat-and-raise-quarter/566928/.

Kolata, G., S. Wee, and P. Belluck. "Chinese Scientist Claims to Use Crispr to Make First Genetically Edited Babies." *New York Times*, November 26, 2018. https://www.nytimes.com/2018/11/26/health/gene-editing-babies-china.html.

Marchione, M. "Chinese Researcher Claims First Gene-Edited Babies." *AP News*, November 26, 2018. https://www.apnews.com/4997bb7aa36c45449b488e19ac83e86d.

Mullin, E. "FDA Approves Groundbreaking Gene Therapy for Cancer." *MIT Technology Review*, August 30, 2017. https://www.technologyreview.com/s/608771/the-fda-has-approved-the-first-gene-therapy-for-cancer/.

Reedy, C. "Kurzweil Claims That the Singularity Will Happen by 2045." Futurism, October 5, 2017. https://futurism.com/kurzweil-claims-that-the-singularity-will-happen-by-2045.

Kirkland, G. "What Are the Levels of Autonomy for Self-Driving Vehicles?" *Robotics Business Review*, July 26, 2019. https://www.roboticsbusinessreview.com/unmanned/unmanned-ground/what-are-the-levels-of-autonomy-for-self-driving-vehicles/.

Topol, E. J. Deep Medicine: How Artificial Intelligence Can Make Healthcare Human Again. New York: Basic Books, 2019, pp: 86–87.

Locker, M. "This AI Breast Cancer Diagnostic Tool Is the First to Get FDA Clearance." *Fast Company*, July 17, 2019. https://www.fastcompany.com/90377791/quantx-is-first-ai-breast-cancer-diagnostic-tool-cleared-by-fda.

Gordon, R., and A. Conner-Simons. "Using AI to Predict Breast Cancer and Personalize Care." *MIT News*, May 7, 2019. https://news.mit.edu/2019/using-ai-predict-breast-cancer-and-personalize-care-0507.

Real Engineering. "How Machine Learning is Fighting Cancer." *YouTube* video, 13.34. October 19, 2018. https://youtu.be/ALQ_RNSRE40.

Grady, D. "A.I. Took a Test to Detect Lung Cancer. It Got an A." *New York Times*, May 20, 2019. https://www.nytimes.com/2019/05/20/health/cancer-artificial-intelligence-ct-scans.html?module=inline.

"FDA Approvals for Smart Algorithms in Medicine in One Giant Infographic." *The Medical Futurist*, June 6, 2019. https://medicalfuturist.com/fda-approvals-for-algorithms-in-medicine/.

Salzman, S. "Why 100,000 Poop Photos May Bring the next Big Thing in Fitness Tracking." *NBC Universal News Group*, October 29, 2019. https://www.nbcnews.com/mach/science/why-100-000-poop-photos-may-bring-next-big-thing-ncna1072726.

Kelly, S. "Medtronic Rolls Out AI-Assisted Colonoscopy System in Europe." *MedTech Dive*, October 21, 2019. https://www.medtechdive.com/news/medtronic-rolls-out-ai-assisted-colonoscopy-system-in-europe/565431/.

Diamandis, P., and S. Kotler. "The Future Is Faster Than You Think: A New Book by Peter Diamandis and Steven Kotler." Last Accessed February 28, 2020. https://futurefasterbook.com/.

Leichman, A. K. "Is the Microbiome about to Change Medicine for Good?" Israel21c, October 15, 2019. https://www.israel21c.org/is-the-microbiome-about-to-change-medicine-for-good/.

"Human Microbiome Market to Be Worth US$3.2 Billion by 2024: Rising Investments by Angel Investors and Venture Capital Firms to Drive Growth, Says TMR." *PR Newswire*, April 3, 2017. https://www.prnewswire.com/news-releases/human-microbiome-market-to-be-worth-us32-billion-by-2024-rising-investments-by-angel-investors-and-venture-capital-firms-to-drive-growth-says-tmr-617961033.html.

Kinthaert, L. "Is The Future of Microbiome Research Already Here?" KNect365 LifeSciences, December 11, 2017. https://knect365.com/next-generation-therapeutics/article/9832cfd5-7d3b-46eb-b5f5-dcca604fafb9/is-the-future-of-microbiome-research-already-here.

Murison, M. "Health IoT: New Wearable Can Diagnose Stomach Problems." *Internet of Business*, April 3, 2018. https://internetofbusiness.com/us-researchers-stomach-wearable-health/.

"Will Ingestibles Be the Next Big Thing after Wearables?" PreScouter Journal, *Medium*, January 8, 2019. https://medium.com/@prescouter/will-ingestibles-be-the-next-big-thing-after-wearables-e25a377e9ba9.

Ross, C. "In Health Care, the Race Is on to Put Sensors in Your Gut." *STAT News*, January 29, 2019. https://www.statnews.com/2019/01/29/ingestibles-gut-sensors-health-care-entrepreneurs/.

Simon, M. "Soon You'll Swallow Origami Pills and Get Magnetic Colonoscopies." *Wired*, May 3, 2017. https://www.wired.com/2016/05/soon-youll-swallow-origami-pills-get-magnetic-colonoscopies/.

Diamandis, P. "VR & Technology Convergence." Diamandis.com (blog), n.d. Last Accessed November 26, 2019. https://www.diamandis.com/blog/vr-technology-convergence.

Minai, H. "8K Endoscopes Making Surgery Safer and Less Painful." *Nikkei Asian Review*, November 27, 2017. https://asia.nikkei.com/Business/Biotechnology/8K-endoscopes-making-surgery-safer-and-less-painful.

Farr, C. "Amazon Launches Amazon Care, a Virtual Medical Clinic for Employees." *CNBC*, September 24, 2019. https://www.cnbc.com/2019/09/24/amazon-launches-employee-health-clinic-amazon-care.html.

"The Potential of Telemedicine in Digestive Diseases." *Lancet Gastroenterology and Hepatology* 4, no. 3 (March 2019). https://doi.org/10.1016/s2468-1253(18)30359-5.

Helsel, B. C., Williams, J. E., Lawson, K. et al. *Dig Dis Sci* 63 (2018): 1392. https://doi.org/10.1007/s10620-018-5054-z.

Wikipedia, "FODMAP," last accessed December 9, 2019, https://en.wikipedia.org/w/index.php?title=FODMAP&oldid=929595760 .

"Tellspec." Last Accessed November 26, 2019. http://tellspec.com/.

"Nima." Last Accessed November 26, 2019. https://nimasensor.com/.

Carlota, V. "A Guide to 3D Printed Food—Revolution in the Kitchen?" 3Dnatives, February 4, 2019. https://www.3dnatives.com/en/3d-printing-food-a-new-revolution-in-cooking/.

Cho, J. Y., J. H. Yoo., D. H. Kim., K. Wonhee., K. H. Ko., K. B. Hahm., S. Hong., P. W. Park., J. Cho., and W. Ko. "Mo1520 New Technique for GI Endoscopy Using 3D Printing." *Gastrointestinal Endoscopy* 81, no. 5 (April 27, 2015). https://doi.org/10.1016/j.gie.2015.03.850.

Nawrat, A. "3D Printing in the Medical Field: Four Major Applications Revolutionising the Industry." Verdict Medical Devices, August 7, 2018. https://www.medicaldevice-network.com/features/3d-printing-in-the-medical-field-applications/.

Dragolea, N. "9 Drones That Will Revolutionise Healthcare." *Doctorpreneurs*, September 2, 2016. http://www.doctorpreneurs. com/9-drones-that-will-revolutionise-healthcare/.

"Drone Deliveries Are Advancing in Health Care." *The Economist*, June 11, 2019. https://www.economist.com/business/2019/06/11/ drone-deliveries-are-advancing-in-health-care.

McFarland, M. "UPS Broke into Drone Deliveries Shuttling Medical Samples. Now It's Ready to Take Off." *CNN*, October 1, 2019. https://edition.cnn.com/2019/10/01/ tech/ups-drones-faa/index.html.

Reader, R. "Drones from CVS and Walgreens Are Finally Here—And They're Bringing Band-Aids." *Fast Company*, October 21, 2019. https://www.fastcompany.com/90419596/ cvs-and-walgreenss-drones-are-finally-here-and-theyre-bringing-bandaids.

"Endoscopy Care Pathways." *Rx.Health*, January 29, 2019. https://rx.health/ endoscopy-care-pathways/.

Mark Stenhouse (Exact Sciences), interview with author, November 26, 2019.

Dr. Paul Limburg (Exact Sciences), interview with author, November 26, 2019.

Dr. Michael Byrne (Satisfai Health Inc & ai4gi), interview with author, June 27, 2019.

Ira Bahr (AliveCor), interview with author, November 22, 2019.

CHAPTER 2

"Audax Private Equity Portfolio." Accessed December 4, 2019. https://www. audaxprivateequity.com/portfolio.

Herschman, G. W., Y. Shtern, H. M. Torres, A. Newman, N. B. Davis, and C. McGuine. "Insight: Deals Galore–Health Care Transactions See Strong Third Quarter." *Bloomberg BNA News*, October 17, 2019. https://news.bloomberglaw.com/health-law-and-business/ insight-deals-galore-health-care-transactions-see-strong-third-quarter.

Patel S. N., S. Growth, and P. Sternberg. "The Emergence of Private Equity in Ophthalmology." *JAMA Ophthalmol* 137, no. 6 (2019): 601–602. doi: https://doi. org/10.1001/jamaophthalmol.2019.0964.

Tan. S, K. Seiger, P. Renehan, and A. Mostaghimi. "Trends in Private Equity Acquisition of Dermatology Practices in the United States." *JAMA Dermatol* 155, no. 9(2019):1013–1021. doi: https://doi.org/10.1001/jamadermatol.2019.1634.

Konda, S. "The Landscape of Private Equity in Dermatology and Concerns about Private Equity–Backed Models." Next Steps in Dermatology, November 14, 2018. https://nextstepsinderm.com/navigating-your-career/the-landscape-of-private-equity-in-dermatology-and-concerns-about-pe-backed-models/.

Hafner, K. "Why Private Equity Is Furious over a Paper in a Dermatology Journal." *New York Times*, October 26, 2018. https://www.nytimes.com/2018/10/26/health/private-equity-dermatology.html.

"Private Equity Acquisition of Ophthalmology Practices Poised to Explode in 2019." *Insights* (Blog). Physicians First Healthcare Partners. Last accessed December 4, 2019. https://www.physiciansfirst.com/blog/private-equity-acquisition-of-ophthalmology-practices-poised-to-explode-in-2019.

Lowes, R. "Physician Practice Management Companies...Going...Going..." Medical Economics, March 5, 2001. https://www.medicaleconomics.com/article/physician-practice-management-companies-goinggoing.

Dr. Lawrence Kosinski (SonarMD), interview with author, August 26, 2019.

Dr. Michael Dragutsky (Gastro One), interview with author, August 3, 2019.

Dr. Naresh Gunaratnam (Huron Gastroenterology Associates), interview with author, May 2019.

Sid Sahni (Prime Therapeutics), interview with author, February 2019.

Dr. Kadirawelpillai Iswara (Maimonides Medical Center), interview with author, 2019.

CHAPTER 3

"UnitedHealth's Optum to Acquire Surgical Care Affiliates for $2.3 Billion." *Modern Healthcare*, January 9, 2017. https://www.modernhealthcare.com/article/20170109/NEWS/170109936/unitedhealth-s-optum-to-acquire-surgical-care-affiliates-for-2-3-billion.

Digestive Health Network Fall Meeting 2019.

Japsen, B. "Buying Binge for UnitedHealth's Optum Is Only Just Beginning." *Forbes Magazine*, April 18, 2018. https://www.forbes.com/sites/brucejapsen/2018/04/18/the-buying-binge-of-unitedhealths-optum-is-only-just-beginning/#293c76de192d.

Dyrda, L. "Optum Has 50,000 Employed, Affiliated Physicians, and a Vision for the Future." *Becker's ASC Review*, September 17, 2019. https://www.beckersasc.com/asc-transactions-and-valuation-issues/optum-has-50-000-employed-affiliated-physicians-and-a-vision-for-the-future.html.

Creek, W., and E. Prairie. "John Muir Health and Optum Launch New, Comprehensive Relationship to Advance Quality Care and Experiences for Patients in Bay Area." Optum.com, July 17, 2019. https://www.optum.com/about/news/john-muir-health-optum-new-relationship-bay-area.html.

Wolff, T. "OptumCare Can Reach 70 Percent of the US Population." *Health Care Blog*, December 13, 2017. https://thehealthcareblog.com/blog/2017/12/13/optumcare-can-reach-70-percent-of-the-us-population/.

"Humana Pushes Deeper into Health Care Delivery." *Insurance News Net*, December 19, 2017. https://insurancenewsnet.com/oarticle/insurer-humana-pushes-deeper-into-delivery-of-health-care.

Livingston, S. "Cigna and Express Scripts Close on $67 Billion Merger." *Modern Healthcare*, December 20, 2018. https://www.modernhealthcare.com/article/20181220/NEWS/181229999/cigna-and-express-scripts-close-on-67-billion-merger.

Wikipedia, "Ouroboros," accessed December 4, 2019, https://en.wikipedia.org/w/index.php?title=Ouroboros&oldid=927944752.

LaPointe, J. "What Is Value-Based Care, What It Means for Providers?" *RevCycleIntelligence*, June 7, 2016. https://revcycleintelligence.com/features/what-is-value-based-care-what-it-means-for-providers.

Kacik, A. "Hackensack Meridian Health Commits $400M to Englewood Health in Proposed Merger." *Modern Healthcare*, October 15, 2019. https://www.modernhealthcare.com/mergers-acquisitions/hackensack-meridian-health-commits-400m-englewood-health-proposed-merger.

Sitrin, C. "Hackensack, Meridian Merger Yields NJ's 2nd Largest Hospital System." *NJ Spotlight*, June 22, 2016. https://www.njspotlight.com/2016/06/16-06-22-hackensack-university-meridian-health-merger-yields-nj-s-2nd-largest-hospital-system/.

Livio, S. K. "Hackensack Meridian Now N.J.'s Largest Hospital Chain." NJ.com, January 3, 2018. https://www.nj.com/healthfit/2018/01/hackensack_meridian_is_njs_largest_hospital_chain.html.

Kacik, A. "Hackensack Meridian Health Commits $400M to Englewood Health in Proposed Merger." *Modern Healthcare*, October 15, 2019. https://www.modernhealthcare.com/mergers-acquisitions/hackensack-meridian-health-commits-400m-englewood-health-proposed-merger.

LaPointe, J. "A Provider-Sponsored Health Plan Is a Hospital's Natural Next Step." *RevCycleIntelligence*, July 16, 2018. https://revcycleintelligence.com/news/a-provider-sponsored-health-plan-is-a-hospitals-natural-next-step.

"Big Business Is Beginning to Accept Broader Social Responsibilities." *The Economist*, August 22, 2019. https://www.economist.com/briefing/2019/08/22/big-business-is-beginning-to-accept-broader-social-responsibilities.

Huynh, N. "How the 'Big 4' Tech Companies Are Leading Healthcare Innovation." *Healthcare Weekly*, February 27, 2019. https://healthcareweekly.com/how-the-big-4-tech-companies-are-leading-healthcare-innovation/.

"Where Tech Giants Are Betting on Digital Health." CB Insights Research, October 28, 2019. https://interactives.cbinsights.com/tech-giants-digital-healthcare-investments.

Huynh, N. "How the 'Big 4' Tech Companies Are Leading Healthcare Innovation." *Healthcare Weekly*, February 27, 2019. https://healthcareweekly.com/how-the-big-4-tech-companies-are-leading-healthcare-innovation/.

Gurdus, L. "Tim Cook: Apple's Greatest Contribution Will Be 'about Health'." CNBC, January 8, 2019. https://www.cnbc.com/2019/01/08/tim-cook-teases-new-apple-services-tied-to-health-care.html.

Elias, J., and C. Farr. "Google Has a Trust Problem, and It Could Kill the Company's Cloud Ambitions." CNBC, November 13, 2019. https://www.cnbc.com/2019/11/13/google-trust-deficit-could-kill-the-companys-cloud-ambitions.html.

Chen, A. "What the Apple Watch's FDA Clearance Actually Means." *The Verge*, September 13, 2018. https://www.theverge.com/2018/9/13/17855006/apple-watch-series-4-ekg-fda-approved-vs-cleared-meaning-safe.

Thorne, J. "Judge Allows Ex-UnitedHealth Exec to Join Amazon Healthcare Joint Venture." *GeekWire*, February 22, 2019. https://www.geekwire.com/2019/judge-allows-ex-unitedhealth-exec-join-amazon-healthcare-joint-venture/.

Griggs, M. B. "Amazon Is Now Offering Virtual Health Care to Its Employees." *The Verge*, September 24, 2019. https://www.theverge.com/2019/9/24/20882335/amazon-care-telemedicine-employees-healthcare.

Quirk, J. "Big Tech Advance in Healthcare Rolls On with Amazon, JPMorgan Insurance Alliance." *Karma*, November 4, 2019. https://karmaimpact.com/big-tech-advance-in-healthcare-rolls-on-with-amazon-jpmorgan-insurance-alliance/.

Farr, C., and E. Kim. "Inside Amazon's Grand Challenge—a Secretive Lab Working on Cancer Research and Other Ventures." *CNBC*, June 5, 2018. https://www.cnbc.com/2018/06/05/amazon-grand-challenge-moonshot-lab-google-glass-creator-babak-parviz.html.

Sullivan, M. "Amazon Prime Health Is Coming, According to an Early Investor." *Fast Company*, November 30, 2018. https://www.fastcompany.com/90274630/amazon-prime-health-is-coming-according-to-an-early-investor.

Huynh, N. "How the 'Big 4' Tech Companies Are Leading Healthcare Innovation." *Healthcare Weekly*, February 27, 2019. https://healthcareweekly.com/how-the-big-4-tech-companies-are-leading-healthcare-innovation/.

Lee, P. "Microsoft and Partners Combine the Cloud, AI, Research and Industry Expertise to Focus on Transforming Health Care." *Official Microsoft Blog*, February 16, 2017. https://blogs.microsoft.com/blog/2017/02/16/microsoft-partners-combine-cloud-ai-research-industry-expertise-focus-transforming-health-care/.

Novet, J., and J. Fortt. "Microsoft Signs a Huge Deal with Walgreens, as Amazon's Growing Interest in Health Care Looms Large." *CNBC*, January 15, 2019. https://www.cnbc.com/2019/01/14/walgreens-is-microsofts-next-big-cloud-customer.html.

O'Shea, D. "Walgreens Partners with Microsoft to Develop Digital Healthcare." *Retail Dive*, January 16, 2019. https://www.retaildive.com/news/walgreens-partners-with-microsoft-to-develop-digital-healthcare/546266/.

Coombs, B. "Why Walmart May Have Designs on Humana, and What It Thinks It Could Get from a Deal." *CNBC*, April 1, 2018. https://www.cnbc.com/2018/04/01/walmart-may-have-designs-on-humana-heres-what-could-happen-with-a-deal.html.

Oliver, E. "Walmart Is Coming to Gastroenterology—5 Insights." *Becker's ASC Review*, October 3, 2019. https://www.beckersasc.com/gastroenterology-and-endoscopy/walmart-is-coming-to-gastroenterology-5-insights.html.

Souza, K. "Walmart to Pilot Expanded Healthcare Benefits in 2020." *Talk Business & Politics*, October 2, 2019. https://talkbusiness.net/2019/10/walmart-to-pilot-expanded-healthcare-benefits-in-2020/.

Sherman, E. "U.S. Health Care Costs Skyrocketed to $3.65 Trillion in 2018." *Fortune*, February 21, 2019. https://fortune.com/2019/02/21/us-health-care-costs-2/.

Dr. Raffaele Gibilisco, interview with author, January 31, 2020.

Jeff Griffin (Digestive Disease Specialists), interview with author, July 16, 2019.

Dr. Mehul Lalani (US Digestive Health), interview with author, October 5, 2019.

CHAPTER 4

Duhaime-Ross, A. "A Bitter Pill." *The Verge*, May 4, 2016. https://www.theverge.com/2016/5/4/11581994/fmt-fecal-matter-transplant-josiah-zayner-microbiome-ibs-c-diff.

Paunescu, D. "Responsible Biohacking: Is It Possible?" *Vox*, October 15, 2019. https://www.vox.com/recode/2019/10/15/20915402/biohacking-josiah-zayner-crispr-ethics-gene-editing-reset-podcast.

Patricio, M. "How Mindfulness Became a Billion Dollar Industry." *Medium*, November 14, 2018. https://medium.com/@actuallyme/how-mindfulness-became-a-billion-dollar-industry-61acb50fd436.

"Buy Classes." MNDFL. Last accessed December 5, 2019. https://www.mndflmeditation.com/buy.html.

Monroe, R. "The Bulletproof Coffee Founder Has Spent $1 Million in His Quest to Live to 180." *Men's Health*, January 23, 2019. https://www.menshealth.com/health/a25902826/bulletproof-dave-asprey-biohacking/.

Samuel, S. "How Biohackers Are Trying to Upgrade Their Brains, Their Bodies—and Human Nature." *Vox*, November 15, 2019. https://www.vox.com/future-perfect/2019/6/25/18682583/biohacking-transhumanism-human-augmentation-genetic-engineering-crispr.

Hu, C. "Investors Are Pouring Money into Startups That Are Trying to Find a Cure for Aging." *Business Insider*, October 26, 2018. https://www.businessinsider.in/science/health/investors-are-pouring-money-into-startups-that-are-trying-to-find-a-cure-for-aging/articleshow/66382981.cms.

Scialom, M. "Living to 1,000: The Man Who Says Science Will Soon Defeat Ageing." *Cambridge Independent*, June 17, 2018. https://www.cambridgeindependent.co.uk/business/living-to-1-000-the-man-who-says-science-will-soon-defeat-ageing-9050845/.

Brodwin, E. "The Founder of a Startup That Charged $8,000 to Fill Your Veins with Young Blood Says He's Shuttering the Company and Starting a New One." *Business Insider*, August 14, 2019. https://www.businessinsider.in/tech/the-founder-of-a-startup-that-charged-8000-to-fill-your-veins-with-young-blood-says-hes-shuttering-the-company-and-starting-a-new-one/articleshow/70682419.cms.

"Home." Alkahest. Last accessed December 5, 2019. https://www.alkahest.com/.

"Human Plasma-Derived Therapeutics Market Size, Status and Global Outlook—Alkahest, Baxter, CSL Behring, Entegrion, Inc., Gammagard, Grifols." *Market Research Journals*. Accessed December 5, 2019. https://marketresearchjournals.com/2019/10/15/human-plasma-derived-therapeutics-market-size-status-and-global-outlook-alkahest-baxter-csl-behring-entegrion-inc-gammagard-grifols/.

Diamandis, P., and S. Kotler. "The Future Is Faster Than You Think, a New Book by Peter Diamandis and Steven Kotler." Last Accessed February 28, 2020. https://futurefasterbook.com/.

"Top 25 Anti-Aging startups." MedicalStartups, February 19, 2020. https://www.medicalstartups.org/top/aging/.

Devlin, H. "The Cryonics Dilemma: Will Deep-Frozen Bodies Be Fit for New Life?" *The Guardian*, November 18, 2016. https://www.theguardian.com/science/2016/nov/18/the-cryonics-dilemma-will-deep-frozen-bodies-be-fit-for-new-life.

Buder, E., M. Kane, and J. Koury. "Die. Freeze Body. Store. Revive." *The Atlantic*, June 20, 2019. https://www.theatlantic.com/video/index/591979/cryonics/.

Diamandis, P. H. "Merging Mind with Machine." Peter Diamandis. Accessed December 5, 2019. https://www.diamandis.com/blog/brain-computer-interfaces-neuralink.

Vitallife. Accessed December 9, 2019. https://www.vitallifeintegratedhealth.com/.

Dr. Jeffrey Gladden (Apex HHPLO), interview with author, October 31, 2019.

CHAPTER 5

Mahoney, D. "What's Love Got to Do with Health Care? Everything, Says Christiana Care CEO." *Industry Edge*, no. 21, October 2017. https://www.pressganey.com/docs/default-source/industry-edge/issue-21---october/what-39-s-love-got-to-do-with-health-care__everything-says-christiana-care-ceo.pdf.

"Exponential Organizations Book—OpenExO: Transforming the World for a Better Future." OpenExO. Accessed February 28, 2020. https://www.openexo.com/exponential-organizations-book.

Dr. Jay Underwood (GI Associates & Endoscopy Center), interview with author, July 18, 2019.

Todd Warren (GI Associates & Endoscopy Center), interview with author, July 18, 2019.

Dr. Reed Hogan (GI Associates & Endoscopy Center), interview with author, July 18, 2019.

Dr. Reed Hogan III (GI Associates & Endoscopy Center), interview with author, July 18, 2019.

Dr. Louis Wilson (Wichita Falls Gastroenterology Associates), interview with author, July 15, 2019.

Dr. Jared Hossack (Mid-Atlantic GI Consultants), interview with author, October 2, 2019.

CHAPTER 6

Shore, Neal D. "The Present and Future of LUGPA," Grand Rounds in Urology, January 27, 2018. https://grandroundsinurology.com/The-Present-and-Future-of-LUGPA/.

CHAPTER 7

Murali, N. S. "Vitals." Last accessed on December 12, 2019. https://www.vitals.com/doctors/Dr_Narayanachar_Murali.html.

Dr. Narayanachar Murali (Gastroenterology Associates of Orangeburg), interview with author, May 28, 2019.

Jeremy Watkins (Wichita Falls Endoscopy Center), interview with author, July 15, 2019.

Brandon Beshear (United Regional Health Care System), interview with author, July 15, 2019.

Krista Zimpel (Wichita Falls Gastroenterology Associates), interview with author, July 15, 2019.

CHAPTER 8

Dr. Scott Ketover (MNGI), interview with author, October 8, 2019.

Lisa Jordan (GI Associates & Endoscopy Center), interview with author, July 19, 2019.

CHAPTER 9

Dr. James Leavitt (Gastro Health), interview with author, August 2, 2019.

Jerry Tillinger (US Digestive Health), interview with author, November 27, 2019.

CHAPTER 10

"Physicians Endoscopy Attracts Growth Investment from Pamlico Capital." Pamlico Capital, September 3, 2013. https://www.pamlicocapital.com/news/physicians-endoscopy-attracts-growth-investment-from-pamlico-capital.

"PE (Physicians Endoscopy) and Capital Digestive Care Announce Strategic Partnership." *PR Newswire*, August 1, 2019. https://www.prnewswire.com/news-releases/pe-physicians-endoscopy-and-capital-digestive-care-announce-strategic-partnership-300894380.html.

OptumCare Specialty Practices (OSP). PDF file. July 2019. https://www.optumcare.com.

Dan Murrey's LinkedIn page. Last Accessed December 5, 2019. https://www.linkedin.com/in/dan-murrey-3b088b8/.

Google. "Google Health—Helping you get the most out of healthcare" YouTube video, 2:12. November 19, 2019. https://www.youtube.com/watch?v=Q2UeoWow8yA&feature=youtu.be.

Kwon, S. "In 'Drop Out Club' Doctors Counsel One Another on Quitting the Field." *Scientific American*, May 25, 2017. https://www.scientificamerican.com/article/in-drop-out-club-doctors-counsel-one-another-on-quitting-the-field.

Lee, J. "47% Of Early Career Doctors and Pharmacists Are Interested in Tech Careers." LinkedIn, December 17, 2018. https://www.linkedin.com/pulse/47-early-career-doctors-pharmacists-interested-tech-careers-jaimy-lee/.

Dr. John Allen (University of Michigan Health System), interview with author, January 13, 2020.

Dr. James Burdick (Baylor University Medical Center), interview with author, July 17, 2019.

Kevin Harlen (Capital Digestive Care), interview with author, September 27, 2019.

Dr. Michael Weinstein (Capital Digestive Care), interview with author, September 27, 2019.

Barry Tanner (Physicians Endoscopy), interview with author, July 23, 2019.

PART 4

I first heard Barry Tanner, chairman of Physicians Endoscopy, use the term "GI 2.0" in our meeting. It made a lot of sense as something that the entire industry can aspire to.

CHAPTER 11

Flaccus, G. "Oregon Blockbuster Outlasts Others to Become Last on Earth." *AP News*, March 18, 2019. https://apnews.com/e543db5476c749038435279edf2fd6of.

Johnston, C., and A. Technica. "Netflix Never Used Its $1 Million Algorithm Due to Engineering Costs." *Wired*, April 16, 2012. https://www.wired.com/2012/04/netflix-prize-costs.

"To Reinvent Healthcare, Cambia First Reinvented Itself: How They Built a Culture of Innovation." Alpha UX. Last Accessed February 28, 2020. https://exec.alphahq.com/to-reinvent-healthcare-cambia-first-reinvented-itself-how-they-built-a-culture-of-innovation/.

Kafka, P. "Netflix Thought It Would Have 5 Million New Subscribers This Quarter. Instead It Added 2.7 Million." *Vox*, July 17, 2019. https://www.vox.com/recode/2019/7/17/20698370/netflix-q2-earnings-miss-5-million-2-7-million-content-disney-hbo-att-nbc-streaming.

Hankin, A. "A Dozen or So Companies Amazon Is Slaying This Year." *Investopedia*, December 4, 2019. https://www.investopedia.com/news/5-companies-amazon-killing/.

CHAPTER 12

Kannan, N. "Doctors Are Practicing Reimbursement Based Medicine and Not Evidence Based Medicine." *h+ Media*, November 26, 2013. https://hplusmagazine.com/2013/11/26/doctors-are-practicing-reimbursement-based-medicine-and-not-evidence-based-medicine/.

Toy, S. "Livongo Health IPO: 5 Things to Know about the Digital-Health Startup." *MarketWatch*, July 22, 2019. https://www.marketwatch.com/story/livongo-health-ipo-5-things-to-know-about-the-digital-health-startup-2019-07-05.

Kuchler, H. "How Digital Health Apps Are Leading the Fight against Diabetes." *Financial Times*, July 16, 2019. https://www.ft.com/content/0fee5b5c-a357-11e9-974c-ad1c6ab5efd1.

Muoio, D. "Livongo Credits Recent Partnerships, Integrations for Its Strong 2019 Growth; Aims for Nearly $300M Revenue in 2020." Mobihealthnews, March 03, 2020. https://www.mobihealthnews.com/news/livongo-credits-recent-partnerships-integrations-its-strong-2019-growth-aims-nearly-300m.

"Vivante Health." Crunchbase. Last Accessed June 30, 2020. https://www.crunchbase.com/organization/vivante-health-inc.

"The 'Sick Care' Approach to Digestive Health Isn't Working. We Can Do Better." Oshi Health. Last Accessed June 30, 2020. https://www.oshihealth.com/about/.

"ModifyHealth™ Aims to Help Millions of IBS Patients as the First Meal Delivery Service to Ship Low-FODMAP and Gluten-Free Meals Nationwide." ModifyHealth. Last Accessed June 30, 2020. https://modifyhealth.com/blogs/newsroom/modifyhealth-aims-to-help-millions-of-ibs-patients-as-the-first-meal-delivery-service-to-ship-low-fodmap-and-gluten-free-meals-nationwide.

"Ro." Crunchbase. Last Accessed June 30, 2020. https://www.crunchbase.com/organization/roman-2.

"Vida Health." Crunchbase. Last Accessed June 30, 2020. https://www.crunchbase.com/organization/vida-health.

Azevedo, M. A. "Digital Therapy Startup Talkspace Raises $50M In Revolution-Led Series D." Crunchbase News, May 29, 2019. https://news.crunchbase.com/news/digital-therapy-startup-talkspace-raises-50m-in-revolution-led-series-d/.

"Nurx." Crunchbase. Last Accessed June 30, 2020. https://www.crunchbase.com/organization/nurx.

CHAPTER 13

Robbins, T. "Business Mastery." TonyRobbins.com. https://www.tonyrobbins.com/events/business-mastery. The concept of determining the life cycle of a business and industry are covered really well in this seminar, among several other strategies.

CHAPTER 14

Robbins, T. *The Time of Your Life*. TonyRobbins.com. https://store.tonyrobbins.com/products/the-time-of-your-life. The concepts of identifying what truly matters through questions are dealt well in this audio program.

AFTERWORD

"United States." Worldometer. Last Accessed May 29, 2020. https://www.worldometers.info/coronavirus/country/us/.

Welna, D. "Coronavirus Has Now Killed More Americans Than Vietnam War." NPR, April 28, 2020. https://www.npr.org/sections/coronavirus-live-updates/2020/04/28/846701304/pandemic-death-toll-in-u-s-now-exceeds-vietnam-wars-u-s-fatalities.

Kimball, S. "Doctors Face Pay Cuts, Furloughs and Supply Shortages as Coronavirus Pushes Primary Care to the Brink." CNBC, May 25, 2020. https://www.cnbc.com/2020/05/25/coronavirus-family-doctors-face-pay-cuts-furloughs-and-supply-shortages.html.

Miller, S. "The Secret to Germany's COVID-19 Success: Angela Merkel Is a Scientist." *The Atlantic*, April 20, 2020. https://www.theatlantic.com/international/archive/2020/04/angela-merkel-germany-coronavirus-pandemic/610225/.

Oliver, E. "Exact Sciences Pivots to Telemedicine in a COVID-19 World—4 Quotes on the Company's Q1 Performance." *Becker's ASC Review*, May 8, 2020. https://www.beckersasc.com/gastroenterology-and-endoscopy/exact-sciences-pivots-to-telemedicine-in-a-covid-19-world-4-quotes-on-the-company-s-q1-performance.html.

Sugathan, S. "AI Stepping up against COVID-19." LinkedIn, May 22, 2020. https://in.linkedin.com/in/suzettesugathan.

Simonite, T. "Chinese Hospitals Deploy AI to Help Diagnose Covid-19." *Wired*, February 26, 2020. https://www.wired.com/story/chinese-hospitals-deploy-ai-help-diagnose-covid-19/.

Pennic, J. "Exscientia to Screen 15,000 Drugs in Search for Coronavirus Treatment." *Healthcare IT News*, April 7, 2020. https://hitconsultant.net/2020/04/07/exscientia-to-screen-drugs-in-search-for-coronavirus-treatment/.

Byrne, M. "SI: Artificial Intelligence in Gastroenterology." *TIGE Journal*, April 2020. https://www.tigejournal.org/issue/S2590-0307(20)X0002-X.

Farr, C., and A. Levy. "Digital Health Stocks Are Surging Because 'Suddenly Now We're in the Future.'" CNBC, May 23, 2020. https://www.cnbc.com/2020/05/23/digital-health-stocks-are-surging-amid-coronavirus-pandemic.html.

The Editorial Board. "Opinion | The Doctor Will Zoom You Now." *Wall Street Journal*, April 26, 2020. https://www.wsj.com/articles/the-doctor-will-zoom-you-now-11587935588.

Chinni, D. "Hertz, JCPenney, JCrew Join List of Businesses Filing Bankruptcy." *NBC News*, May 24, 2020. https://www.nbcnews.com/politics/meet-the-press/hertz-jcpenny-j-crew-join-list-businesses-filing-bankruptcy-n1213961.

Ellison, A. "Walmart Health Expands as Physician Practices Face Cash Crunch." *Becker's Hospital Review*, May 6, 2020. https://www.beckershospitalreview.com/finance/walmart-health-expands-as-physician-practices-face-cash-crunch.html.

Newton, C. "How COVID-19 Is Changing Public Perception of Big Tech Companies." *The Verge*, March 26, 2020. https://www.theverge.com/interface/2020/3/26/21193902/tech-backlash-covid-19-coronavirus-google-facebook-amazon.

Koons, C. "The Amazon-Berkshire-JPMorgan Health Venture Fails to Disrupt." *Bloomberg*, May 21, 2020. https://www.bloomberg.com/news/articles/2020-05-21/bezos-buffett-dimon-joint-venture-fails-to-disrupt-health-care.

Reader, R. "Drones from CVS and Walgreens Are Finally Here—and They're Bringing Band-Aids." Fast Company, October 21, 2019. https://www.fastcompany.com/90419596/cvs-and-walgreenss-drones-are-finally-here-and-theyre-bringing-bandaids.

"Coronavirus: Robot Dog Enforces Social Distancing in Singapore Park." *BBC News*, May 11, 2020. https://www.bbc.com/news/av/technology-52619568/coronavirus-robot-dog-enforces-social-distancing-in-singapore-park.

Wason, E. "The Snake That Ate the Dinosaur: U-M LSA Museum of Paleontology." LSA, February 4, 2014. https://lsa.umich.edu/paleontology/news-events/all-news/search-news/the-snake-that-ate-the-dinosaur.html.

ABOUT THE AUTHOR

PRAVEEN SUTHRUM is the co-founder and president of NextServices. The company provides a platform that medical practices need to thrive while facing tougher reimbursements, higher operating costs, and increased regulation. Under his leadership, the company developed a cloud-based GI EHR and endoscopy report writer called enki. Additionally, NextServices serves as a bridge between GI practices and private equity.

Praveen has been featured in *Forbes, Inc.*, the *Economic Times*, the *Detroit News*, *STAT News*, *Huffington Post*, *Becker's ASC*, and India's *National Geographic Traveler*. *Scope Forward* is Praveen's second book and his follow-up to the Amazon number one new release *Private Equity in Gastroenterology*.

He has an engineering degree from Manipal Institute of Technology and an MBA from the University of Michigan's Ross School of Business. He also completed the Exponential Medicine program at Singularity University. Additionally, he studied sculpture at the New York Studio School and music at Trinity Laban.

He serves on the board of Dr. Mohan's Diabetes Centre, one of the largest VC-funded diabetic chains in India. Previously, he served as the Chairman of the Michigan-Ross Alumni Board of Governors. Praveen is based in Mumbai and the New York region.

Made in the USA
Monee, IL
09 September 2020

41891496R00194